FROM WESLEY TO ASBURY

FROM WESLEY TO ASBURY

STUDIES IN EARLY AMERICAN
METHODISM *by* FRANK BAKER

DUKE UNIVERSITY PRESS   DURHAM, N.C.   1976

© 1976, Duke University Press
L.C.C. card no. 75–39454
I.S.B.N. 0–8223–0359–0
Printed in the United States of
America by Heritage Printers, Inc.

TO THE OFFICERS AND MEMBERS
OF THE
COMMISSION ON ARCHIVES AND HISTORY
OF THE UNITED METHODIST CHURCH
FOR
"THE FELLOWSHIP OF KINDRED MINDS"

CONTENTS

INTRODUCTION

Imagine yourself spirited back to an English Methodist circuit of two hundred years ago. It would take some time for you to recover from the initial shock of the simplicity—even the crudeness—of living standards, the differences in food and clothing, in speech and manners, the comparative stillness of the narrow streets in the tiny towns, the absence of any paved roads. If you were removed to London, Bristol, Oxford, or a handful of other places, of course, it would be slightly different, though even there living for the majority was hard, manners coarse, and the streets both narrow and for the most part paved with cobblestones. The present-day English Methodist whisked back to the America of two hundred years ago would experience a similar shock, accentuated by the vast and alien wilderness beyond the sparse settlements, and the far fewer centers of modest culture, notably the largest and greatest city, Philadelphia, and a rapidly developing New York.

Both you and your English counterpart would receive a warm welcome from his Methodist cousins over the waters and over the centuries. As each visitor became more familiar with his surroundings, grimly adjusting to life out of a story book, he would surely wish himself back in the twentieth century as speedily as possible—though (if sufficiently hardy and adventurous) not until he had learned something about what made these distant ancestors tick. He would probably be somewhat embarrassed at the lack of restraint in discussing personal religion in private, and troubled in public by the fervent singing and the outpourings of extempore prayer. The measure of embarrassment would depend upon his age and upon the kind of church in which he had been reared: the old would feel more comfortable than the young, the Blacks more comfortable than the whites. In any case, however, he would surely realize and respect the deep sincerity of a simple faith and a genuine piety in these enthusiastic Methodist pioneers.

Then, for the persistent, would follow a period of adjusting to the outward patterns of Methodist activity—ways of worship, of fellowship, of organization. And here there would be a significant difference between the reactions of the Englishman and the American.

The twentieth-century American transported to eighteenth-century English Methodism would find its customs completely baffling, but the twentieth-century Englishman going back to eighteenth-century American Methodism would slip fairly easily into familiar ways. In both Britain and the U.S.A. Methodism has inevitably—and rightly— undergone a transformation through two centuries. In conservative England, however, this has been so minor as to leave clear traces of the past. In America Methodism has changed out of all recognition. American Methodism was of enormous social and spiritual signifi- cance in large measure because it so flexibly adapted itself to an ad- vancing physical frontier. In so doing, however, it accepted and fur- thered certain pioneering elements in the American way of life which create problems as well as opportunities—mobility of population, re- placement rather than renovation, and even planned obsolescence. Certainly one result was that the past of American Methodism, both in its buildings and its culture, tended to be torn down and rebuilt, or altered so many times that its origin can no longer be deduced from the vestigial remains. For the most part it is impossible to understand early American Methodism in terms of modern American Method- ism. It is only to be understood fully by bearing constantly in mind that Methodism was a British import, adapted to its original Ameri- can setting chiefly by British laymen and preachers.

Take, for instance, The Case of the Missing Class-Ticket. The class-ticket was a method devised by John Wesley in 1741 for rec- ognizing the members of the Methodist societies who were in good standing—it also provided a very handy method of dramatizing and enforcing Methodist discipline. A new ticket, complete with a fresh serial letter and a different scriptural text, was written out for each approved member every three months, and if you did not receive one you would not be admitted to the private meetings of the society nor to the popular love-feasts. The class-ticket was familiar in early Ameri- can Methodism, also. When in 1784 Methodists were organized as a church rather than a society, however, there was an increasing ten- dency not to set strict standards for membership—or at any rate not to enforce those standards. The class-ticket, the symbol of membership, therefore diminished in importance, though it lingered on for many years as a means of screening the love-feasts from disruptive elements— hence its American name of "love-feast ticket." The love-feasts also, which during Asbury's day were popular features of most gatherings attended by Methodists from a wide area, gradually fell into disrepair, and with them the tickets used for admittance. For well over a century, therefore, the class-ticket has been almost forgotten in America, as a rare museum piece, and even then under a name which obscures its origin. In Britain, on the other hand, it continued to be of such importance throughout the nineteenth century that many loyal Methodists would save every quarterly class-ticket they received, and at their death either bequeath them to their heirs or have them placed in their coffins—a kind of passport to heaven! Although class-tickets have been somewhat under fire within recent years, and their disciplinary value is now almost nil, they still remain in use.

Other customs, events, and personalities of early American Methodism can similarly be better understood by an acquaintance with transatlantic Methodism. What I am trying to do in this book is to bring to life some aspects of early Methodism in this great country, and to do so especially in the light thrown by early Methodism in the British Isles. The volume does not set out to be a "history" of early American Methodism, but simply an examination of some persons, events, and emphases which were important to its development during the years between the first coming of John Wesley to colonial America and the departure of Francis Asbury from a maturing independent nation for a heavenly reunion with Wesley—the man whom above every other he seems to have admired and copied, though admiration did not always mean agreement, no more than copying implied an attempt at slavish reproduction.

Each chapter (except the one on the forgotten man of American Methodism, Thomas Coke) was originally prepared for separate presentation as a paper or publication in its own right. Three have never been published, however, and three have been almost completely rewritten in ampler form. All have been revised, sometimes extensively, to play their part in this volume, so that in combination they do indeed cover much of the excitement of the pioneering story of early American Methodism. Some slight overlapping remains, for I found it impossible to remove all repetition except at the expense of the integrity of the individual chapters, though to avoid serious overlapping it did seem desirable to omit several passages, as well as two papers which fitted the theme, one on "The Wesleys and America," and the other on "The Americanizing of Methodism." I believe that many new insights are here offered, perhaps especially because of my own somewhat unusual status and background. I am an Englishman, whose major field of research and writing over thirty-seven years has been British Methodist history, but who during fifteen years' residence in this country has sought to familiarize himself with the figures and events and documents of early American Methodist history.

We look first at the Wesleys in Georgia, where much that later seemed unique in British Methodism was in fact the subject of experiment during a ministry fraught with error and frustration, but by no means the dismal failure that it is sometimes made out to be. An attempt is then made to define Methodism, as a movement, as a society, as a church, comparing the varying progress made through these stages in Britain and in America, and drawing attention to the key role of Wesley's pupil, colleague, and successor, George Whitefield, in bridging the wide gap between the embryo Methodism in Wesley's Georgia and the rise of Methodist societies farther north a generation later. We turn then to the lay pioneers of American Methodism, mostly immigrants from Ireland, but also some who received their inspiration here, from Whitefield. Next follows a biography of Captain Thomas Webb, who more than any other man brought encouragement to these scattered groups, and fostered a sense of belonging to something much larger than any tiny forgotten handful of spiritual survivors—or explorers—in a hostile environment. Then comes the documented story of how these pioneers appealed to Wesley for help, and of Wesley's response in sending a succession of his experienced itinerant preachers to organize American Methodism after the tried British patterns. From this we turn to the real founder of American Methodism, Francis Asbury, one chapter being devoted to his years of training in England, and another to the fulfilment of that training in America. We then study Thomas Coke—the first Methodist bishop. After looking mainly at people and events we turn to the ideas which motivated those people, and see how in doctrine as well as in discipline the Methodist Episcopal Church was founded solidly upon the teachings and publications of John Wesley. The closing chapter examines various essential features of early American Methodism —piety, evangelism, worship, fellowship, discipline, lay leadership, and community service—and adds a brief comment about the relevance of each for Methodism today.

Clearly there are dangers in an attempt like this: the danger to which Englishmen are especially prone of assuming their own obvious rightness; the danger of using English words with an English rather than an American nuance; the danger of an approach to history which might turn off more people than it turns on; and I do indeed realize also that a little learning may be a dangerous thing when not based upon a lifetime's acquaintance with the subject under review. Nevertheless, though it would have been folly for me to write such a book when I came to live permanently in America in 1960, I believe that by now I know both my American Methodist history and my American Methodist brethren far better, and if my publishers are prepared to make the venture, "Barkus is willing!"

Perhaps it would be well, however, in order that I do not have to make too heavy inroads into the capital of the known generosity of my many American friends, that I should "come clean" about my approach to historical writing, or rather to delivering historical addresses to denominational audiences with greatly varying backgrounds of historical awareness. In this pursuit I recognize in myself many elements: the research detective, enjoying the elusive chase for the sake of the chase; the earnest seeker after truth; the entertainer, striving to select points and present those points in such a way as will most interest hearer or reader, and perhaps even merit the occasional appreciation of a happy phrase, the chuckle at a touch of humor. What will also sometimes be seen, however—and this in general will not be so welcome to the professional historian, nor to me personally when writing for the general public rather than speaking to fellow-Methodists—is the fact that I am a preacher, seeking not only an understanding of the human situation in history, but also the bearing of that understanding upon the human situation today. This is especially true in the final chapter, which may be considered the homiletic application of the preceding historical research—and may therefore be skipped by the true-blue dyed-in-the-wool professional historian.

Those who seek "straight" history only, therefore, may not find it here—though I have a sneaking suspicion that completely impartial history, uncolored by either prejudice or purpose in their most pastel shades, is nowhere to be found, and if discovered would probably prove extremely dull reading. I must claim, however, that my desire to entertain or to exhort never consciously interferes with my determination to find and honestly to present what I conceive to be the truth. My statements of fact are always based on careful research, normally with primary sources, and usually documented so that the curious reader may follow my tracks. A mere hypothesis is never disguised as a dogma, but is introduced with a "probably" or a "perhaps." Not, alas! that every statement which I here set down as a fact will necessarily remain such in a century's time. I write in the light of available evidence, and with a realization of my own fallibility, and would indeed be grateful if manifest errors were pointed out, though I hope and believe that they are few. As hinted earlier, the book has an underlying theme which has undoubtedly colored my approach, though I hope not distorted my interpretation of the events, namely a conviction of the essential oneness of early British and American Methodism from Wesley to Asbury. It would indeed prove an immense source of joy to me if my work helped to further transatlantic understanding, which is at least one important element in forwarding the aim of the World Methodist Council to make fully true once more the words of John Wesley himself—"The Methodists are one people in all the world."[1]

Duke University, Durham, North Carolina   Frank Baker
Thanksgiving, 1975

1. Letter to Ezekiel Cooper in Philadelphia, Feb. 1, 1791, original at Garrett Theological Seminary, Evanston, Illinois.

FROM WESLEY TO ASBURY

1. THE WESLEYS IN GEORGIA

Contrary to what some have claimed I believe both that Georgia meant much to the Wesleys and the Wesleys to Georgia. Their brief pioneering mission can in one sense be dismissed as a failure, but it was by no means a complete failure, and in it were many elements of success—success both immediate and on the spot, and also the seeds of the immense worldwide success which eventually came to the Methodist movement. Fully to realize both failure and success we must dig below surface appearances and exercise historical imagination—and both are difficult.

As Oxford undergraduates neither John nor Charles Wesley seems to have bothered his head much about America. They came out as missionaries almost on the spur of the moment, and during a comparatively brief stay they both suffered severe hardship and disappointment. Yet strangely enough both planned to return, and to their dying day both retained a deep affection for America and its people. At least a small measure of the phenomenal growth of Methodism in the U.S.A., and therefore in the world at large, can be traced to this affection, while the distinctive quality of American Methodism is in turn indebted to American affection for "Mr. Wesley." The Wesleys' mental pictures of America were always colored by what they personally experienced in the newly founded colony of Georgia, where they spent most of their time, or in South Carolina's proud Charleston, though Charles Wesley also spent a month in Boston en route to England.

It may be claimed that the Blacks were indirectly responsible for bringing the Wesleys to America. In 1730, a year after the formation of the Holy Club in Oxford, a group of London philanthropists were pondering a way of utilizing £1000 bequeathed in trust for the purpose of converting Negroes.[1] They decided to seek more funds, and

Delivered before the South Georgia Annual Conference of the United Methodist Church, June 5, 1972, and before the North Georgia Annual Conference, June 19, 1972. First published in *Historical Highlights*, II, No. 1 (June, 1972), 6–13, by the Commission on Archives and History, South Georgia Conference, the United Methodist Church.

1. Leslie F. Church, *Oglethorpe: A Study of Philanthropy in England and Georgia*, pp. 47–51; cf. John Wesley, *Journal*, Standard Edition, ed. Curnock (henceforth "Wesley, *Journal*"), VIII, 287.

to expand the trust into a scheme to help ablebodied and industrious poor people to remove themselves from debtors' prisons and the charity rolls in order to set up in a new country—where they might incidentally furnish a buffer between the Carolinas on the one hand and the Spanish and the Indians on the other. In 1732 King George II granted a charter to this projected new colony, which was loyally named after him, "Georgia." The first group of settlers, including a minister sponsored by the Society for the Propagation of the Gospel, was taken over that year by James Oglethorpe, and arrived at Charleston, South Carolina, in January 1733. Soon they were at work building the first town, Savannah, which by that summer numbered forty houses. Oglethorpe managed to make friends of the local Indians, with whom he entered into a treaty. When he returned to England in 1734 he brought with him the chief, Tomochichi, and members of his family.[2]

Samuel Wesley, the rector of Epworth, greatly admired the philanthropist's work, and told him so. For his part Oglethorpe subscribed to Wesley's massive tome on Job.[3] Oglethorpe was especially friendly with Wesley's eldest son, another Samuel, who published several poems praising his work both in prison reform and in the establishment of the new colony. He also raised subscriptions for the venture and was responsible for securing the silver chalice used in the church in Savannah.[4] It may very well have been Samuel Wesley junior who suggested his younger brothers as possible replacements for the first missionary, Samuel Quincey, who proved unsatisfactory.

John Wesley's Oxford friend Dr. John Burton, Fellow of Corpus Christi College, one of the original Georgia Trustees, seems to have been "commissioned" (the word is his) to enlist the Holy Club for the Georgia enterprise.[5] He arranged for Wesley to meet Oglethorpe in August, 1735, and followed this up with several letters.[6] When John Wesley asked his mother whether she would be prepared to lose Charles and himself to America she replied: "Had I twenty sons I should rejoice that they were all so employed, though I should never see them more."[7] The upshot was that four members of the Holy

2. Church, op. cit., pp. 51–140.

3. Luke Tyerman, *The Life and Times of the Rev. Samuel Wesley*, pp. 425–7.

4. Wesley, *Journal, VIII*, 283.

5. John S. Simon, *John Wesley and the Religious Societies*, pp. 110–12; cf. Wesley, *Journal*, VIII, 285.

6. Simon, op. cit., pp. 110–12; cf. Wesley, *Journal*, VIII, 285–91.

7. Henry Moore, *The Life of the Rev. John Wesley*, I, 234.

Club agreed to go out to Georgia as a missionary team under the leadership of John Wesley, at first to work together in Savannah, and then to spread out to different tasks. Charles Wesley, though officially appointed "Secretary for Indian Affairs," served as a kind of private secretary to Oglethorpe—though not a very good one. In order that he too might share more fully in the pastoral oversight of the colony he was persuaded to enter Holy Orders shortly before embarking.

GEORGIA IN 1736

It is enormously difficult for us to put ourselves in the buckled shoes and kneebreeches of these two young clergymen and their still younger companions, the Rev. Benjamin Ingham and the sugar merchant Charles Delamotte, as on February 6, 1736, they set foot on American soil—on Cockspur Island near where Fort Pulaski now stands—and gained their first impressions of the marshes, the swamps, the pine barrens, and what Charles Wesley calls the "vast impervious forests"[8] of Georgia. Nor is it easy to imagine the manner of their coming, by tiny sailing boat during a voyage of over three months; nor of their journeying around Georgia, on foot, on horseback, or in flat-bottomed boat.

Up to 1733 the only inhabitants of this huge wilderness were a few tribes of Indians and an occasional Indian trader or runaway slave from South Carolina. In 1736 the only clear boundary was the Atlantic on the east, along which Oglethorpe had purchased a six-mile strip from the Indians. Here a handful of villages and plantations were strung together with the only town, Savannah, by a lacework of waterways, though Oglethorpe did try, unsuccessfully, to build an arterial road. The only penetration inland was along the River Savannah, to the Swiss township of Purysburg and the neighboring Salzburger settlement of New Ebenezer, about twenty miles north of Savannah. Atlanta and Macon were not dreamed of, and Augusta, a hundred and fifty miles north of Savannah, was a mere plot of land with no houses—not even the fort had yet been built.

By 1736 Savannah itself contained about two hundred houses and seven hundred inhabitants. John Wesley found a minister's house ready for him. Charles Wesley was not so fortunate in Frederica, a garrison town being built as an outpost against the Spanish. He was

8. Frank Baker, *Charles Wesley as Revealed by his Letters*, p. 23.

not only the first minister there but one of the very first batch of about a hundred and twenty people to lay it out, meantime sleeping in a boat, a tent, or a hut—plagued by sandflies wherever he was.

England was flooded with romantic literature about Georgia, the latest—and last—British colony in North America, but actual conditions were grim. The idealism of the charitable founders, in seeking to help unsuccessful debtors find a new start, served to cut its own throat. Although the settlers sent over at the cost of the Georgia Trustees were handpicked, they were after all mostly misfits, those who had failed to make a living in England, but were now expected to be successful under far harsher conditions. Nor did the subsidized industries of silk and wine prove practicable for them. On the other hand the large proportion of more affluent freeholders who paid their own passage out—a thousand during the first ten years against eighteen hundred sent by the charity[9]—served to aggravate the situation, making a division between rich and poor, so that Oglethorpe complained to the Trustees, "the people who come at their own charge live in a manner too expensive."[10] Thomas Causton, the storekeeper and chief magistrate at Savannah, proved to be a tyrant and a swindler. A bitter trade war developed with South Carolina, as well as political rivalries and deepseated personal animosities in Savannah itself. Added to this was the confusion of tongues and of religions. Even from Britain the nominal Anglicans with their Cockney background would certainly find it almost impossible to understand either the dialect or the point of view of the harsh Presbyterians from the highlands of Scotland; and with these were mingled groups of French Huguenots, German Lutherans, Moravians, a few Portuguese, Italians, and Dutch, and even some Jews—a bewildering mixture for a colony which still numbered fewer than two thousand when John Wesley left in 1737!

THE YOUNG MISSIONARIES

Undoubtedly the Wesleys were not the ideal men for this very unideal pioneering situation. The marvel is, however, that they did so well.

9. E. Merton Coulter and Albert B. Saye, eds., *A List of the Early Settlers of Georgia*, p. x.

10. Public Records Office, London, C.O. 5/639, p. 336, Feb. 13, 1735/6, in Charles Wesley's hand.

John Wesley was a man approaching thirty-three when he set foot in Georgia, Charles just turned twenty-eight. Both were slim and small in stature: John was 5 feet 3 inches tall and weighed 122 pounds in his later years;[11] Charles was no taller, though unlike John he turned portly in old age. John was an omnivorous scholar, a keen and logical thinker, a born organizer, and an ordained clergyman of ten years' standing. Charles leaned heavily on his brother, partly because he was so much older, partly because of his superior gifts of leadership, partly because Charles himself suffered from the ups and downs of a fiery artistic temperament. At this time both were in the midst of what we might call identity crises, both seeking the perfect life of religion by ever-increasing self-discipline in devotional practices, in denying themselves most bodily comforts, in service to the needy. And yet these pastors whom others accounted saints knew that their own religion lacked something vital.

This is what John Wesley meant when he told Dr. John Burton about his reasons for coming to Georgia: "My chief motive, to which all the rest are subordinate, is the hope of saving my own soul. I hope to learn the true sense of the gospel of Christ by preaching it to the heathen." Let us not overlook his second avowed motive, however— "to impart to them what I have received, a saving knowledge of the gospel of Christ." Here is absolute honesty: he knows himself called to be an evangelist, but before he can preach his message with conviction he must know from personal experience that what he offers is indeed the genuine gospel of Christ. Georgia was to be his testing-ground, where he believed the Indians to be the noble savages later idealized by Jean Jacques Rousseau. Said Wesley: "They are as little children, humble, willing to learn, and eager to do the will of God, and consequently they shall know of every doctrine I preach whether it be of God."[12]

Charles was almost equally idealistic and devoted to God, though it was only reluctantly that he had agreed to ordination just before they set sail in order that he might better assist his brother's mission. On the *Simmonds* he transcribed some of John's sermons so that he could preach them both on shipboard and in Georgia.[13] On the threshold of the New World his lack of spiritual certainty plunged him to

11. Wesley, *Journal*, VI, 462, VII, 461n.
12. Ibid., VIII, 289–90.
13. *Proceedings of the Wesley Historical Society* (henceforth *WHS*), XXXVII (Feb., 1970), 113.

greater depths of self-despair than John's, and on the day they first anchored in the River Savannah he wrote back home: "In vain have I fled from myself to America. . . . If I have never yet repented of my undertaking, it is because I could hope for nothing better in England —or Paradise. Go where I will, I carry my hell about me." Yet his truly pastoral heart shines forth from that same letter: "Give God your hearts; love him with all your souls; serve him with all your strength. . . . Let God be your aim, and God only! . . . To love God, and to be beloved of him, is enough."[14]

THE MISSION TO THE INDIANS

The mission to the Indians did not work out as the Wesleys had hoped. In Frederica Charles seems to have had little personal contact with them, though as Secretary for Indian Affairs he spent much of his time issuing licenses to Indian traders, especially during his brief later stay in Savannah. John found his hands full with the many and varied problems of his duties as minister of Savannah, meeting with such success that Oglethorpe tried to hold him back from the Indians. In July, 1736, Oglethorpe reported to the Trustees: "The change since the arrival of the mission is very visible with respect to the increase of industry, love, and Christian charity. . . . But on their removal to the Indians we shall be left entirely destitute, and the people by a relapse if possible worse than before."[15] Nor were the Indians as receptive to new ideas as Wesley had believed, though he was impressed by the Chickasaws, and planned to learn their language. He sent to the prestigious *Gentleman's Magazine* an account of an interview with five Chickasaws on July 20, 1736, in which he faithfully recorded their religious views. This was printed with an introduction pointing out "what a deep and habitual sense of a divine providence is imprinted on the minds of those ignorant heathens, and how excellently they are prepared to receive the gospel."[16] By the time it was published, however, almost a year later, Wesley had become thoroughly frustrated and disillusioned about the Indians in general. His attempts to convert Tomochichi were met with a proud refusal

14. Ibid., XXV (June, 1945), 17–20, (Sept., 1946), 97–102.
15. Public Records Office, London, C.O. 5/636, p. 353, July 26, 1736, in Charles Wesley's hand.
16. *The Gentleman's Magazine*, VII (May, 1737), 318–19.

(which remained, however, one of Wesley's chief weapons against merely nominal Christianity): "Why, these are Christians at Savannah! Those are Christians at Frederica! Christians drunk! Christians beat men! Christians tell lies! Me no Christian."[17] Thus rebuffed, Wesley went from one extreme of naïveté to the other, accepting as truth many of the evil rumors that he heard, and reporting to the Trustees: "They are all, except perhaps the Choctaws, gluttons, drunkards, thieves, dissemblers, liars. They are implacable, unmerciful; murderers of fathers, murderers of mothers, murderers of their own children. . . . Whoredom they account no crime. . . ."[18]

It was left to their ministerial companion and fellow Oxford Methodist, twenty-three-year-old Benjamin Ingham, to keep the Indian venture alive. He lived for many months among the Yamacraws, at Musgrove's trading post, became reasonably proficient in their language and customs, and (encouraged by Tomochichi) ran a school for their children. This faded out, however, in February, 1737, when he left for England to seek replacements, nor did his intention of returning materialize.[19] All things considered the Indian mission must be adjudged a failure. Yet its influence remained with John Wesley to the end of his life, and his sermons and other writings frequently drew upon illustrations—usually favorable—from Indian culture.

PASTORAL SUCCESS AND FAILURE

The Wesleys' work among the whites seemed at first more promising. Oglethorpe wisely warned the brothers against a superficial emotional approach, advising them to "beware of loghouse converts."[20]

17. Charles C. Jones, *Historical Sketch of Tomo-Chi-Chi*, p. 103. Jones cites no authority, but apparently derived the quotation from Robert Wright, *A Memoir of General James Oglethorpe*, p. 183. Wright similarly cites no authority, but appears to have combined for greater dramatic force two quotations from Thaddaeus Mason Harris, *Biographical Memorials of James Oglethorpe*, p. 164. These two statements in their turn (though Harris likewise cites no source) derive (a) from Wesley's sermon, "The Mystery of Iniquity," §32, "Why, these are Christians at Savannah! These are Christians at Frederica," and (b) from *A Farther Appeal to Men of Reason and Religion*, Pt. I, VII.4, where Wesley speaks of "the very savages in the Indian woods" crying out, "Christian much drunk; Christian beat men; Christian tell lies; devil Christian! Me no Christian!"

18. Wesley, *Journal*, I, 407. Cf. J. Ralph Randolph, "John Wesley and the American Indian: A Study in Disillusionment," pp. 3–11.

19. Church, op. cit., pp. 246–9.

20. Baker, *Charles Wesley*, p. 24.

Both threw themselves into steady pastoral work and found in it great promise and fulfilment. When Charles Wesley arrived in Frederica to serve the "fifty poor families" there his depression lifted, and he wrote in his *Journal*: "Tuesday, March 9. About three in the afternoon I first set foot on St. Simon's Island, and immediately my spirit revived. No sooner did I enter upon my ministry than God gave me, like Saul, another heart. . . . At seven we had evening prayers in the open air. . . ." And so it continued.

The same was true to a larger degree in the case of John. Granted that his approach was unduly ritualistic for the rough pioneer settlers, nevertheless he proved a faithful pastor whose energy and dedication commanded the respect of the unprejudiced majority. Faithfully he conducted baptisms, weddings, funerals, prepared wills, and administered first aid. Every day in town he spent three hours in visiting from house to house, and in order to converse with his widely scattered and immensely diverse flock he added to the French which he already knew and the German which he had learned aboard the *Simmonds* at least a smattering of Spanish and Italian. Every day he read public prayers morning and evening, and expounded the Second Lesson. He conducted weekly catechism classes for children and adults, administered the Lord's Supper every Sunday and Saint's day, and carried the elements to the sick and dying, whom he visited daily. Methodically he maintained mountains of statistics, as well as keeping his finger on his own spiritual pulse in a diary recording the religious mood and activities of every hour.[21] He not only preached without a manuscript,[22] but experimented with new forms of worship and fellowship. Especially noteworthy were the regular meetings for Christian fellowship apart from public worship, forerunners of the Methodist society and band meetings in England, together with the singing of hymns—in 1737 he published America's first hymnbook (the first, that is, as opposed to a book of metrical psalms only).[23] He even had the

---

21. Frank Baker, *John Wesley and the Church of England*, pp. 45–6. A valuable clue to Wesley's indefatigable labors can be found in the pastoral schedule which George Whitefield inherited from him. After a month in Savannah he wrote: "I visit from house to house, catechise, read prayers twice and expound the two second lessons every day; read to a houseful of people three times a week; expound the catechism to servants, etc., at seven in the evening every Sunday." See Whitefield, *Works*, I, 44; cf. his *Journals*, p. 155.

22. Egmont, Earl of, *Diary of Viscount Percival, afterwards First Earl of Egmont*, II, 313–14.

23. See *John Wesley's First Hymn-book: A Facsimile with Additional Material*.

joy of experiencing a spiritual revival among the young people of Savannah.[24]

Nevertheless the promise was not immediately fulfilled. Both brothers suffered from the fact that they were earnest and eligible bachelors, becoming focal points for dissimulation, jealousy, intrigue, and gossip. Both refused to pay court to the wealthier and more influential colonists, but served where they felt the need was greatest, thus gaining the love of the poor and the active enmity of some of the rich. Both were inexperienced in the ways of the world, both committed serious errors of judgment and of tact. The work of both became so undermined that retreat was inevitable, especially after both committed the cardinal sin of antagonizing the most influential members of their flocks.

Charles fell victim first. He rebelled in any case against wearing his official hat, as secretary to Oglethorpe, and entered in his *Journal* for March 16, 1736: "I was wholly spent in writing letters for Mr. Oglethorpe. I would not spend six days more in the same manner for all Georgia."[25] Worse still, Charles not only found himself in the bad books of Thomas Hawkins, doctor and chief magistrate at Frederica, but of Oglethorpe himself. A malicious gossip told Charles that Oglethorpe had committed adultery with Mrs. Hawkins, and to even things out Oglethorpe himself was informed that she had committed adultery with Charles. Unfortunately both men believed what they were told, and Oglethorpe became so bitter towards Charles that he refused him even a board to sleep on, largely as a result of which he contracted the dysentery which broke down his health.[26] John Wesley came down from Savannah to investigate, managed to reassure Oglethorpe, and brought about a reconciliation. He then stayed on in Frederica, likewise incurring the wrath of Mrs. Hawkins, who on one occasion requested a pastoral visit—and then attacked him with a pistol and a pair of scissors.[27] Meantime Charles recuperated in Savannah, but remained frustrated, so that in July, 1736, Oglethorpe granted him an

24. Wesley, *Journal*, I, 358–9, 361; cf. his letters of March 29, 1737, to Mrs. Chapman, and June 16, 1737, to James Hutton, in *Letters*, I, 220, 222.

25. Six of these letters (including one to John Wesley) are preserved in the Public Records Office, London.

26. Charles Wesley, *Journal, 1736–39*, ed. Telford, pp. 9–11, 14, 17–18, 35–9, 41; Wesley, *Journal*, I, 188–9, 193–5; *The Georgia Historical Quarterly*, XL (Sept., 1956), 209–10.

27. Wesley, *Journal*, I, 263–4 (Aug. 22, 1736).

honorable discharge, sending him back with official despatches to England. He had been four and a half months in Georgia—about the same length of time that he had spent on board the *Simmonds*.

After a year in Georgia Benjamin Ingham also returned.[28] John's turn was next. The eventual crisis is well known—his infatuation with young Sophy Hopkey; his announcement that he must remain celibate; her sudden and irregular marriage to William Williamson, giving the lie to some of her solemn declarations to Wesley; his correct but tactless refusal to serve communion to her, followed by the fury of her uncle and guardian Thomas Causton, who rigged a grand jury against Wesley, and thus effectively drove him from America. John had been just under two years in Georgia, spending fourteen months in Savannah and the surrounding area, a total of three months during three periods in Frederica, and the remainder in wide travels, including two intermediate visits to Charleston, S.C.

THE FINAL ACCOUNTING

His spiritual work had undoubtedly been of value, as Oglethorpe reported to the Trustees, and as Whitefield was to reiterate when at Wesley's request he took over as one of the Holy Club volunteers canvassed in turn by Charles Wesley and Benjamin Ingham. After visiting in the Savannah area Whitefield testified that his name was "very precious among the people." This was on June 2, 1738, just after he had bidden "Bon voyage!" to Wesley's lay companion from England, Charles Delamotte, who had been caring for the Methodist society and school which Wesley had founded in Savannah. Whitefield reported that "the poor people lamented the loss of him" also, just as they had lamented Wesley's departure.[29] He, too, had to a large extent been a victim of Causton's enmity.[30] Henceforth the Wesleys were represented in Georgia only by Whitefield and these humble followers.

A few tangible links with those pioneering days remain, such as Whitefield's orphanage and some buildings and sites both in Savannah and on St. Simon's Island. The spiritual links, however, are almost impossible to trace, though one suspects that some of these same poor

28. Ibid., I, 320–1.

29. George Whitefield, *Journals*, p. 157. Whitefield himself walked cautiously, and ingratiated himself with many of those whom Wesley had offended. His preaching drew increasing numbers. See Arnold Dallimore, *George Whitefield*, I, 202–3.

30. Wesley, *Journal*, VIII, 308–10; Coulter and Saye, op. cit., p. 13.

people kept alive a flickering flame of devotion which was eventually rekindled by the visits of Wesley's preachers a generation later, to result in the beginnings of official Methodist history in Georgia.

In fact, however, this early Georgian Methodism is hardly the greatest element of success in the Wesleys' missionary sojourn, though it constitutes a mysterious and fascinating element which may yet be more fully documented. Of greater importance is the fact that in this pioneer setting both John and Charles Wesley came more clearly to realize the nature of that additional something which was needed for a dynamic fruitful ministry—a personal assurance of salvation. This they had already suspected; this their Georgia ministry fully confirmed. And especially through some of their Moravian parishioners, both on board the *Simmonds* and in Savannah, their feet were set on the path that led to the warmed hearts of May 21 and May 24, 1738.

Not only can the motive power of later worldwide Methodism be traced to Georgia, however, but many of its methods. It was in Georgia, both in Savannah and in Frederica, that John Wesley began to hold the regular meetings for Christian fellowship outside church hours which later he termed "the second rise of Methodism"—the first being the formation of the Holy Club at Oxford.[31] It was in Georgia that he made his first experiments in the use of lay leaders in parish work, in the appointment of women as "deaconesses," in extempore prayer, in itinerant preaching, preaching in the open air, early morning services before the beginning of the working day, the use of hymns in public worship, even at the Lord's Supper.[32] Georgia furnished John Wesley both with the opportunity for pioneer experimentation in church work and a guiding thread leading him to the all-important spiritual experience which transformed him into one of the world's greatest religious leaders.

---

31. John Wesley, *A Concise Ecclesiastical History*, IV, 175; cf. *Works*, XIII, 307.
32. Baker, *John Wesley*, pp. 48–52.

2. THE BEGINNINGS OF METHODISM IN AMERICA

When did Methodism really begin in America? And where? I have in my files a large parcel of documents labeled "Priority of North or South in American Methodism," material collected by Dr. John S. Simon, a fellow-Englishman, whom Dr. A.B. Sanford and Dr. L.R. Streeter were trying with some success to convert to their own view that the first American Methodist Society was formed in New York. Hundreds of pages generated a little light, but—I am afraid—too much heat! Before we are in a position to discuss the "When?" and the "Where?" it would be wise to ask a preliminary question, the answer to which is too often taken for granted: "What, after all, is Methodism?"

WHAT IS METHODISM?

"What is Methodism?" Clearly the essential Methodism which links us to our distant beginnings is not the totality of that sprawling, many-tentacled monster which we criticize—and which we love—as "the Methodist Church," or more recently, since the enrichment of our joint traditions by union with another early branch of the family, as "the United Methodist Church." This was born in 1939 and entered into a new partnership in 1968, though most of its general features had been laid down long before, and had been remoulded —sometimes out of all recognition—by each passing generation. But what is the essential purpose that directed this long and painful process of experimentation, this constant trying on of new suits for a rapidly growing child in a world of constantly changing fashions? What is the inner genius of Methodism, its essence? Is it to be found in doctrinal teaching, in a moral code, in forms of worship, in evangelistic methods, in social service, in ecclesiastical organization—or in a peculiar combination of some or all of these features? "What is Methodism?"

Delivered before the Association of Methodist Historical Societies, Philadelphia, April 24, 1963, and before the Western North Carolina Annual Conference of the Methodist Church, June 3, 1963. Published in *Methodist History*, II, No. 1 (Oct., 1963), 1–15.

This, I believe, is the question that John Wesley would urge upon us. Did he not warn his own contemporaries to be sure that they knew what they were talking about, mentioning the case of an Irishman who remarked: "Methodists? Ay, they are the people who place all religion in wearing long beards!"[1] Wesley's own definition, as given in his *Complete English Dictionary*, was disarmingly simple: "A Methodist—one that lives according to the method laid down in the Bible." For our particular purposes this will hardly suffice, though as sheer propaganda we cannot afford to discard it. A brief analysis of early Methodism in Britain may help us to see our own historical problems more clearly—always a useful step towards finding a solution. There is no doubt that England was the birthplace of Methodism, in its generally accepted meaning of the family of Protestant Christian denominations arising from the religious activities of John and Charles Wesley. (Here you notice that I have slipped in, very cautiously, a rough working definition, which may at least introduce us to our major problem.) Even in England, however, there has been much difficulty in deciding in what year Methodism really began, the chief contestants being 1738 and 1739, though a good fight has been put up for 1729, and some backers would favor 1725 or 1744, while even 1784 and 1795 have their supporters. We bypass the tortuous arguments in favor of these varied claims and take to the throughway of a generalization: British Methodism can be divided into three main categories, which are also to some extent chronological stages—the *movement*, the *society*, and the *church*.

THE STAGES OF BRITISH METHODISM

Although itself one example of a much larger spiritual movement, the *Methodist movement* in Britain may be said to have begun with the group of Oxford students gathered around the Wesley brothers in 1729. Their main theme was the pursuit of holiness, whence their familiar title of "The Holy Club." They were methodical in their private and public devotions, in serious study of the Bible, and in service to the community, and so earned the more lasting nickname of "Methodists." Soon anyone who sought energetically to know and to do the will of God was termed a Methodist. This remained John Wesley's basic understanding of Methodism, as we have seen from

1. Wesley, *Works*, VIII, 347.

his dictionary definition, even after the movement had been tightly organized into co-ordinated societies.

Along with the pursuit of piety was later combined the conviction that a devout Christian could personally *know* that he was saved from the penalty and from the power of sin. This emphasis came into the Methodist movement by way of the Moravians and John Wesley's Aldersgate experience. These twin emphases upon piety and spiritual experience normally revealed themselves in a desire for Christian fellowship, in evangelical preaching, and frequently in a highly developed social conscience. Taken as a whole this movement was a stirring of the dry bones of conventional "churchianity," and especially of the Church of England, though the new spirit spread also to the Nonconformists. In its later manifestations it could be described as German Pietism translated into vernacular Puritan English. The term "Methodist" was widely used all over the English-speaking world to denote this spiritual awakening in general, and this continued long after the formation of Wesley's societies.

The *Methodist Society* can be said to have originated in England in 1739, although Wesley had used the term "society" of the Holy Club at Oxford. The membership of the 1729 Oxford society, however, was limited to members of the university, even though it was their intention to serve the community and even to revitalize religion in general. The societies which Wesley organized in London and Bristol in 1739, on the other hand, were for all seeking Christians. They were formed partly from older Anglican societies which had been revived under Methodist and Moravian influence, but were now splitting over theological issues, and partly from Wesley's own converts. These Methodist societies could clearly be distingushed from the older religious societies in that they looked to Wesley alone for leadership. His driving genius organized them into a tightly knit "connexion" by means of carefully chosen lay leaders and lay preachers, while at the same time preserving the devotional spirit, the high moral standards, and the program of social service that had characterized the Methodist movement. Throughout his life Wesley maintained that these societies were not churches, nor their preachers "ministers." Methodism was not a sect, an independent denomination. Loyal Methodists, he insisted, would regularly attend their parish churches—or their dissenting meeting-houses—for public worship and

the sacraments, for marriages and burials. The Methodist societies offered extra preaching-services out of church hours, and the extra fellowship of the weekly class-meeting, for those who were prepared to
place themselves under Wesley's spiritual oversight. As a society within
the church Methodism had its own rules, its own conditions of membership, though these were simple—simple to understand, at least, if
not to practice. There was no doctrinal test, nor did the Methodist
society insist upon an experience of conversion before granting membership. The only condition of membership was "a desire to flee from
the wrath to come," the sincerity of which must be confirmed by avoiding evil, by doing good, and by using the means of divine grace.

The *Methodist Church* arose in Britain when the people called
Methodists no longer depended on their parish church for worship
and sacraments. Although Wesley maintained to his death that he
was a loyal communicant of the Church of England, in fact strand by
strand he had been severing the ties which attached his societies to the
parent body. As early as 1743 he had leased a disused Huguenot chapel
in London, and in this consecrated building he was able without
qualms of conscience to administer communion to his followers. (Indeed on this evidence we could make out a case for marking 1743 as
the birth of Methodism as an independent denomination.) The year
1784, however, should probably be regarded as the date of Wesley's
implied Declaration of Independence. In that year he not only legally
incorporated the annual Methodist Conference as a self-perpetuating
body in complete charge of the Methodist Societies, subject to no oversight by any Anglican bishop or court, but also himself assumed episcopal functions by ordaining preachers to administer the sacraments
in America. Charles Wesley echoed the dictum of his old schoolfellow
Lord Chief Justice Mansfield, "Ordination is separation." John Wesley still tried to make the best of both worlds, but British Methodism
had in effect become a church in 1784, even though there was a show
of remaining a society within the Church of England.[2] After Wesley's
death, at the cost of several severe agitations and continued compromise, the separation became obvious and tacitly admitted, though the
use of the term "church" by Methodism was long deferred, and there
was no legal declaration setting up a Methodist Church until the
present century.

2. See Baker, *John Wesley*, espec. chapters 13–15.

THE STAGES OF AMERICAN METHODISM

Turning from our analysis of Methodist history in Britain we are comforted by at least one fact. If we look for the same three categories in American Methodism there can be no hesitation in declaring that in the U.S.A. Methodism entered its final church phase in 1784. The group of preachers summoned to the Lovely Lane meeting-house in Baltimore that Christmas apparently went beyond Wesley's intentions for them when they officially adopted the title of the Methodist Episcopal Church. Nevertheless they acted along lines that he himself had laid down. In Thomas Coke he had sent them a "superintendent" empowered to ordain, and had nominated Francis Asbury for ordination as a fellow-superintendent. (The word "superintendent" suffered a sea-change into "bishop," as happens to so many English words in transatlantic usage.) Wesley himself ordained other elders for service in America. He sent over a revision of the Book of Common Prayer for the use of American Methodists, once more without the *imprimatur* of any Anglican bishop. Even so the ecclesiastical status of American Methodism might well have remained as ambiguous as that of British Methodism but for the cleancut decisions of that momentous Christmas Conference, which constitutes an incontrovertible landmark in American Methodist history.

If for the beginnings of the church phase the American Methodist historians are in a better position than are their British counterparts, the situation is much more complicated when we consider the Methodist movement and the Methodist society, both of which existed here as well as in England. Once more it is necessary to ask a number of preliminary questions before we are in a position to offer any definitive answers, and to ask these questions in the context of the differing aspects of Methodism as movement and as society which we discover from our study of early British Methodism. And we must begin at the beginning.

WAS WESLEY A METHODIST IN GEORGIA?

The first question should be: Was John Wesley a Methodist in 1735 when he came to Georgia as a missionary of the Society for the Propagation of the Gospel? The answer must unhesitatingly be "Yes," for according to his own definition a Methodist was a spiritual seeker rather than a converted sinner. Even if we ask, "Was Wesley a converted man at this time?" our answer might well be the same, though (as he later explained) he then possessed the faith of a servant of God rather than the assured faith of a son which came to him at Aldersgate. He was a devout Christian seeking a deeper personal experience of God, in other words a true "Oxford Methodist." Indeed the Georgia mission was quite clearly a Holy Club project, absorbing four of the group's key members, and gaining the intended support of at least two others.

John Wesley's spiritual status during 1736 and 1737, the larger part of which years he spent in America, may be gauged by his closing manifesto, that pioneer *Collection of Psalms and Hymns* which he published at Charleston, S.C., in 1737, but which had been prepared and used in Georgia. The hymns for Sunday (at the beginning of the book) and for Saturday (at the end) are mainly hymns of praise. The middle section of twenty for use on Wednesdays and Fridays, however, all emphasize personal salvation from sin, and most of them claim that this can come only by the free grace of God in Christ. Most of the items which Wesley chose or translated for this section were already in the form of personal prayers addressed to God in the second person, and he amended others in order to transform them also into prayers. Assuredly the editor of this volume was no cold formal cleric, however naïve and tactless he might have been in his High Church enthusiasm—and however inept at handling a love affair.

The second question is this: Did Wesley begin any typically Methodist practices in Georgia? Once more the answer is "Yes." America witnessed at least a strengthening of Methodist hymn-singing, if not its birth, and the first published Methodist hymnbook. Germ ideas for other practices later developed more fully in the British Methodist societies were first tried out in Georgia, such as extempore prayer and preaching, the use of laymen and women. Most important of all, however, was the fact that in Georgia Wesley clearly developed the practice of forming societies of Christian seekers to meet for prayer and fellowship (including the singing of hymns) quite apart from their regular worship in the church. It was no looking back through rose-colored spectacles that led Wesley to claim in 1781: "The first rise of Methodism, so called, was in November, 1729, when four of us met together at Oxford; the second was at Savannah, in April, 1736, when twenty or thirty persons met at my house; the last was at London, on [May 1, 1738], when forty or fifty of us agreed to meet together every Wednesday evening, in order to a free conversation, begun and ended with singing and prayer."[3]

Clearly if Wesley had defined Methodism in a more specific manner the organized fellowship of a society would have formed a main feature of such a definition. We should therefore look more closely at what was involved in this "second rise of Methodism," namely the society in Savannah. Wesley writes in his *Journal*: "We considered in what manner we might be most useful to the little flock at Savannah. And we agreed, (1), to advise the more serious among them to form themselves into a sort of little society, and to meet once or twice a week, in order to reprove, instruct, and exhort one another." He went on to describe how this society was divided into bands on the Moravian pattern: "(2), to select out of these a smaller number for a more intimate union with each other, which might be forwarded, partly by our conversing singly with each, and partly by inviting them all together to our house."[4] They met on Wednesday, Friday, and Sunday evenings. Within a few weeks a similar society was meeting on the same evenings in the southern outpost of Fort Frederica.[5] The members attending spent "about an hour in prayer, singing, and mutual exhortation."[6] The *Collection of Psalms and Hymns* affords a sample of what they sang on those occasions.

Thus Wesley clearly introduced Methodism as a movement and even as an embryo society to America, and indeed in some features of the experiment America seems to hold priority over Great Britain. But our next major question would seek to discover whether in fact these experiments which certainly proved fruitful in England bore any kind of fruit in America. Was there any continuity between this experimental introduction of Methodism to Georgia in 1736 and its permanent establishment in other parts of America thirty years later? This major question can best be approached by way of several minor questions, but even so it must be confessed that no complete nor com-

3. Wesley, *Works*, XIII, 307.
4. Wesley, *Journal*, I, 197–205; Luke Tyerman, *The Oxford Methodists*, p. 79. Cf. p. 189 for a similar but independent account of these events.
5. Wesley, *Journal*, I, 226–30, 232.
6. Wesley, *Letters*, I, 214.

pelling answer can be given. Enough for our pressent purpose that some doubts are raised about the common assumption that the only link between the American Methodism of 1736 and that of 1766 was that they both originated in the British Isles, though quite independently of each other.

DID WESLEY FAIL IN GEORGIA?

And first, was Wesley's Georgia mission a failure? The answer seems to be both "Yes" and "No." Even some of the practices charged against him, such as his rigorous but faithful pastoral visitations, proved in fact of real spiritual value, and the lives of some of his parishioners were certainly altered for the better. The pietist pastor of the Salzburger community at New Ebenezer, Martin Bolzius, paid high tribute to Wesley, though he was not blind to the fact that Wesley's personal faith needed deepening: "He does the work of the Lord, and since he is most affectionately disposed towards his Saviour and the souls of his congregation, the true and chief Shepherd will surely supply him with a greater measure of the *Spiritus Evangelici.* He performs the duties of Christianity very earnestly, and visits his people industriously, and is well received by some."[7] We note that last phrase, "well received *by some,*" not only for its limitations, but also for its positive content. Wesley himself could conscientiously claim: "All [i.e., all the English-speaking settlers] in Georgia have heard the word of God. Some have believed, and begun to run well. A few steps have been taken towards publishing the glad tidings both to the African and the American heathen"[8]—i.e., the Blacks and the Indians.

But he antagonized a ruling faction—not the first minister to commit this cardinal sin, nor the last—and so was lost to those whom he had already served and might well have served far better. Charles Delamotte, who accompanied Wesley as a schoolmaster and became a lay preacher in Savannah, stayed behind when Wesley left, and after a few weeks of despondency reported that the Savannah society was continuing to meet for prayers and fellowship in his home, having been turned out of Wesley's. Renewed persecution drove some away,.

7. Martin Schmidt, *John Wesley: A Theological Biography,* I, 180.
8. Wesley, *Journal,* I, 435.

but united the remainder, a few becoming "zealous advocates for the Lord God of Hosts."[9] Delamotte thus became public enemy No. 1 for the ruling clique, headed by Sophy Hopkey's uncle and guardian, Thomas Causton, who held the strategic position of chief magistrate, and was determined to "break the neck of" the society. Evil rumors were spread about "that monster Wesley and his crew." Causton interviewed every member of the society, with both promises and threats. A lawsuit was begun. This time the grand jury dismissed the charges against Delamotte, as motivated merely by "spite and malice against Mr. Wesley."[10] The effect was similar, however. Six months after Wesley himself Charles Delamotte also was frozen out of Savannah and returned to England. But not before he passed on the torch of evangelism to George Whitefield, another member of the Oxford Methodists come to succeed the Wesleys. Whitefield arrived in Savannah on May 7, 1738, and sadly noted the "many divisions among the inhabitants."[11] When Delamotte set sail on June 2 Whitefield remarked how at least "the poor people lamented the loss of him, and went to the waterside to take a last farewell."[12]

It was in this context that Whitefield crowned a tribute to the labors of his "worthy predecessors" in Georgia with this testimony: "The good Mr. John Wesley has done in America, under God, is inexpressible. His name is very precious among the people; and he has laid such a foundation, that I hope neither men nor devils will ever be able to shake." Whitefield was unduly optimistic in his exuberance, of course, as well as more than a little naïve. Powerful men like Causton did in fact join forces with the devil to shake the foundations of devout Christian living and evangelical fellowship laid by Wesley and his Oxford Methodist companions. As a result history has not been able to point to any dramatic fruits of Wesley's labors in Georgia. Fruits, however, there certainly were. When in 1778 Wesley preached on "the late work of God in North America" he spoke of the "Great Awakening" under Jonathan Edwards in New England, and in the same breath of a simultaneous "work of grace in the newly-planted colony of Georgia . . . both at Savannah and Frederica; many inquiring what they must do to be saved, and 'bringing forth fruits meet for

9. Ibid., VIII, 308–10, a letter from Charles Delamotte to Wesley, dated Savannah, Feb. 23, 1738, the original being in the Methodist Archives, London.

10. Loc. cit.

11. Whitefield, *Journals*, p. 155.

12. Ibid., p. 157.

repentance.' "[13] For this he gave much credit to the Moravians, though this could hardly be true—except indirectly—in Frederica. Whitefield himself echoed that early tribute in the last message which he sent to Charles Wesley in 1770: "Do pray. I am sure prayers put up above thirty years ago are now being answered; and, I am persuaded, we shall yet see greater things than these."[14] Yet when all the tributes have been paid to Wesley's early American ministry it is probably fair to say that the influence of Wesley on Georgia was of less importance than the influence of Georgia on Wesley.

FROM 1737 TO 1766

Another question affecting this problem of continuity is this: Did Wesley shake the dust of America from his feet in 1737 until his immigrant followers revived his interest in the 1760's? By no means. Both brothers maintained a warm interest in America, and both hoped to return. Wesley's links with Jonathan Edwards, for instance, are in themselves sufficient for a chapter, or even a book. Wesley edited and republished more of Edwards's writings than of any other man.[15] He was on terms of warm friendship with Edwards' successor as President of Princeton College, Samuel Davies, and from 1755 onwards sent parcels of his own publications to Davies in Virginia, the most useful being his hymnbooks. These proved so popular that Davies reported that the Negroes would sit up for whole nights singing them.[16] Wesley did not forget America, nor did America forget him. Several of his publications were sold and reprinted in Philadelphia from 1739 onwards, by the Bradfords, by Benjamin Franklin, and by Christopher Saur, for whose German-speaking public Wesley's extract from William Law entitled *The Nature and Design of Christianity* proved most popular.

Nevertheless all this does not seem to have led to the establishment of any other specific Methodist societies between those in Georgia and those founded farther north in the 1760's by Methodist immigrants. The Methodist *movement*, however, in the broader sense, continued long after the Wesleys left America, and long after in England it had

---

13. Wesley, *Works*, VII, 410.
14. Thomas Jackson, *Life of the Rev. Charles Wesley*, II, 243.
15. See below, p. 71.
16. Wesley, *Journal*, IV, 101, 125–6, 194–5.

been overshadowed by the Methodist *society*. The title "Methodist" was used not only of Whitefield, to whom it clearly belonged, but of many evangelical leaders walking in the steps of Frelinghuysen, Edwards, the Tennents, and Davies. The "enthusiasm" of these so-called Methodists aroused the same kind of antagonism as that faced by their fellows in England, including persecution from the American members of the Church of England. The Anglican missionaries of the S.P.G. sent a joint report in 1747 stating that it was "a matter of great comfort . . . to see in all places the earnest zeal of the people in pressing forward into the Church from the confusions which Methodism had spread among them."[17] In 1763–4, the Anglican itinerant missionary Thomas Barton, who served in Pennsylvania from 1754, reported that "the Church of England . . . has hitherto stood her ground amidst all the rage and wildness of fanaticism, . . . whilst Methodists and New Lights have roam'd over the country, 'leading captive silly women', and drawing in thousands to adopt their strange and novel doctrines."[18]

The focal point of the term "Methodist" in its general sense and to some extent at least in its specific sense, both in England and in America, was George Whitefield. He was Wesley's pupil, and a member of the Holy Club, summoned by Wesley to help him in Georgia. In large measure he succeeded in accomplishing in America what Wesley returned to accomplish in Britain. The fire of the Great Awakening—and of the Georgia awakening—was continually dying down for want of fuel, but it was rekindled and spread by Whitefield. Not only did he help America to maintain the spiritual glow. He also exercised a constantly mellowing effect on the tendencies towards harsh puritanism and dry orthodoxy among the evangelical dissenters on the one hand, and on the religious formalism and political Toryism of the Anglican ministers on the other. Certainly the Holy Club played an important role in spreading vital religion throughout eighteenth-century America, even though this was brought about by a Methodist movement rather than by means of Methodist societies organically linked with those in England.

It has often been claimed, indeed, that Whitefield formed no so-

17. C. F. Pascoe, *Two Hundred Years of the S.P.G.*, p. 45. Cf. the rash of printed attacks by ministers and ministerial associations in New England on Whitefield in 1745, as evidenced by Charles Evans, *American Bibliography*, Nos. 5534, 5551, 5563, 5589, 5592, 5605, 5609, 5617, 5643, 5668, 5670, 5678, 5680, 5690.

18. Pascoe, op. cit., p. 37.

cieties in America. This is not quite true. Both in England and America he stressed the value of Christian fellowship. His first visits to Philadelphia in 1739 were consummated by the formation of two societies, and the society which he formed at Lewes was still rousing the ire of the local Anglican missionary in 1741.[19] Nevertheless he organized no "connexion" in America, either in Wesley's name or his own. The Methodism that he had learned at Oxford was diffused through existing and newly created churches of other denominations. In this process Wesley thought that Whitefield squandered his spiritual fruits, yet in order to preserve similar fruits in England Wesley himself was led into forming a rival denomination to the Church of England. In this respect it could be argued that Whitefield was a better Methodist than Wesley. In spite of their differences, however, both ecclesiastical and theological, they remained close friends and colleagues until Whitefield's death in 1770. Nor is there any more sincere or discerning tribute to Whitefield's evangelism than Wesley's funeral sermon, preached at Whitefield's request both in his own London headquarters and in Wesley's Foundery.

As an evangelist-at-large Whitefield helped to keep alive a spiritual expectancy in America which both stabilized the Christian denominations already in being and kept the soil in condition for the coming of Wesley's preachers. This was the Methodist movement. Whitefield did even more, nurturing individuals and groups who later formed the nuclei of more specifically Methodist societies. There are hints of this in what became the main centers of Methodist influence. In Maryland the Bayards of Bohemia Manor were among Whitefield's disciples and seem to have become supporters of Wesley's societies.[20] In Philadelphia the little group that gathered around Captain Thomas Webb in 1767 apparently numbered two of Whitefield's converts, Edward Evans and James Emerson, the latter of whom is supposed to have held together a group of "Methidies" for a generation.[21] In New York Whitefield helped to keep alive at least a flicker of evangelism,

19. Whitefield, *Journals*, pp. 420–1; article by the Rev. John N. Link, "Was Lewes before Philadelphia?," *Christian Advocate*, June 24, 1961.

20. James Bayard wrote to Whitefield, May 10, 1749, "O that the midnight state of the Church of England might be remembered by our Dear Emmanuel." (George Whitefield Correspondence, Library of Congress). Joseph Everett of Queen Anne's County, Maryland, was converted under Whitefield, became a Presbyterian, but later served as a Methodist itinerant (W. W. Sweet, *Religion on the American Frontier, 1783–1840*, Vol. IV, *The Methodists*, p. 8on.).

21. Francis H. Tees, *The Beginnings of Methodism*, pp. 89–91.

and a revival on Long Island in 1764 died down only to be quickly rekindled by Captain Thomas Webb, leading to the organization of Methodist societies in organic touch with Wesley.[22] Jesse Lee claimed that Whitefield opened the way for the later Methodist preachers such as himself.[23]

By the 1760's the desire for evangelical preachers could be heard on every side, and Whitefield was probably the first to ask Wesley to send men over to help. In September, 1764, he wrote from Philadelphia: "Here is room for a hundred itinerants. Lord Jesus, send by whom Thou wilt send."[24] In answer to such pleas Wesley replied that he could spare no itinerants, but that "some of the local preachers [were] equal both in grace and gifts to most of the itinerants," recommending to Whitefield one man in particular.[25]

Already a few other Methodist local preachers and class-leaders had come out to America for various personal reasons, especially Irish Methodists seeking a new economic start. During the 1760's these men were encouraged to make ventures in holding fellowship groups and preaching in a small way, particularly Robert Strawbridge in Maryland and Philip Embury in New York. Their efforts were co-ordinated and new evangelism was begun by the most mobile of all the local preachers, Captain Thomas Webb. Letters from these and others— especially Thomas Taylor—made it clear to Wesley that he must send out itinerants and take some responsibility for organizing societies.[26] The first two itinerants came out in 1769, and Wesley asked Whitefield to keep a fatherly eye on them. American Methodism, in its society phase, after a lengthy gestation and prolonged and complicated labors, had at last been born.

Where does this leave us in our discussion of the beginnings of American Methodism? With two clear dates at the outer extremes and much uncertainty in the middle. I think that we can claim that

22. James Waddell of Lancaster County, Virginia, wrote Whitefield August 5, 1766, asking whether the Long Island revival had been "injured or interrupted by the Stamp Act," and requesting Whitefield to send one of his "flaming preachers" to itinerate through Virginia (Whitefield correspondence, Library of Congress). For Webb, see below, chap. 4.

23. Jesse Lee, *A Short History of the Methodists*, p. 38. This was perhaps especially true in New England, where Whitefield began his labors in 1740 by successfully pleading with the ministerial students at Harvard and Yale for a converted ministry. See Dallimore, *Whitefield*, I, 547–62. See also pp. 30–2 below.

24. *Arminian Magazine*, V (Aug., 1782), 439.

25. Letter to Whitefield, March 21, 1767 (*Letters*, V, 44–5).

26. See below, chap. 5.

Methodism as a movement began with the Wesleys in 1736 and as a church in 1784. Methodist societies of a kind existed from 1736 and remained a feature of the movement, though subject to much fluctuation and offering little concrete proof of real continuity in any area. The frame of mind and heart which Wesley thought of as Methodism, however, was kept alive by scattered evangelical leaders, and especially by his former spiritual lieutenant George Whitefield, whose coordinating labours for the specifically Methodist societies were taken over by Captain Webb in 1766 or early 1767.

We all like to have something tangible to celebrate, of course, and we prefer it to be as clearcut as possible. It seems to me that although the birth of the Methodism movement in America must be dated in 1736, the conscious formation of groups of converted and converting Christians into Methodist societies looking to John Wesley as their exemplar and leader began in 1766. It seems quite clear that Robert Strawbridge's first Maryland society was in operation at the latest by June of that year, and in October Philip Embury began to preach in New York. The society at Leesburg, Virginia, can even point to a chapel deed dated 1766. Much homework remains to be done before a clearer picture emerges, as I believe it eventually will.

There is one further comforting and challenging consideration, however. Far more important than these *dates* of Methodist beginnings are the *data* in the literal sense of that Latin word, the "things given" by God for the enrichment of this great nation through Methodism. John may have planted, and George may have watered, but through the nurture of Robert and Philip and Thomas, and especially of Francis, God eventually gave a wonderful increase.

3. THE LAY PIONEERS OF AMERICAN METHODISM

The year 1766, as we have seen, was epochal in the history of American Methodism. It forms a highly visible landmark in the era of the lay pioneers of the Methodist Society in America, an era which lasted for about two decades, until the itinerant preachers sent by Wesley to consolidate these beginnings eventually took charge. Then in 1784 Methodism became a church, in which the laity were regarded as helpers rather than as leaders. These lay pioneers, quite naturally, were British immigrants, although they were highly successful in recruiting native Americans as colleagues. It is therefore fitting that we should study them against the background of earlier British Methodist laity.

During the winter of 1711–12 the father of the Wesleys was in London fulfilling his duties as a member of the Convocation of the Church of England, leaving a somewhat ineffective curate in charge of the parish of Epworth. Susanna Wesley not only conducted prayers and read sermons for her own large family, but threw open her home for as many of the parishioners as wished to crowd into her kitchen. On occasion as many as two hundred assembled on Sunday evenings, most of them standing all the time. Others could not get in, and decided to come earlier the next time. The jealous curate complained to the Reverend Samuel Wesley that his wife was turning the parsonage into a dissenting meeting house. She herself, indeed, spoke of the gathering as "our society." Samuel Wesley wrote asking her to desist. She refused to do so unless he expressly commanded it—as a good seventeenth-century bride she had promised to obey her husband, and was indeed prepared to do so. Having upon his conscience the spiritual impoverishment of his flock, he wisely hesitated to press his authority too far. The meetings continued until his return.[1]

In later years a youthful member of that kitchen congregation was to speak of Susanna Wesley as "in her measure, a preacher of righ-

Delivered at American Methodism's Bicentennial Celebration, Baltimore, Maryland, April 21–4, 1966. Published in Albea Godbold, ed., *Forever Beginning, 1766–1966*, pp. 169–77. Almost completely rewritten for this volume.

1. Wesley, *Journal*, III, 32–4. In his collected *Works* (1771–4) Wesley added asterisks to this passage to emphasize its special importance.

teousness." This was no other than her son John, a very serious eight-year-old when his mother became the first Methodist lay preacher. Thirty years later he must have recalled this unorthodox venture when his widowed mother checked his hasty anger over one of his own lay helpers taking it upon himself to preach—a religious exercise which Wesley at that time considered permissible only for ordained ministers like himself. "Take care what you do with respect to that young man," Susanna Wesley urged, "for he is as surely called of God to preach as you are." After Wesley had heard Thomas Maxfield preach, his strong prejudices were overcome. He was compelled, however reluctantly, to agree with his mother, saying with the aged Eli at the call of young Samuel, "It is the Lord: let him do what seemeth him good."[2]

CHARLES DELAMOTTE

In fact John Wesley had already followed his mother's example some years earlier. In Georgia he had accepted the help of a layman as an assistant pastor. Charles Delamotte was a sugar merchant's son, aged twenty-one, who volunteered to accompany the Oxford Methodists on their mission to the infant colony in 1735. He became the first schoolmaster in Savannah, and gave more time and thought to instilling the principles of religion into the children there than to building up any trade or business for himself. Nor did he seek any payment for his services. So dependable was Charles Delamotte that on one occasion Wesley left the complete care of the parish in his hands for nearly three weeks, and on his return noted, "I found my little flock in a better state than I could have expected, God having been pleased greatly to bless the endeavours of my fellow labourer while I was absent from them." Delamotte played the part of a trusted friend in urging caution on Wesley both in his infatuation with Sophy Hopkey and in his subsequent discipline of her, though to no avail. One by one the Oxford Methodists left Georgia, Charles Wesley after four and a half months, Benjamin Ingham after a year, and John Wesley after nearly two. Delamotte stayed on, the shepherd of the Methodist society, holding his head up in the midst of continued persecution. He maintained fellowship meetings for the members in his own home, and urged his friends in Oxford to send more helpers. Thomas Cau-

2. *WHS*, XXVII, 8.

ston, the chief magistrate, tried to get rid of him as he had done of Wesley, by summoning a grand jury, but his charges against Delamotte were dismissed as caused by "nothing but spite and malice against Mr. Wesley."[3]

For six months Delamotte held together the first experimental Methodist society in America. In June, 1738, he too returned to England, to manage a branch of his father's sugarboiling business in the northern seaport of Hull, where Wesley occasionally met him. He did not leave, however, before the arrival of the pleaded-for reinforcements in the person of George Whitefield. Indeed Delamotte had so spent his funds as well as his thought and energy that he did not have the passage money home until Whitefield pressed it upon him.[4] Whitefield records the leave-taking at the Savannah waterfront: "Friday, June 2, [1738]. This evening parted with kind Captain Whiting and my dear friend Delamotte, who embarked for England about seven at night. The poor people lamented the loss of him, and went to the waterside to take a last farewell. And good reason had they to do so, for he has been indefatigable in feeding Christ's lambs with the sincere milk of the Word, and many of them (blessed be God) have grown thereby. Surely I must labour most heartily, since I come after such worthy predecessors."[5]

And so the first lay pioneer of American Methodism, dedicated and intelligent, eager yet level-headed, departed from these shores, leaving behind him a spiritual challenge not only to a handful of humble settlers in Georgia, but to one of America's greatest roving evangelists, George Whitefield, who kept the Methodist spark alive for a generation until more laymen fanned it into flame.

WHITEFIELD'S CONVERTS

Whitefield was more dramatic as a preacher than his tutor John Wesley, much more emotional, but much less methodical. Those who were converted under his ministry were numbered by the thousands; the societies which he organized to build them up in the faith could be counted on the fingers of two hands. Nor was this only because he wanted to feed the existing churches rather than to found a new one.

3. Wesley, *Journal*, I, 315, 324–5, 356, 361; VIII, 308–10. Cf. John Nayler, *Charles Delamotte*, and Egmont, *Diary*, II, 314, etc.

4. Egmont, *Diary*, II, 513.

5. Whitefield, *Journals*, p. 157.

He realized the value of spiritual fellowship, and encouraged others to follow the example of the Wesleys in forming religious societies, but his own *forte* was oratory rather than organization. Nevertheless Wesley claimed that "by his ministry a line of communication was formed, quite from Georgia to New England."[6] This was echoed by Jesse Lee, who maintained that by means of "Mr. Whitefield's labours as an itinerant preacher . . . the way was opened for our preachers to travel and preach the gospel in different parts of the country."[7] For the most part this influence cannot be charted, though some indications remain. Robert Walker, for instance, was converted under Whitefield at Fogg's Manor, in Chester County, Pennsylvania, and later moved south to Frederick County, Maryland, where he was re-awakened under Strawbridge's ministry, joined his first society, and apparently became a valued local preacher, one of whose sermons Asbury transcribed. He later settled on Sandy River, south of Chester, South Carolina.[8] One of Whitefield's followers in Baltimore was Jesse Hollingsworth, an influential merchant who became a pioneer of Baltimore Methodism, and the Bayards of Bohemia Manor were supporters alike of Whitefield and the later Methodists.[9] The clearest link between Whitefield and the lay pioneers of American Methodism in the 1760's, however, is to be found in Philadelphia.

One of the first fruits of Whitefield's evangelism in Philadelphia was Edward Evans, a cordwainer specializing in high quality shoes for ladies. It seems highly probable that he was a member of the group described in Whitefield's *Journal* for Friday, May 9, 1740: "Preached in the evening, and afterwards began a Society of young men, many of whom I trust will prove good soldiers of Jesus Christ. Amen." When Joseph Pilmore arrived from England in 1769 he testified that Evans had "stood fast in the faith for near thirty years," and that he was "a man of good understanding, and sound experience in the things of God." Becoming distressed by Whitefield's Calvinism, he was associated with the Moravians for about twelve years. Although he believed that his true spiritual affinities were with the Wesleys, he had been dissuaded from writing to them, both by Whitefield and by Peter Böhler. From about 1759 he served as a greatly beloved free-

6. Wesley, *Works*, VII, 411.
7. Lee, *History*, p. 38.
8. Francis Asbury, *The Journal and Letters*, I, 342; II, 272.
9. William Phoebus, *Memoirs of the Rev. Richard Whatcoat*, pp. 79–80; cf. Gordon Pratt Baker, ed., *Those Incredible Methodists*, pp. 42, 47. See also above, p. 25, note 20.

lance evangelist, mainly in the countryside around Philadelphia. With Pilmore's arrival his true spiritual home was discovered, as one of the founding members and leaders of St. George's Methodist Society. He remained an honored preacher, both in Philadelphia and New Jersey, and also served as the pastor of Greenwich Chapel near Gloucester, N.J. On December 4, 1770, at long last, he wrote to John Wesley a lengthy biographical letter to which Wesley replied February 7, 1771. Pilmore preached his funeral sermon to a crowded church on Monday, October 14, 1771.[10]

Another of Whitefield's converts, and probably a member of that same 1740 Philadelphia men's society organized by him, was James Emerson, an Irishman who for a living sold "orange-lemon shrub." The nucleus of the Methodist society which took over the St. George's Church was a fellowship group led by Emerson, which had been meeting for some time (how long no one really knows) in a sail loft on Dock Creek belonging to Samuel Croft. The assertion that he had held together the "Methidies" since 1740 may well be correct.[11] When Pilmore and Boardman arrived in Philadelphia in 1769, planning "to hasten forward to New York as soon as possible," they chanced upon still another Irishman in the street, a Methodist whom Boardman had known in Ireland. It was this unidentified immigrant who persuaded the two missionaries that at least one of them should remain in Philadelphia.[12]

Methodism had come to Ireland from England in 1747, and in that predominantly Roman Catholic country—an impoverished country, too—the Wesleys faced even greater difficulties than they did in England. The rewards were as great as to many they seemed unlikely. John Wesley thought highly of Irish Methodism, and continued to make biennial preaching tours in the island almost to the end of his long life. History has proved him right. The sturdy independence of the Irish, their emotional fervor, their robust physique and dogged endurance, made them tough prospects for the Methodist preachers' evangelism, but valiant champions once won over. Among the waves of Irish immigrants seeking a new opportunity in America during Wesley's day were many Methodists, and their contribution to the

10. Joseph Pilmore, *Journal*, ed. Frederick E. Maser and Howard T. Maag, pp. 24, 105; Tees, op. cit., pp. 89–90; Albert W. Cliffe, *The Glory of Our Methodist Heritage*, p. 17; Edward Evans, letter to John Wesley, Dec. 4, 1770 (Methodist Archives, London).
    11. Cliffe, op. cit., p. 17.
    12. Pilmore, *Journal*, p. 20. His identity is conjectural.

planting of Methodism far outweighed their numbers. As we have already seen, one of the lay pioneers in Philadelphia was an Irishman, James Emerson. So was the key pioneer in the south, Robert Strawbridge. So were the pioneers of Methodism in New York, the Emburys and the Hecks. Robert Williams also, who may be thought of as the father of the Methodist Publishing House as well as the apostle of Methodism in Virginia and North Carolina, came to America from a three-year preaching itinerancy in Ireland. Indeed the only major lay pioneer of early American Methodism who had no strong connection with Ireland was Captain Thomas Webb.

ROBERT STRAWBRIDGE

The most influential of these men, and the first, was Robert Strawbridge. Most of the details surrounding his life in Ireland, and many of those in America, are speculative, and in the past too many dogmatic assertions have been made about such things as his birth, his coming to America, his ventures in preaching and baptizing. Some claims have been made almost solely by calculating backwards or forwards from somewhat imprecise and tentative statements about dates and ages made by people far removed from the events themselves either by time or by distance.

Strawbridge was born on a farm in Drumsna (then "Drummersnave") in County Leitrim, Ireland, perhaps about 1732. As a young man he embarked upon a wandering life, perhaps because he was persecuted as a Methodist, but more probably because of his work in some branch of the building trade. He seems to have gone west to Sligo, then east of Leitrim to Kilmore in Cavan County, then farther east still to Tanderagee in Armagh County, eventually settling among Wesley's followers at Terryhoogan, in the parish of Ballymore, Armagh, from among whom he took a bride, Elizabeth Piper.[13] It seems fairly clear that Robert Strawbridge was a well built man of medium height, with dark silky hair and a dark complexion. Certainly he was of an independent, roving spirit, and just as certainly he had kissed the Blarney stone.[14]

The date of the Strawbridges' arrival in America is uncertain,

13. William Crook, *Ireland and the Centenary of American Methodism*, pp. 149–56.
14. Ibid., pp. 154, 158–9; see also Frederick E. Maser, "Robert Strawbridge," pp. 3–21, espec. pp. 8–9.

though it seems to have been during the early 1760's. (The problem is made the more confusing because others of the same name appear at earlier periods in Maryland records, including a Robert Straw- bridge who was charged in 1753 with pigstealing.)[15] They settled on a fifty-acre farm south of New Windsor, Frederick County, Maryland, rented (and later purchased) from a Quaker neighbor, John En- gland.[16] Almost immediately Robert Strawbridge began a preaching service in his log house on the farm, and a Methodist society was formed, described by Asbury, on a visit in 1801, as "the first so- ciety in Maryland—*and America*."[17] John England's name is included among the members of this first society, and recently discovered evi- dence about him confirms the assertion, about which so much ink has been spilt, that the Maryland society did indeed predate that in New York. For John England's name also occurs in surviving contempo- rary records belonging to the Fairfax (Virginia) Monthly Meeting. The last reference is found in the minutes of June, 1766, stating that "John England had left Friends and joined in society with some other persuasion of people, and desired not to be looked upon a member of our society."[18] Strawbridge's original home is still preserved, as one of the historic shrines of the United Methodist Church, though it is greatly altered in appearance.[19]

It was surely a little later that Strawbridge built for his gradually multiplying followers a log meeting-house, twenty-four feet square, about a mile from his home, "in a meadow near tributaries of both Sam's and Pipe Creeks." This was almost certainly the first American building for purely Methodist purposes. Two of the Strawbridge chil-

15. G. P. Baker, op. cit., pp. 2–3, 5; Maser, op. cit., pp. 5–6.
16. G. P. Baker, op. cit., pp. 4–6.
17. Asbury, *Journal*, II, 294.
18. Edwin Schell, "New Light on Robert Strawbridge," pp. 62–4; cf. G. P. Baker, op. cit., p. 7. This places Strawbridge's society at least a little earlier than that in New York, though not as early as the dates of 1763 or 1764 given for it on the basis of the testimony of John Evans, recorded by Dr. Warfield, for which see a summary in Albea Godbold, "Facts and Thoughts about Robert Strawbridge and his Work," pp. 22–6, espec. p. 23. We still cannot rule out the possibility, however, that the Strawbridge society had in- deed begun much earlier, and that John England was a late recruit. The approximate date suggested by the Evans evidence is confirmed or pushed even farther back by that relating to the baptism by Strawbridge of Henry Maynard, which may possibly have been about 1762, though the date of Maynard's birth (August 12, 1757) appears to be better authenticated than the tradition that he was baptized "when he was but four or five years of age" (Ruthella Mory Bibbins, *How Methodism Came*, p. 29), which appears in John Lednum, *The Rise of Methodism in America*, p. 16, as "but six or seven."
19. G. P. Baker, op. cit., p. 5.

dren were buried beneath the pulpit of this meeting-house, which was dismantled a century later.[20]

Some of the members of this first society in their turn became class-leaders. One class was led by John Evans, meeting in his log cabin, and another in the home of Evans' brother-in-law, Andrew Poulson, on Pipe's Creek.[21] Meantime they looked after his farm while he became an evangelist-at-large, preaching in new places, founding societies, and then encouraging the building of meeting-houses as permanent homes for those societies. Bush Forest Chapel, near Aberdeen, was built in 1769.[22] The class at Andrew Poulson's became a society, still meeting in his large house, but in 1783 needing a new stone chapel.[23] A society was begun in Baltimore County, in Daniel Evans' home, another in Gunpowder Neck at Joseph Presbury's, another at Nathan Perigau's in Patapsco Neck, and still another at the Gatch Farm. At the invitation of Edward Dromgoole, Strawbridge preached in Fredericktown near Frederick City, and in Georgetown, now D.C.[24]

Nor could he be confined within the borders of western Maryland. His many preaching journeys took him far afield, over Chesapeake Bay to begin Methodism on the Eastern Shore, north into Pennsylvania, and west into Virginia.[25] It seems indeed very likely that Strawbridge was responsible for founding the Methodist society in Leesburg, Virginia, where the old stone church was built on land secured May 11, 1766, for "no other use but for a church or meeting house and graveyard"—a building which two years later was described in another contemporary document as "the Methodist meeting house."[26] So numerous became his societies and followers that in 1768 an appeal to Wesley for itinerant preachers went from Maryland as well as from New York, though quite independently.[27]

To a remarkable degree Strawbridge was already helping to supply this need himself, and continued to do so until his death, with enormous success. From among his own converts and disciples he aroused

20. Bibbins, op. cit., 40–4; G. P. Baker, op. cit., p. 9; Maser, op. cit., p. 8.
21. Maser, op. cit., pp. 8, 10; G. P. Baker, op. cit., p. 8; Bibbins, op. cit., pp. 36–8.
22. G. P. Baker, op. cit., pp. 9–10.
23. Ibid., p. 8.
24. Ibid., pp. 8–10; Maser, op. cit., pp. 10–11; Asbury, *Journal*, I, 56, 697.
25. Maser, op. cit., pp. 10–12; G. P. Baker, op. cit., pp. 8–10.
26. William Warren Sweet, *Virginia Methodism*, pp. 46–8; Melvin Lee Steadman, Jr., *Leesburg's Old Stone Church, 1766*, pp. 1–13, espec. pp. 1–3, 8; G. P. Baker, op. cit., pp. 10–11.
27. Pilmore, *Journal*, p. 15.

many to undertake spiritual leadership, either as class-leaders, local preachers, or eventually as itinerant preachers, or in varied combinations of these offices. The class-leaders who had been called into that work by Strawbridge themselves aroused others to service. One of these, Joseph Presbury, was responsible for the conversion of William Watters, the first native itinerant, at least after Edward Evans of Philadelphia.[28] William Watters himself graphically described the process by which in their turn the new converts were divided into little bands of three or four, each sent out to evangelize different areas by singing hymns, praying, reading, talking to the people, and occasionally adding "a word of exhortation."[29] Thus from one center of evangelism the evangelizing wave spread out in all directions. It was enthusiastic converts such as these who opened up new areas. Thus two members of Strawbridge's society came to John Randall's, near Worton, in Kent County on the eastern shore. They talked and prayed with his family to such good effect that Strawbridge himself was asked to come and preach there. He was followed by Robert Williams and Francis Asbury, and the area became a Methodist stronghold.[30]

The opening of homes for preaching sometimes brought the householders or members of their families into the preaching ministry, as in the case of William Durbin, a member of Strawbridge's first society, whose son John became a member of the Baltimore Conference,[31] or of Richard Webster, who first offered his home in Harford County for preaching services, and then himself (briefly) for the itinerant ministry, after which he remained a local preacher (and an occasional supply for itinerants) until his death in 1824.[32] From the conversion of Thomas Bond and his wife there came to Methodist circles Thomas Emerson Bond, the distinguished physician-local preacher who edited the New York *Christian Advocate*, and John Wesley Bond, the preacher who served as Asbury's devoted traveling companion.[33] As in many other cases Daniel Ruff's home was a preaching-place before he himself felt called to preach—a traumatic experience of which Asbury paints a vivid picture.[34]

28. Maser, op. cit., pp. 13–14; G. P. Baker, op. cit., p. 14.

29. William Watters, *A Short Account of the Christian Experience and Ministereal* [sic] *Labours of William Watters*, p. 19.

30. Lee, *History*, p. 39; cf. pp. 41, 49, 50, and Asbury, *Journal*, I, 57.

31. Lednum, op. cit., p. 18, and Asbury, *Journal*, I, 53–4.

32. Lednum, op. cit., p. 20; Asbury, *Journal*, I, 192.

33. Lednum, op. cit., p. 20; Asbury, *Journal*, I, 51.

34. Asbury, *Journal*, I, 92; cf. pp. 67, 91.

Strawbridge was also, as might be expected, the direct spiritual father of a number of preachers, most of them remaining local preachers for most of their careers. The first was Richard Owings, who, like Strawbridge himself, "though encumbered with a family, . . . often left wife and children and a comfortable living and went into many distant parts before we had any traveling preachers among us, and without fee or reward freely published that gospel to others."[35] Others were Hezekiah Bonham, a former Baptist awakened by Strawbridge's preaching, whose son Robert became an itinerant,[36] Sater Stevenson (a member of Daniel Evans' group),[37] and Jacob Toogood, a slave whose master gave him permission to preach to Blacks, apparently the first Negro preacher in Methodism.[38]

Daniel Evans' class, indeed, twice mentioned above, was one of the more fruitful of Strawbridge's ventures, for from it emerged a number of preachers, not only Owings and Stevenson, but Isaac Rollins (whose clouded career ended early, in 1783),[39] and Nathan Perigau, who was the instrument of the conversion of Philip Gatch, who in turn became one of the great leaders of early American Methodism.[40] The snowballing effect of spiritual forces can be seen also in the case of Freeborn Garrettson: Strawbridge was responsible for the conversion of Daniel Ruff, Daniel Ruff of Freeborn Garrettson (among many others), and Garrettson of Ezekiel Cooper (among very many others).[41] Perhaps all this is an oversimplification of the spiritual processes at work, because rarely does one cause alone govern one effect, and spiritual movements both in men and in nations usually consist (whether we can trace them or not) of a complex interweaving of many contributory and even conflicting influences, of which only ambiguous clues often remain for the historian. In this instance, however, clues, dogmatic statements, solid facts, all combine to insist that Robert Strawbridge was the central figure in an epochal spiritual work in the southern states of America before Wesley's itinerant preachers ar-

35. G. P. Baker, op. cit., p. 13.
36. Lednum, op. cit., pp. 17–18; Asbury, *Journal*, I, 54.
37. Lednum, op. cit., p. 19; G. P. Baker, op. cit., p. 8.
38. G. P. Baker, op. cit., pp. 5, 8, 13–14.
39. Asbury, *Journal*, I, 60, 90, 373, 444.
40. Lednum, op. cit., pp. 93–100; cf. John M'Lean, *Sketch of Rev. Philip Gatch*, pp. 9–18.
41. Nathan Bangs, *The Life of the Rev. Freeborn Garrettson*, pp. 37–9, 52–3; cf. J. B. Wakeley, *Lost Chapters Recovered from the Early History of American Methodism*, pp. 56–7.

rived, and that he remained the focal point of that movement long afterwards. In the process such strong personal loyalties were forged among his followers that when the English itinerants sought to bring Strawbridge into line with Wesley's practices they found themselves up against huge obstacles, and even reluctant compromises did not remove the danger of a major split between the northern conservative loyalists, led by Asbury, and the southern radical independents, led by Strawbridge.

In his early years in Maryland, perhaps as early as 1762–3, Strawbridge had taken it upon himself to baptize the infant brother of one of his converts, Henry Maynard.[42] As a layman he also administered the Sacrament of the Lord's Supper, and after the arrival of the itinerant preachers continued to urge that all of them should consider themselves authorized to do so, Church or no Church, Wesley or no Wesley. Some support for this attitude is to be found, of course, in the fact that a far greater proportion of American Methodists came from non-Church of England backgrounds than was the case in England itself, and that during and after the revolutionary period it was quite impracticable for them to receive communion at their parish churches.[43] Strawbridge had no patience with red tape, however, and his concern for sacramental worship was far greater than his concern for ecclesiastical propriety. It was because of Strawbridge's attitude that the first American Conference of 1773 made it quite clear that "every preacher who acts in connection with Mr. Wesley . . . is strictly to avoid administering the ordinances of Baptism and the Lord's Supper," and resolved in addition "in a particular manner to press the people in Maryland and Virginia to the observance of this minute."[44] The supplementary minute was the only printed hint about a secret agreement reached by the preachers upon Strawbridge. Because for so long he had been a law to himself it was deemed wiser (in his case alone) not to enforce the prohibition against preachers administering the sacraments.[45] Neither plea nor reprimand, neither including his name in the printed *Minutes* nor dropping it therefrom, made any

---

42. G. P. Baker, op. cit., pp. 12–13; cf. note 18 above.

43. E.g., John England was a Quaker, Hezekiah Bonham a Baptist, as was Mary Thorne of Philadelphia—apparently the first American woman to be appointed a class-leader (Maser, op. cit., pp. 14–15).

44. *Minutes of the Methodist Conferences, held annually in America, from 1773 to 1794, inclusive* (henceforth "*Minutes* [American, 1975]"), p. 6; cf. Lee, *History*, pp. 41, 47–8.

45. Asbury, *Journal*, I, 85.

difference to Strawbridge: he simply went on in his own gospel way.[46] There can be little question that his unseen hand was behind the southern preachers who in 1779 set up a presbytery of three and ordained each other, though the following year they agreed to accept Asbury's plea to wait until the end of the war, when Wesley's more orthodox help might be forthcoming.[47] It is not altogether surprising that on hearing of Strawbridge's death in 1781 Francis Asbury wrote: "Upon the whole, I am inclined to think the Lord took him away in judgment, because he was in the way to do hurt to His cause."[48] We must not too readily side with Asbury's tart judgment, however, for it was this same stubborn independence which had made Robert Strawbridge the outstanding lay pioneer of early American Methodism apart from Thomas Webb.

Nor in all this must we forget the major importance of Strawbridge's wife. She also was a staunch Irish Methodist, formerly Elizabeth Piper of Terryhoogan, one of the "plain, simple-hearted people" whose society Wesley termed "the mother-church of all these parts."[49] Her probing questions about his spiritual condition apparently led to the conversion of John Evans, the leader of the first society class gathered together by Strawbridge as the nucleus of the first society. Nor could her husband's wide-ranging and fruitful itinerancy have been anything like as successful without her sympathetic encouragement during his brief intervals at home, and her indomitable courage in tending their fields during his absences, aided though she was by friendly neighbors like Evans after her husband himself had left her with the trusting words, "Meat will be sent here today."[50]

The Strawbridge home was the first focal point of organized Methodism in America, and through the efforts of Strawbridge and his associates the South remained the chief stronghold of Methodism. At the first Conference, in 1773, almost half of the membership was to

---

46. Maser, op. cit., pp. 14–19.

47. Sweet, *Virginia Methodism*, pp. 79–85; Bucke, Emory Stevens, ed., *History of American Methodism* (henceforth *HAM*), I, 177–80. That the presbytery comprised the traditional number of three, rather than four, is shown by the fact that Leroy Cole was to be included only "in case of necessity."

48. Asbury, *Journal*, I, 60, 411; cf. pp. 88, 120. Strawbridge died at the home of one of his converts, Joseph Wheeler. His remains and those of his wife were later removed from Wheeler's orchard to the "Bishops' Lot" in Mount Olivet Cemetery, Baltimore (G. P. Baker, op. cit., p. 15).

49. Wesley, *Journal*, V, 114, 202.

50. Crook, op. cit., p. 154, 159; G. P. Baker, op. cit., p. 154; Bibbins, op. cit., p. 35.

be found in Maryland, and with the addition of adjoining Virginia more than half; together they surpassed the combined numbers of New York, New Jersey, and Pennsylvania.[51] With the discovery by the Reverend Edwin Schell of the Quaker records testifying to John England's status in early 1766 the sometimes bitter controversies over the priority of the North or the South may be considered settled. Nevertheless New York remains of key importance, not only because of its later significance as the capital city of the United States of America, but because it was the society there which stirred Wesley to send out his itinerant preachers as missionaries, thus strengthening American ties with the parent body, and ensuring that American Methodism (for better or worse) developed along very similar lines. Here the key lay persons were two—a man, the preacher, and a woman, the prompter.

BARBARA HECK AND PHILIP EMBURY

We are all the more appreciative of Strawbridge when we turn from him to Philip Embury, another Methodist preacher from Ireland, the one a powerful dynamo of evangelism, the other a slow-burning fuse. It seems clear that Embury emigrated to America at about the same time as Strawbridge, perhaps earlier, yet for one reason or another he failed to do the work of an evangelist for several years. We can sympathize with him, of course, and perhaps claim that Embury's mixed background offers at least a partial reason. His Irish enthusiasm was strongly tempered with slower-moving German piety. His was one of over a hundred Palatine families which in 1709 fled from the armies of Louis XIV of France, then invading southern Germany, and settled on the estates of Lord Southwell in County Limerick, Ireland, where they came under Wesley's evangelizing influence. For the most part they were sober, industrious farmers.[52]

Philip Embury was born in Ballingrane (or "Ballingarrane"), near Rathkeale, County Limerick, in 1728. He was educated by Philip Guier in German, then sent to an English school, probably in Rathkeale, where he seems to have attended the Protestant Church, and

---

51. *Minutes* (American, 1795), pp. 6–7.
52. Crook, op. cit., pp. 19–33, and Walter Allen Knittle, *The Early Eighteenth Century Palatine Emigration*, espec. pp. 1–27, 82–98, 302–3. See also Wesley, *Journal*, IV, 275–6, 397–8, V, 131.

later trained as a carpenter. On Christmas Day, 1752, he was converted, possibly as a result of hearing John Wesley preach in Limerick that August. He became both a class-leader and a local preacher among the Methodists, who had formed a society in the neighboring Palatine village of Courtmatrix, where Embury was employed as a carpenter in building the Methodist church. Here also he found a bride, Margaret Switzer, whom he married in November, 1758. Earlier that year he had been placed on Wesley's reserve list as a possible itinerant preacher.[53] In the summer of 1760, however, a group of Palatine families from the area emigrated to America in the hope of bettering their harsh lot, and Embury's last sermon in Ireland was preached from the deck of the S.S. *Perry* just before she cast off from Limerick quay for New York.[54]

Barbara Ruckle also was born in Ballingrane, at Ruckle Hill (named for her family), in 1734, six years later than her cousin Philip Embury. In the year of Embury's conversion, 1752, she also appears to have been converted and become a member of the Methodist society, at the age of eighteen.[55] While still in Ballingrane she married Paul Heck of the same village—when is not known. He also was a Methodist, and a year or two older than his wife.[56] They emigrated to New York with the same group as Embury.

After a nine-week crossing the S.S. *Perry* arrived in New York on Monday, August 11, 1760.[57] Finding no Methodist society, these four and others gravitated to their ancestral Lutheran Church, though perhaps after they had first attended one or more of the churches of the Church of England, of which they had been communicants in Ireland, as of course were most members of the Methodist society. The records of Trinity Lutheran Church list among "first communicants" at Christmas, 1760, the names of Philip Embury, Barbara Heck, and Paul Heck, and show also that children of both families were baptized during the following years.[58] Forsaking his trade as a carpenter— ac-

53. Crook, op. cit., pp. 75–81; Samuel A. Seaman, *Annals of New York Methodism*, pp. 3–9. See also Samuel J. Fanning, "Philip Embury, Founder of Methodism in New York," pp. 16–25, and p. 73, note 12, below.

54. John Atkinson, *The Beginnings of the Wesleyan Movement in America*, pp. 47–8.

55. Crook, op. cit., pp. 78–79; Charles H. Crookshank, *History of Methodism in Ireland*, I, 96.

56. Atkinson, op. cit., p. 57.

57. Ibid., p. 48.

58. Bibbins, op. cit., pp. 92–5. Another Barbara Heck is also recorded therein as communicating Sept. 25, 1757.

cording to Thomas Bell, an English Methodist immigrant, New York was overstocked with tradesmen[59]—within a few months Embury secured a livelihood as a teacher, in a schoolhouse adjoining to and apparently associated with the Lutheran Church.[60] He seems to have settled down into a conventional academic and devotional routine, as had the other Irish Palatine Methodists. Late in 1765 more of their relations and friends came from Ireland to join them, including Barbara Heck's older brother, Paul Ruckle.[61] Their arrival finally sparked Embury's call to preach.

A small book could be written about the complex historiography of this event, of which there are scores of accounts varying considerably in detail. They range from that printed by Wesley in 1768[62] to that in Jesse Lee's Short History of the Methodists of 1810, four accounts (all different) by Nathan Bangs, published in 1818, 1823, 1829, and 1838,[63] through to the age of fuller detail and greater controversy, especially over the question whether Embury himself was playing cards at the time of Barbara Heck's outburst. New evidence has continually been brought to light, even as late as 1945. The most useful surveys of the evidence are those of J. B. Wakeley (1858),[64] John Lednum (1859),[65] William Crook (1866),[66] Samuel A. Seaman (1892),[67] John Atkinson (1896),[68] William Warren Sweet (1935),[69] and Ruthella Mory Bibbins (1945),[70] though valuable details are to be found in unexpected places. For the basic outline it seems best to rely upon that given by a descendant of one of the card players, John Lawrence, as set down by Atkinson, corroborated by undocumented memories of a

59. See letter of Thomas Bell, a cabinet maker, May 1, 1769, printed in Methodist Magazine, 1807, pp. 45–6.

60. Bibbins, op. cit., pp. 90–1.

61. Crook, op. cit., pp. 88–9.

62. See Methodist History, III, No. 2 (Jan., 1965), 9–10, and below, p. 76.

63. His dedicatory discourse at the opening of the second John Street Church, New York (Atkinson, op. cit., pp. 49–51); an anonymous article in the Methodist Magazine (New York) for 1823, which Wakeley believed to be by P. P. Sandford (Lost Chapters, p. 38), but which Bangs later claimed for his own (Atkinson, op. cit., p. 60); his Life of the Rev. Freeborn Garrettson (3rd ed., 1832, pp. 13–14); and A History of the Methodist Episcopal Church I, 47–8.

64. Wakeley, Lost Chapters, pp. 34–41.

65. Lednum, op. cit., pp. 24–30.

66. Crook, op. cit., pp. 89–96.

67. Seaman, op. cit., pp. 14–21, 409–14.

68. Atkinson, op. cit., pp. 47–76.

69. William Warren Sweet, Men of Zeal, pp. 48–62.

70. Bibbins, op. cit., pp. 88–103.

contemporary letter written by Barbara Heck herself, also preserved by Atkinson. It is true, however, that both these accounts have probably been affected at some points by the long processes of oral tradition, and should be corrected or supplemented by possibly authentic details gleaned from other sources. The story we present here is composite.

The newcomers from Ireland settled down in the same area as their compatriots. Naturally Barbara Heck went to visit her brother Paul Ruckle, and he and his friends visited the Hecks. In spite of their somewhat puritanical upbringing, some of them had begun to relish card playing. It seems to have been in Barbara Heck's kitchen that a group was playing when she came in and found them at it. According to one of the players, John Lawrence, she indignantly "lifted a corner of her apron, swept the cards from the table into it with her hand, went to the fire, and cast them from her apron into the flames."[71] After delivering a scathing rebuke, "she put on her bonnet and went to Philip Embury, and said to him, 'Philip, you must preach to us, or we shall all go to hell together, and God will require our blood at your hands!'" His faltering, "Where shall I preach?" brought the swift response, "Preach in your own house!" "But who will come to hear me?" he asked. She replied, "I will come to hear you." They fixed the time, and she was as good as her word. His first congregation comprised Barbara Heck and her husband Paul, their Black servant Betty, and one of the card players, John Lawrence. This was apparently about October, 1766. Once aroused to his task, according to the testimony of his own nephew, Embury proved to be "a powerful preacher—a very powerful preacher."[72] Soon the growing congregation outgrew Embury's rented house in Augustus Street.[73] They moved to a large rigging-loft in Horse-and-Cart Street, and enrolled some of the listeners into a weekly class-meeting. Another genuine Methodist society had come into existence. When the rapidly growing society needed a permanent preaching-house, Embury turned his original trade as a carpenter to good effect, personally constructing the high pulpit, from

71. Atkinson, op. cit., p. 51. Barbara Heck's own account, as remembered by her great-grandniece, speaks of the game taking place in another house, while she "took the cards out of their hands and threw them into the fire" (ibid., pp. 67–8).

72. John Carroll, *Case and His Contemporaries*, V, 235.

73. For the location of Embury's house and the rigging loft, see Seaman, op. cit., pp. 17–18, 25.

which he preached the dedicatory sermon on October 30, 1768. Barbara Heck whitewashed the inside of the building with her own hands.[74]

Shortly after the arrival of Wesley's itinerants the tiny group mainly responsible for their coming left the city of New York to settle in Albany County up the Hudson River, in a colony apparently established by the Irish benefactor of Robert Williams, Thomas Ashton. Embury farmed in New Salem, and was Ashton's collaborator in founding the Methodist society in Ashgrove. He died suddenly, of pleurisy, in 1773.[75] His widow married John Lawrence. Almost all these early Methodists from the British Isles were loyal to the British Crown,[76] and with the approach of the Revolution the Lawrences and the Hecks moved farther north still to Canada, living for some years in Montreal, and then settling down in Augusta, Upper Canada (now Ontario), on land awarded them for their loyalty to George III. Here once more they founded a Methodist society, one of the first in Canada.[77]

ROBERT WILLIAMS

The last of the major forerunners of Wesley's regular itinerants—apart from Captain Thomas Webb, who merits a separate chapter to himself[78]—was probably (upon the evidence of his surname) a Welshman, Robert Williams. He was not in quite the same category as the other laymen, however, for he had been listed in the *Minutes* of the British Conferences for 1766, 1767, and 1768, among the itinerant preachers stationed in Ireland. Yet it is clear that he was not recognized as a fully qualified itinerant: Pilmore refers to him as a local preacher, as does Jesse Lee, the *Minutes* make no reference to his admission as an itinerant, and when his name appears in 1767 and 1768 his surname is given by initial only. Nevertheless Wesley clearly recognized in him not only the eloquence so typical of the Welsh, but a deep evangelical sincerity. It was apparently Wesley himself who sponsored a gathering in the marketplace at Whitehaven in June,

74. Seaman, op. cit., p. 39; Carroll, op. cit., I, 126.
75. Asbury, *Journal*, II, 59–60; Seaman, op. cit., pp. 47–56; Atkinson, op. cit., p. 54; Sweet, *Men of Zeal*, pp. 69–70.
76. Seaman, op. cit., pp. 457–9; cf. pp. 64–6 below.
77. Atkinson, op. cit., pp. 54–7.
78. See chap. 4 below.

1766, when Williams "preached . . . to some thousands of people, all quiet and attentive." A month later Wesley wrote to one of the Irish preachers to whom he had sent Williams as a colleague, "He is usually a reviver of the work wherever he comes." When indeed revival broke out in northern Ireland, Wesley gave credit to Williams along with his colleagues, because they were "all men devoted to God, men of a single eye, whose whole heart is in the work, and who 'constantly trample on pleasure and pain.' "[79]

Yet Wesley was not prepared to sponsor Williams for the American cause, perhaps partly because he thought that his limited gifts were best employed as an auxiliary evangelist rather than as an itinerant preacher who needed organizing ability and disciplinary firmness. Another factor was undoubtedly his tactless criticism of the Anglican clergy.[80] Robert Williams did at least succeed, however, in securing Wesley's permission that he should travel at his own expense, provided that he remained subject to the itinerants when they arrived. This agreement was almost certainly reached in early May, 1769, when during his biennial preaching tour of Ireland Wesley came to the Castlebar circuit, where Williams was stationed.[81] Wesley was not to make his final appeal at the Leeds Conference for another three months, by which time Williams was on the high seas. In agreeing to pay his own way Williams apparently had some business venture in mind, in addition to his urge to preach, probably (as William Warren Sweet suggested) the publication and sale of Methodist literature.[82] Eventually he succeeded in persuading another Irish layman, Thomas Ashton, not only to defray the cost of his passage but to emigrate with him. Selling his horse to pay his debts, Williams arrived at the quay carry-

79. Pilmore, *Journal*, p. 25, quoted below, p. 46, and note 87; Lee, *History*, p. 26; for other preachers stationed by initials only, see *WHS* X, 154-7. (Of the preachers there named only George Guthrie was listed among those officially admitted both on trial and into Full Connexion, followed by two years of stationing by initials only, and then his disappearance from the *Minutes*. In one other instance, that of Thomas Vasey, later to be ordained by Wesley for America, three years of stationing by initials was followed in 1778 by his acceptance into Full Connexion and his normal listing on the stations from that time forward.) For Wesley's implied appreciation of Williams see Wesley, *Journal*, V, 173, and *Letters*, V, 23, 46-7. For his continued doubt about Williams' efficacy in the regular pastoral ministry note his remark to Thomas Rankin that Williams would do good in New York "for a little time" (*Letters*, VI, 57).

80. Wesley, *Journal*, V, 315-16. A similar reference to "Mr. W—ms" in 1743 (III, 74-5) probably refers to another Welsh preacher, Thomas Williams.

81. Ibid., V, 315-16.

82. Sweet, *Virginia Methodism*, p. 49n. This certainly occupied a major portion of Asbury's time in winding up Williams' estate (Asbury, *Journal*, III, 61, 355).

ing his saddlebags, a bottle of milk, a loaf of bread, and an empty purse.[83]

Williams and Ashton apparently disembarked in Philadelphia, and were welcomed by the Methodist society there, who on September 2 both contributed towards Williams' shipboard expenses and saw to washing his clothes before he set out for New York. Before leaving he also set in hand his first publication, from the press of John Dunlap of Philadelphia—the same printer who later issued the first copies of the Declaration of Independence.[84] Arriving in New York early in September, he took pastoral charge of the John Street society, and remained in fairly close touch with them (apart from frequent excursions to the South) for two years, as witness items of expenditure for him in the old account book there, stretching from September 20, 1769, to August 30, 1771.[85] In New York also he issued what was surely one of the first class-tickets in America, dated October 1, 1769.[86] As soon as Richard Boardman reached the city at the end of October, Williams left on a visit to Baltimore via Philadelphia, where the newly arrived Pilmore was able to assess his worth: "He came over to America about business, and, being a local preacher in England, Mr. Wesley gave him a license to preach occasionally under the direction of the regular preachers. During his stay in the city he preached several times, and seemed to have a real desire to do good. His gifts are but small, yet he may be useful to the country people, who are, in general, as sheep without shepherds."[87]

Robert Williams did indeed preach with good effect down much of the eastern seaboard. Strawbridge's hands were strengthened in Maryland, and new opportunities were opened up in Virginia and North Carolina. During the summer of 1770 he continued to itinerate between New York, Philadelphia, and Maryland. Tradition tells of

83. Lee, *History*, pp. 26–7.
84. Tees, op. cit., pp. 102–4, and illustration facing p. 104. Cf. Lee, *History*, p. 27. Although Lee does not specifically mention Philadelphia as the place from which he "went to New York," this would be the normal port of entry, and according to a tradition preserved by Josias Dallam he carried commendatory letters to people in Philadelphia and Baltimore (Atkinson, op. cit., pp. 102–4). The other part of Dallam's tradition, however, that he was on a Baltimore-bound vessel which was forced by bad weather to put in at Norfolk, Virginia, surely refers to a later voyage. Cf. Sweet, *Virginia Methodism* pp. 49–51, and G. P. Baker, op. cit., p. 18.
85. Wakeley, *Lost Chapters*, pp. 192–4.
86. Ibid., pp. 194–6; cf. pp. 414–25.
87. Pilmore, *Journal*, p. 25. The "license" mentioned here almost certainly does not imply a formal document, but probably a commentatory letter from Wesley.

his preaching from a fallen tree trunk in Harford County, Maryland, where one of those greatly moved was Freeborn Garrettson.[88] He warmed Pilmore's heart with stories of the spiritual awakening in Maryland, so that Pilmore referred to this as the area where "the sacred fire is continually spreading wider and wider."[89] He preached the first Methodist sermon in Norfolk, Virginia, of which an eyewitness account survives in the diary of John Littlejohn: "He came in a boat from Craney Island, mounted the highest steps of the courthouse, and commenced singing, 'Come sinners, to the gospel feast,' and I looked out at the door and said to my shop mates, 'There is a crazy fellow at the courthouse. I will go and see him.' . . . Mr. Williams had a very large concourse to hear him, and when he had done they opened to the right and left and he walked through them, . . . having made an appointment to return in a few weeks. This was the commencement of Methodist preaching in this place." He was followed by William Watters, and then by Joseph Pilmore, who organized societies there and in Portsmouth.[90]

Pilmore seems to have revised his views of Williams' gifts, for he gladly welcomed him to his own pulpit whenever he was in town.[91] Williams, indeed, was even such a reformed character that he managed not only to remain on good terms with the evangelical Virginia clergyman, Devereux Jarratt, but to secure his hearty co-operation with Methodism, a major factor in spreading the great spiritual awakening in Virginia.[92] Jarratt described Williams (apparently choosing his adjectives very carefully) as "a plain, artless, indefatigable preacher of the gospel."[93] Jesse Lee, the apostle of New England Methodism, counted himself one of Williams' spiritual children.[94]

Like Strawbridge before him, however, Robert Williams remained too independent of control for Francis Asbury, who was especially troubled by his ventures as publisher and bookseller "for the sake of

88. Atkinson, op. cit., pp. 198–200.

89. Pilmore, *Journal*, p. 48; cf. p. 46.

90. Sweet, *Virginia Methodism*, pp. 49–54.

91. Pilmore, *Journal*, pp. 61, 85, 96.

92. Lee, *History*, pp. 42–3; Wesley M. Gewehr, *The Great Awakening in Virginia, 1749–1790*, pp. 143–7; Sweet, *Virginia Methodism*, pp. 60–71.

93. *A Brief Narrative of the Revival of Religion in Virginia*, p. 6. This pamphlet, originally published by John Wesley (Frank Baker, *Union Catalogue of the Publications of John and Charles Wesley*, No. 330), was incorporated in Asbury's *Journal* (I, 209). In his *History* (p. 43), Jesse Lee uses exactly the same words, without indicating that he is quoting.

94. Lee, *History*, p. 53.

gain," rather than solely for the benefit of the Methodist societies.[95] Although he never put his own name as publisher on the title pages, he seems to have reprinted at least ten of Wesley's publications before the British Conference rule about preachers not printing anything without Wesley's approval was reinforced by the 1773 American Conference.[96] Until that time, however, Williams was in an anomalous position, as in part a local preacher seeking to support himself. Nor is there any doubt that he did concentrate upon dispersing literature which directly supported his ministry, and which proved generally helpful.

Williams relied greatly upon song as the spearhead of evangelism (as did Wesley), and it is therefore appropriate that his first publication was Charles Wesley's *Hymns for the Nativity of our Lord,* for three hundred copies of which the Philadelphia Society paid the local printer John Dunlap, October 7, 1769. It was probably Williams also who was responsible for Dunlap's reprint of Wesley's *Hymns and Spiritual Songs* in 1770, as well as for his *Hymns for those that seek, and those that have, Redemption,* and four sermons printed by James Adams of Wilmington, Delaware, also in 1770. In all probability he also sponsored the printing by Isaac Collins of Burlington, New Jersey, in 1771 and 1773, of Wesley's *Collection of Psalms and Hymns,* along with reprints of the other two major hymnbooks. None of these suggestions, however, are so far susceptible of absolute proof.[97]

From 1773 onwards Williams was listed as one of the itinerant preachers, both in the British and the American *Minutes,* and therefore came under the printing prohibition, except that by a special American minute he was allowed to sell the books he still had on hand. He did more than that, however. Later that year he secured (though apparently never utilized) Wesley's permission to print his *Explanatory Notes upon the New Testament*—though on Wesley's account, not his own. He also printed (surely again with permission) Wesley's editions of Kempis' *Christian's Pattern* (of which no copy seems to have survived), and of Baxter's *Saints Everlasting Rest,* of

95. Asbury, *Journal,* I, 742.

96. *Minutes of the Methodist Conference,* I (1744–98), 51 (1765); *Minutes* (American, 1795), p. 6.

97. Baker, *Union Catalogue,* Nos. 84 (and Tees, op. cit., pp. 102–4), 30, 33, 33A, 56, 105, 165, 200.i, 266, and the sermon, *The Great Salvation,* by the Irish preacher, Thomas Walsh, printed by Adams in 1770. Fuller details will be presented in my forthcoming *Bibliography* of Wesley's publications. Cf. also James Penn Pilkington, *The Methodist Publishing House: A History,* I, 26–36.

which four extant copies are known.[98] This was printed in 1774 by Collins of Burlington—which tends to confirm our suggestion of Williams' responsibility for the hymnbooks printed earlier by Collins.

Both as publisher and as preacher Robert Williams played an important part in the opening years of American Methodism, for most of that time as a layman, and in preaching his funeral sermon in 1775 Asbury paid him high tribute: "Perhaps no one in America has been an instrument of awakening so many souls as God has awakened by him."[99]

What a stirring pageant rolls before our eyes as we recall these lay pioneers of American Methodism! Yet we have only touched all too briefly upon a fraction of those whose names we know, let alone the many whose names are unknown to historians, though not to their Maker. Some have long had the spotlight of attention playing upon them; more deserve it. There were unknown preachers such as the Methodist ship's carpenter who preached in Philadelphia while his ship was docked there.[100] Others were helpful in a more general way, like John Evans of Frederick County, Maryland, who both opened his home for Methodist meetings and looked after Strawbridge's farm while he was away on his preaching journeys. Many gave the support of their money, like Thomas Ashton, the Irish layman who paid for Robert Williams' passage to America, and later became the mainstay of the Methodist cause at Ashgrove to which for a time the Emburys and the Hecks gravitated. Sometimes these supporters were apparently not Methodists themselves, like Joseph Forbes, the simple-minded young gentleman who lent his established credit to the infant Methodist cause in New York to enable them to purchase land for their first chapel.[101] Still others worked as quiet encouragers behind the scenes. Such was Thomas Taylor, whose written appeal for help not only proved most influential in recruiting itinerant preachers for America, but also supplies us with our most vivid contemporary account of American Methodist beginnings before their arrival.[102] These and many others, men and women, old and young, rich and poor, educated and influential, illiterate and humble, were alike in one thing—their

98. Asbury, *Journal*, III, 61; Baker, *Union Catalogue*, Nos. 26 and 131.ix.
99. Asbury, *Journal*, I, 164.
100. Lednum, op. cit., p. xiv.
101. See *Methodist History*, III, No. 2 (Jan., 1965), 12. Pilmore (*Journal*, p. 28), describes Forbes as "non compos mentis."
102. Ibid., pp. 13–15, and chap. 5 below.

readiness to spend of themselves for the good of their neighbors and the glory of God. They waited for no directives from above, no organization by full-time ordained ministers, no financial sponsors, but answered the call of God in simple yet mighty faith, conscious of their own limitations, but conscious even more of the unlimited resources of their almighty Father.

4. CAPTAIN THOMAS WEBB, CONSOLIDATOR

Captain Thomas Webb is familiar to all students of early Methodism in America, though too little is known about the man himself. He strides onto the pages of our history books, a green patch covering the socket of the right eye lost under General Wolfe; he lays his sword by the open Bible and announces himself as a soldier of the cross and a spiritual son of John Wesley. He builds a chapel for the Methodists, and is gone. He comes from nowhere and disappears into oblivion.

True, he finds a niche in the *Dictionary of American Biography* (not, be it noted, in its older British counterpart), but the information given is meager and somewhat misleading. What manner of man was he? What were his actual connections with the British army? With the American revolutionaries? When, where, and to whom was he married? Did he leave any family? What kind of a preacher was he? What happened to him after he left America? Why has no biography of him ever been written?

The last question is perhaps the easiest to answer first. As a matter of fact some memoirs were prepared upon his death in 1796, as part of a funeral oration (of thirty-two printed pages) by a Methodist preacher named John Pritchard, a work now extremely rare. Several later writers have set out to prepare a biography, but many of the seeds of desire have fallen upon the stony ground of lack of evidence, or have been choked by the discouraging weeds of inaccuracy in the traditional evidence that is readily available; still others have been devoured by the birds of the air in the shape of descendants of Webb who appear to have destroyed papers that might be interpreted to his discredit. I confess that I too have for years been gathering material about him, and have at times been greatly discouraged. The evidence keeps accumulating, however, and a full biography remains a possibility. This study attempts something much more modest, a snapshot rather than a portrait.

Thomas Webb was extremely reticent about his family background. Clearly he was an Englishman, and apparently a west country man,

Read before the Northeastern Jurisdiction of Methodist Historical Societies, Washington, D.C., April 16, 1962. Published in *Religion in Life*, Summer, 1965, pp. 406–41.

both Bath and Salisbury offering themselves as possible parental homes. The year of his birth has previously been guessed from the date of his death and his reported age at the time. Ten years before his death, however, he felt himself failing, and wrote a letter to his eldest son containing such rare personal details that Charles Webb endorsed it: "This letter contains my Father's age." What Thomas Webb wrote on April 15, 1786, was this: "I have no reason to believe that I shall tarry many years here, as I am 61 years of Age the 31st of next May, and I find that I grow weaker and weaker every day; therefore I would not have you be surprised if you hear of my death, as all mankind must pay their debt on account of sin."[1] Thus he was born on May 31, 1725, and at his death on December 20, 1796, he was not in fact "aged 72" (as his memorial tablet states—there is no record of age in the burial register) but in his seventy-second year.[2]

THE WOUNDED SOLDIER

The twenty-nine-year-old Webb secured a commission as quartermaster in the 48th Regiment of Foot on October 29, 1754. The following year, on November 9, he was promoted to lieutenant in the same regiment, which was transferred two days later to a new colonel, Daniel Webb.

"Webb's" regiment (regimental numbers were rarely used), with Thomas Webb as one of its handful of lieutenants, was among the reinforcements brought to America in 1758 to stem the advance of the French in the north as the Seven Years' War, begun in 1756, extended itself across the Atlantic. On July 26, 1758, the tide turned with the capture of Louisburg by Generals Amherst and Wolfe; Webb's memorial tablet claims that "at the siege of Louisburg" he lost an eye. The following year, on September 18, Quebec surrendered to the British, both Wolfe and Montcalm losing their lives. This even more famous engagement has also been pointed out as the occasion when Webb lost his eye, though one version credits him with a mere wounded arm at the scaling of the Heights of Abraham.

The legends surrounding General Wolfe baffle readers eager to dis-

1. MS letter in Methodist Archives, 25–35, City Road, London, England.
2. Tablet and register formerly at Portland Methodist Chapel, Bristol, England, now at John Wesley's Chapel ("The New Room"), Bristol. For an illustrated account of Portland Chapel, see a valuable article on Webb by Marvin E. Harvey in *Together*, Oct., 1963, pp. 26–9. For a full history see A. J. Lambert, *The Chapel on the Hill*, illus.

cover what kind of a man and a general he really was. Legends have also grown up around that very junior officer in his army named Thomas Webb, sometimes even to the point of hinting that he was Wolfe's righthand man. Perhaps this is partly Webb's own fault. The heats of war distort men's recollections. Particularly is this true when events are recalled through the haze of distant memory, after separate happenings have flowed together into a unity, and tiny dramatic embellishments have disguised themselves as truth. It is true that the 48th Regiment of Foot was present at both actions; indeed, Thomas Webb volunteered for the hazardous task of carrying scaling ladders at the storming of Louisburg. He was not present, however, when Wolfe conquered Quebec. The truth is romantic, but slightly less romantic than the legend. He lost his eye during the Battle of Montmorency on July 31, 1759, a year after Louisburg and almost two months before Quebec, though still in the same campaign under General Wolfe. It is understandable that Montmorency was not greatly publicized in the English press, and that Webb's memory of the specific engagement was occasionally submerged in the general campaign, for Montmorency was a devastating French victory which certainly delayed the capture of Quebec, and did not show Wolfe at his best as a general.[3]

From his camp six miles north of Quebec, on the far side of the Montmorency River, Wolfe had long been wondering how to secure a foothold nearer the city. At length he took to boats and attacked the French entrenchments along the cliffs lining the junction of the Montmorency and the St. Lawrence. The men climbing the steep slopes were mowed down so that many of the wounded had to be left behind—for scalping by the waiting Indians. Only a thunderstorm prevented the defeat from becoming a massacre. Wolfe recorded 210 killed and 230 wounded, including one colonel and 27 junior officers. Among these was Webb. A musket ball hit the socket of his right eye, was diverted through the eyeball, passed through his palate into his mouth, and was then swallowed. His only recollection was a flash of light as his eye was destroyed. He was one of the fortunate men carried to a boat. With help, all were landed except Webb. Looking at him one of the men said, "He needs no help; he is dead enough." Just then Webb's senses returned for a moment and he croaked, "No, I am not dead." They struggled ashore with him, but it was three months

3. Marvin E. Harvey, "The Wives of Thomas Webb and Their Kin," 154.

before he was fit to carry out any duties. Not for him the task of scaling the Heights of Abraham![4]

That summer of 1759 was memorable for Lieutenant Thomas Webb for another reason. He became an author. While in winter quarters he had prepared a volume which was intended as a stepping stone to military promotion. The work was advertised in the issues of the *Pennsylvania Journal* for May 24 and 31 as "in the press, and will speedily be published by subscription." It was printed by William Dunlap of Philadelphia—a slight book of 112 pages entitled *A Military Treatise on the Appointments of the Army*. Webb offered "many hints, not touched upon before by any author," and proposed "some new regulations in the army, which will be particularly useful in carrying on the war in North-America." His observations included the criticism that British weapons were generally too heavy for American service, and that one of the chief problems was securing good flints. The dedication to Admiral Boscawen sought pardon for any shortcomings, assigning as a reason what was also a broad hint: "humbly relying on your well known goodness, that you will pass over those defects of observation, whose origin may perhaps be the want of a more enlarged sphere of action." There is an interesting sequel. In 1774, when General Washington needed a treatise on military discipline in anticipation of war with Britain, the only one that his aide-de-camp could discover in Philadelphia was this by Webb, which Washington therefore read, and presumably turned to good service against the British. His copy now reposes in the Boston Athenaeum.[5]

Five years went by, and the Seven Years' War (or French and Indian War) had been over for a year before Webb was finally recommended for a captaincy and the command of a company in "Webb's" regiment—whether as a reward for scholarship, bravery, or seniority, or a combination of all three, we do not know. By that time, however, his circumstances had altered. He was a married man. The bond for his marriage with Mary Arding of New York, dated August 29, 1760, has been discovered by Dr. Marvin E. Harvey in New York's colonial records, badly damaged by a disastrous fire in 1911. Rather than re-

---

4. *Wesleyan Methodist Magazine*, 1849, pp. 385–90, from the recollections of Joseph Sutcliffe, who heard Webb tell his own story many years earlier. Cf. *Wes. Meth. Mag.*, 1844, pp. 518–26, 647–58, for some literary embellishments.

5. For Washington's purchase, see *A Catalogue of the Washington Collection in the Boston Athenaeum*, p. 220. The copy itself is in crisp condition, apparently not much used.

turn to the British Isles with his regiment, even as a captain, he refused the promotion, and shortly afterwards retired from active duty on half a lieutenant's pay. He was, however, accorded the courtesy title belonging to the proffered captaincy. To augment his income, on July 2, 1764, he took over nominal duties as barrack master at Albany. The next we know is that the man who sacrificed promotion to stay in America with his wife and child did in fact return to his native land. This may well have been because of the death of his wife, though so far no record of this has been discovered. In any case he wanted to sell his army commission, and this could best be done in England. His infant son (and possibly his wife) would be in good hands with the Arding family.[6]

THE SOLDIER PREACHER

The sober man of thirty-nine or forty who returned to England was very different from the boisterous youth who had set out on high adventure in a new land six years earlier. Webb was certainly maimed in body, and apparently maimed in spirit by bereavement. From our vantage point after the event we can see that he was ripe for conversion. During the winter of 1764–5 he underwent a lengthy period of deep depression, so convinced that he was a sinner past redemption that he contemplated suicide. In a dream he was directed to a Moravian minister named Cary, who invited Webb to hear him preach the following day—apparently March 24, 1765. While the minister discoursed on the sufferings of Christ—it was Passion Sunday—Webb experienced a vision of the Saviour bearing his sins on the Cross, and "in a moment his burden was removed, peace and joy through believing filled his mind." Soon afterwards (according to Pritchard) "it pleased the Lord to strengthen him with repeated tokens of His favour; giving him a full assurance of hope that he should one day be with Him in glory, which assurance he enjoyed to the day of his death."[7]

Cary introduced Webb to the Rev. James Rouquet, one of Whitefield's converts, who in his turn recommended him to the Method-

6. *WHS*, XXXIII, 155–6.

7. John Pritchard, *Sermon Occasioned by the Death of the late Capt. Webb*, Bristol, Edwards, 1797, p. 13. Pritchard says the occasion was March 23; Charles Atmore, *The Methodist Memorial*, p. 445, states that it was the twenty-fifth; in fact the nearest Sunday was the twenty-fourth.

ists, whom Webb found so spiritually congenial that he determined to live and die with them.[8] His debut as a public speaker occurred at Bath. When the expected preacher did not arrive for a service Webb was prevailed upon to recount in public what he had often told in private, the story of his own conversion. The romantic appeal of the scarred warrior's dramatic narrative, coupled with a rough eloquence, ensured his instant success.

His army commission sold, in 1766 Webb returned as a civilian to resume his modest duties at Albany. He tried to make the best of both worlds by retaining his military uniform and the courtesy title of captain—an ostentation which during the War of American Independence caused him serious embarrassment. Nevertheless his had been a genuine conversion, and he carried his religion and his Methodist practices back with him. Many features of his second sojourn in America are obscure, but these six years constituted probably the most fruitful period of his life, when crucial steps were taken to consolidate the feeble and scattered beginnings of American Methodist activity. At Albany he made a point of holding family prayer meetings for his household, to which he invited friends and neighbors. Once more he recited his spiritual experience, adding a word of exhortation. Once more his rough-hewn preaching touched people's hearts and proved a means of conversion, so that soon "he was encouraged to go farther still, even into the highways and hedges" —according to tradition as far as Schenectady. He proclaimed the central evangelical truths, with especial emphasis upon Christian perfection.[9]

Thomas Webb's wife Mary had a brother, Charles Arding. In June, 1766, Arding married Abigail Van Wyke, and they settled on a sixty-acre farm at Jamaica on Long Island, a few miles north of what was to be Kennedy Airport. Early in 1767 Webb himself took a house nearby, apparently in order to be close to his young son Charles, who either then or later was informally adopted by the childless couple, was set up in business by his uncle Charles, and was eventually made sole executor of his will and residuary legatee after the death of his aunt Abigail.[10] Webb now had a new territory for his Methodist evan-

8. For Rouquet, incumbent of St. Werburgh's, see A. Barrett Sackett, *James Rouquet and His Part in Early Methodism.*

9. Pritchard, op. cit., p. 15; Asbury, *Journal,* II, 542.

10. *WHS,* XXXIII, 155. Cf. Webb's correspondence with his son Charles, in the Methodist Archives, London.

gelism. He preached in his own house "and several other places on Long Island" to such good effect that within six months twenty-four people had been converted, "near half of them Whites, the rest Negroes." This he spoke of figuratively as "felling the trees on Long Island."[11]

From Long Island Webb was able to spend a good deal of time in New York. Hearing of the infant Methodist society there, in February, 1767, he sought them out in the hired room near the barracks, to which they had moved from Embury's home. His appearance in full regimentals before the small company must have constituted something of a shock, but after the service they found that he was truly one of them. They invited him to preach. It was Webb's preaching, indeed, that necessitated the move to the rigging loft in Horse-and-cart Street—in more sophisticated days renamed William Street.[12]

Webb was also one of the prime movers behind the purchase by lease and re-lease on March 29 and 30, 1768, of two lots of land on John Street where a chapel could be built. The final conveyance of the John Street property to permanent trustees was not effected until late in 1770, after Richard Boardman and Joseph Pilmore had arrived from England. Once again Webb was one of the signatories. Already the chapel had been built, and Webb's contribution of £30 headed the subscription list, though a later gift of his former military colleague William Lupton brought his offering also up to this sum, and James Jarvis gave two amounts of £10. Webb added the interest of £3 4s. which he had received on a further £200 lent for the building expenses. He also begged £32 from his friends of Philadelphia, and apparently raised money for building the chapel by selling books. Undoubtedly he was the strong pillar on which the New York society was raised to eminence.[13]

Even in his semi-retirement Thomas Webb was an energetic man. Long Island and New York could by no means hold him. In 1767 we find him in Philadelphia—far more the metropolis of those days than New York. Here again a small group was already meeting, keeping alive the evangelical flame kindled by George Whitefield. Once more the group worshiped in a rigging loft—on Dock Creek. Again Webb's bustling enthusiasm soon had them organized into a lively Methodist

11. See Thomas Taylor's letter to Wesley, April 11, 1768, *Methodist History*, III, No. 2 (Jan., 1965), 10.

12. Loc. cit.; see p. 76 below.   13. Ibid., p. 13.

society, which moved to more commodious quarters in a tavern in Loxley Court. In October, 1769, Boardman and Pilmore arrived to find a society a hundred strong and ripe for building a chapel. A month later, with encouragement and active support from Webb, Miles Pennington purchased on their behalf a half-finished meeting-house which had proved a white elephant for the German Reformed congregation. On November 26, 1769, Captain Webb preached the opening Sunday morning sermon in this chapel, which became St. George's Church, and when Pennington conveyed the property to nine Methodist trustees the following year Webb's name came next after the two itinerant preachers from England. A year later still he was one of the key figures trying to liquidate the debt on St. George's by ventures in state lotteries in England, in which evangelical ministers like John Newton and William Grimshaw had participated without undue qualms, and in which John Wesley also was indirectly concerned, as Grimshaw's agent.[14]

By this time Webb had moved to new headquarters, though they appear to have been only temporary. The letter about the lottery was written from Trenton, New Jersey, where Webb was laid up with gout, but redeeming his enforced immobility by preaching in his lodgings. He may well have preached in Trenton earlier, and the formation of the Methodist society there was at least partially due to his enthusiasm, though the credit is also given to one of his converts, Joseph Toy, who had moved from Burlington. Webb had preached in the market place and also in the courthouse at Burlington in 1770, and on December 14 formed there the first Methodist society in New Jersey, leaving Toy in charge.[15] A rival claimant for the honor of being the first New Jersey society is Pemberton, then called New Mills. Once more it was Webb who founded the cause, about 1769 or 1770. Here he later made one of his permanent homes—if a wanderer such as he can be said ever to have had a permanent home.[16]

Almost wherever we turn along the central eastern seaboard we hear of Captain Thomas Webb, as pioneer preacher, as founder or stabilizer of the Methodist societies. In New York state he had

14. Letter from Webb to Daniel Montgomery, another trustee of St. George's, Dec. 27, 1771, of which a copy is preserved at Drew University. Cf. Cliffe, op. cit., pp. 32–3.
15. *Methodist Magazine* (New York), 1826, pp. 438–9.
16. Lednum, op. cit., pp. 49–51; Asbury, *Journal*, I, 29, 31.

preached at Albany and apparently at Schenectady, though any societies that he founded there did not survive the Revolution. In addition to his support of the infant New York society and the founding of one in Jamaica, Long Island, he also preached the first Methodist sermon in Newton, Long Island, and founded a society there in the home of James Harper, whose grandsons built up the publishing firm of Harper and Brothers.[17] He was the pioneer in New Jersey, especially in Trenton, Burlington, and Pemberton. Similarly he was the constructive leader in Philadelphia and the pioneer in other areas of Pennsylvania, such as the oldest town, Chester, and Bristol, where he preached under a tree which became a Methodist landmark.[18] He led the way also in Delaware, both at Wilmington, where he formed the first society after preaching in the open air and in Jacob Stedham's home, and at New Castle, where the society organized in Robert Furness' tavern was at first more prosperous than that in Wilmington.[19] Joseph Pilmore even claimed Webb as the fellow pioneer with Robert Strawbridge in Maryland, writing in 1769: "The work that God began by him and Mr. Strawbridge, a local preacher from Ireland, soon spread through the greatest part of Baltimore County, and several hundreds of people were brought to repentance, and turned to the Lord."[20]

RETURN FOR REINFORCEMENTS

Webb did much, but more was needed. In April, 1768, Thomas Taylor wrote to John Wesley from New York the letter which we have briefly noted. Boardman and Pilmore answered the call, and were welcomed to Philadelphia by Webb, who may well have added his own plea to Wesley.[21] He certainly seems to have valued their cooperation, and even their leadership. Further help was slow in arriving, in spite of renewed appeals, but in 1771 two more preachers came, Richard Wright and Francis Asbury. Early in 1772 Webb him-

---

17. Asbury, *Journal*, I, 540n. 19. Ibid., pp. 55–9.
18. Lednum, op. cit., pp. xiv–xvi. 20. Pilmore, *Journal*, p. 25.
21. Thomas Coke and Henry Moore, *Life of the Rev. John Wesley*, p. 449, claims as much, and this seems most likely. They do not mention Taylor's letter, however, and no trace of Webb's appears to have survived, so that we cannot be certain that he wrote to Wesley. Who else, however, was more likely to send the appeal for the Methodists in Maryland, as noted in Pilmore, *Journal*, p. 15?

self returned to England once more, apparently with the set purpose of pleading the cause of American Methodism in person.

When the Methodist Conference assembled in Leeds on August 4, 1772, Thomas Webb was there. The published *Minutes*, as usual, furnish little more than an outline of administrative arrangements, and make no reference either to Webb or America. George Shadford's journal takes us behind the scenes: "When he [Captain Webb] warmly exhorted preachers to go to America, I felt my spirit stirred within me to go; more especially when I understood that many hundreds of precious souls were perishing through lack of knowledge, scattered up and down in various parts of the woods, and had none to warn them of their danger. . . . Accordingly, Mr. Rankin and I offered ourselves to go the spring following."[22] Rankin's own journal shows that he had several conversations with the enthusiastic captain about America, but he was a little skeptical, realizing that Webb "had a lively imagination and was always ready to dwell upon the marvellous."[23]

For a few months Webb served Wesley as an itinerant preacher at large. His fame mushroomed. In spite of himself even John Wesley was impressed, writing in his *Journal*: "I admire the wisdom of God in still raising up various preachers according to the various tastes of men. The Captain is all life and fire; therefore, although he is not deep or regular, yet many who would not hear a better preacher flock together to hear him. And many are convinced under his preaching, some justified, a few built up in love."[24] He even hinted that Webb's popularity might have a salutary effect on the well known Calvinist minister Rowland Hill, by forcing him into the background, and in fact according to Charles Wesley when Webb preached in Bath—one of Hill's favorite stamping grounds—the people deserted the Countess of Huntingdon's chapel to hear him.[25] Nevertheless Charles Wesley was far less impressed than was his brother. In the secrecy of shorthand he added a passage to one letter from Bristol: "Your captain has done much good; because God sends by whom he will. He is a strange man, and very much of an enthusiast. Cannot you persuade him to

22. Thomas Jackson, ed., *Lives of Early Methodist Preachers*, VI, 162.

23. Thomas Rankin, MS Journal, at Garrett Theological Seminary, Evanston, Illinois, p. 3.

24. Wesley, *Journal*, V, 497.

25. Wesley, *Letters*, VI, 8; MS letter of Charles Wesley to Joseph Benson, Jan. 19, 1773, at Duke University, Durham, N.C.

keep his abundance of visions and revelations to himself? At least not to publish them indifferently to all. I have heard him myself. He has much life and zeal, though far from being a clear or good preacher." To which John in London replied laconically: "He has been long enough with you; send him to us."[26] John Wesley even despatched Webb to Ireland to clear up some Methodist problems there by his fiery evangelism, and Mrs. Bennis wrote gratefully from Limerick: "Our society is once more more readjusted; we all seem to be in love and in earnest. Captain Webb's visit has proved a blessing; our house was not large enough for the congregations."[27] In Dublin also he reclaimed for Wesley's society a crowd of hearers who had been drawn away by one of the Countess of Huntingdon's preachers.[28]

The activity of the Calvinistic Countess and her preachers, indeed, became a major reason for securing further reinforcements for America in addition to Shadford and Rankin. In October, 1772, Lady Selina had sent over the Reverend William Piercy (or Percy)[29] and some of her students to Philadelphia, and Webb wanted an adequate counterattraction. He set his heart on Joseph Benson, a scholarly level-headed man, as well as a warmhearted evangelist. Indeed Webb was sure by a divine impression that Benson *must* be the man, and managed to persuade John Fletcher of Madeley that he was right. Benson demurred, and found an ally in Charles Wesley, who compared Webb to a former Methodist preacher who had caused a tremendous furore by prophesying the end of the world on February 28, 1763: "The Captain's impressions are no more (or very little more) to be depended on than George Bell's. He is an inexperienced, honest, zealous, loving enthusiast."[30] Even John Wesley concurred, telling Benson: "An impression on the mind of another man is no rule of action to you."[31] Frustrated, Webb turned to Joseph Yerbury (or Yearbry), a local preacher from Bradford-on-Avon, who unofficially accompanied the party, found that he was not cut out to be a Method-

26. MS letter of Charles Wesley to John Wesley, Dec. 8, 1772, at Methodist Archives, London; Wesley, *Letters*, VI, 6.

27. Wesley, *Letters*, V, 343.

28. MS letter, Charles Wesley to Joseph Benson, Jan. 19, 1773, at Duke University, Durham, N.C.

29. Later minister of St. Michael's, Charleston, S.C.; see George Walton Williams, *Early Ministers at St. Michael's, Charleston*, pp. 65–78.

30. MS letter, Charles Wesley to Joseph Benson, March 6, 1773, at Duke University, Durham, N.C.

31. Wesley, *Letters*, VI, 20.

ist preacher, and returned to England in 1774 with Richard Wright, having prudently taken along with him sufficient broadcloth to defray the cost of his return passage.[32]

Personal as well as public concerns brought Thomas Webb into touch with the Reverend John Fletcher of Madeley. Webb was preparing to marry his second wife, Grace Gilbert, sister of Nathaniel Gilbert, the pioneer of Methodism in Antigua. Maybe he had known her before coming to England; just possibly he was connected with some of the Webbs of Antigua. At any rate the following record was entered in the parish register at Whitchurch: "Thomas Webb Esq., of the City of New York, widower, and Grace Gilbert of this parish of Whitchurch, Spinster, were married in this Church (by licence) this twelfth day of February in the year of our Lord 1773, by me, John Fletcher, vicar of Madeley." Webb was forty-seven, his bride probably about forty. She was not too old to bear him two children—a son, given her family name of Gilbert, and a daughter Mary, named after one of the numerous Marys in her own family, one suspects, rather than after her husband's first wife.

THIRD AMERICAN CAMPAIGN

Captain Thomas Webb, experienced traveler and ex-quartermaster, took charge of all the outfitting for the little Methodist expedition to America. On Good Friday, April 9, 1773, he and his new bride, together with Rankin, Shadford, Yerbury, and another gentleman named Rowbotham about whom nothing is known, set sail from Pill near Bristol in the *Sally*, commanded by Captain Young. After a "comfortable passage of eight weeks," during which Webb shared preaching duties with the others, on June 1 they arrived safely to a warm welcome in Philadelphia. Rankin summoned the first American Conference in July, and commented wryly on what he considered the slipshod state of American Methodism, so different from "the wonderful accounts [he] had heard in England, and during [their] passage."[33] He also wrote critically of Webb to Wesley, who replied: "Dear Tommy, Captain Webb does not wilfully tell lies, but he speaks incautiously; so that we must make large allowances for this whenever he speaks, otherwise we shall be deceived. But where is

32. Jackson, *Early Methodist Preachers*, V, 185, and Rankin, MS Journal, p. 105.
33. Ibid., V, 183, 185-7, 193.

he now, and what is he doing? I fear his wife will have need of patience."[34]

Captain Webb had apparently taken his wife to a home "on the Green Bank" at Burlington, New Jersey. Here they struck up warm friendships with their Quaker neighbors the Morrises and the Dillwyns.[35] Another Quaker numbered among their friends was Anthony Benezet. It is not altogether surprising that young Charles Webb, who came to live with his father and stepmother for a time, became a Quaker preacher.[36] Grace Webb needed friends, for her husband was frequently away from home on preaching trips. We catch interesting glimpses of him in the journals of Asbury, Pilmore, and Rankin, and, indeed, of future President John Adams. All, with the strange exception of Adams, shared the Wesleys' perplexity at the impact of Webb's unmethodical sermons. In 1769 Pilmore wrote: "His preaching, though incorrect and irregular, is attended with wonderful power."[37] Some months later he claimed: "He is a genuine Wesleyan and labours hard to promote the cause. His gifts are small; but he is very zealous and honest."[38] In March, 1774, at Baltimore, Asbury observed that Webb preached "an animating discourse from Rev. 6:17" (i.e., the Day of Wrath), and remarked two days later: "There is something very singular in his manner; nevertheless the Lord owns and blesses his labours." The two men shared the responsibility for building the first Methodist meeting house in Baltimore, Lovely Lane. Asbury laid the foundation stone in April, 1774, and in October Webb preached the first sermon in the building. Webb accompanied Asbury on some of his preaching journeys, and seems to have taken Asbury's part in the friction that developed with Rankin, who felt that Baltimore did not really need the tender loving care that Asbury lavished upon the cause.[39]

It was on Sunday, October 23, in that same year of 1774, that the redoubtable John Adams, an inveterate sermon-taster, heard Webb

34. Wesley, Letters, VI, 56-7.

35. See the correspondence between Mrs. Webb and the two families, 1775-85, preserved in the Historical Society of Pennsylvania, Philadelphia.

36. George S. Brookes, Friend Anthony Benezet, pp. 305, 308, 313; Wakeley, Lost Chapters, p. 153.

37. Pilmore, Journal, p. 30.

38. John P. Lockwood, The Western Pioneers, p. 177. When William Duke, as a young preacher, heard Webb, he "was tempted to laugh at his odd expressions" (Duke, MS Journal, 1774-1776, Peabody Institute, Baltimore, abstracted by Edwin Schell, April 15, 1774).

39. Asbury, Journal, I, 117, 139, 140, 147.

preach in Philadelphia. In the morning he listened to the Countess of Huntingdon's emissary William Piercy, whom he dismissed in his diary as "No genius—no orator." In the afternoon he heard a Virginian Baptist, about whom the only saving grace he could find was "honest zeal." Over Webb, however, he went into raptures: "He is one of the most fluent, eloquent men I ever heard. He reaches the imagination and touches the passions very well, and expresses himself with great propriety."[40] Webb was apparently a layman's preacher rather than a preacher's preacher.

In spite of some awkward moments, Webb got along reasonably well with that thorny disciplinarian Thomas Rankin. During the summer of 1775 he accompanied Rankin on his preaching circuit around Chesapeake Bay, taking in the lower counties on the eastern shore. Eventually Webb wilted in the heat and turned back—it was the middle of July, and then as later he seems to have been corpulent. In 1776 also Webb worked with Rankin in Philadelphia, and then "promised to supply the Trenton circuit in the best way he could." Rankin shared the hospitality not only of Webb's chaise (somewhat more comfortable than the circuit rider's traditional horse) but also of the new home to which the Webbs had moved this year, in the comparatively rural seclusion of Pemberton, New Jersey. War with Britain inevitably curtailed their preaching activities, even though (as Rankin's diary makes clear) the Methodists officially espoused neither side and tried to avoid carrying arms. Throughout December, 1776, and January, 1777, Rankin stayed with Webb, occupying his time in compiling a natural history of America, to the accompaniment of the sound of cannon and small arms, "the noise and din of war."[41] After the following Conference in May, 1777, he and the remaining British preachers, with the single exception of Asbury, bade farewell to their younger American brethren and returned home. Within a year all were gone. Webb's own attempted departure was both prolonged and painful.

TRIALS OF A LOYALIST

For some years Webb had tried to keep his finger on the pulse of the American people, as is revealed by his letters to the Earl of Dart-

40. L. H. Butterfield, ed., *Diary and Autobiography of John Adams*, II, 156.
41. Rankin, MS Journal, p. 205 (Jan. 1–29, 1777).

mouth, Colonial Secretary and Lord Privy Seal of England during the fateful years 1772–82, and a warm friend of the Methodists. In September, 1774, Webb reported unfavorably on the first Congress, assembled in Philadelphia. In March, 1775, writing from New York, he expressed his belief that the American people were now more friendly to Britain, particularly in view of the New York Assembly's rejection of Congress's measures. If the king's standard were raised, he claimed, about three-fourths of the people would rally round. He passed a suggestion that closing the ports might bring the rebels back into line.

Clearly Webb was not in sympathy with the restless spirit of independence, and it is not surprising that eventually he was caught up in serious trouble at the hands of the patriots. Henry Dawson, in that monumental adventure, *The Historical Magazine*, printed an interesting letter written to General Schuyler from Baltimore on May 1, 1777. Samuel Purviance, Jr., an American spy, told Schuyler that Webb was a British spy, "a half pay officer in the British service" using the disguise of a Methodist preacher. Indeed, he went on, "It is a certain truth that all the denomination called Methodists almost to a man (with us [i.e., in Baltimore]) are enemies to our cause under the mask of religion, and are countenanced by the Tories."[42] Webb was arrested and "transported to the back parts of Pennsylvania"— in fact to the Moravian center of Bethlehem. Many Moravian families were moved out of their homes to make room for prisoners of war. The Webbs lodged first in the house of Brother Lindemeyer, and later in that of William Böhler—shades of Methodist beginnings! The captain served the prisoners as chaplain, preaching for them and burying their dead.[43]

Altogether Webb's family was detained in Bethlehem for nearly fifteen months. Webb himself, however, secured a passport releasing him from his parole of not venturing more than six miles from the town. Thus armed, on February 22, 1778, he set out for Philadelphia, in order to hasten his exchange for an American prisoner of war. His

42. *Historical Magazine*, Morrisania, N.Y. (1866), 361–8. Cf. John W. Jackson, *Margaret Morris, her Journal*, pp. 69–70. For Webb's letters to the Earl of Dartmouth see *Historical Manuscripts Commission. . . . The Manuscripts of the Earl of Dartmouth*, II. 145, 160, 190, 276.

43. Diary of the Moravian Church, Bethlehem, quoted in Bulletin No. 7 of the Association of Methodist Historical Societies, 1939.

passport scorned, he was held prisoner in Philadelphia for months while he attempted to prove that he was in fact not a soldier but a civilian. His wife interceded for him even with George Washington. Eventually the exchange was effected, but Webb does not seem to have rejoined his wife and family until they reached New York on their way to England, towards the end of August, 1778.[44]

Arrived in England, Webb found himself in some financial distress, though not quite penniless. His wife's little fortune of £2,000 was tied up in the Gilbert estates in Antigua, and some time after her brother Nathaniel's death in 1773 her annual interest of £120 ceased. For a decade and more they kept hoping for a restoration of the annuity if not of the capital. For some years Webb had fruitlessly complained in official quarters that he was almost the last of the neglected veteran officers of the Seven Years' War to receive a suitable reward. Now he began again, mustering support for his claims as a civilian loyalist actively engaged in forwarding British aims, who had been dispossessed and suffered loss through the Revolution. In support of his memorial to "the Honourable Commissioners appointed . . . to inquire into the losses and services of the American Loyalists" he secured recommendations from several people prominent in public affairs. John Wesley lent his aid, as did two of his preachers, Thomas Rankin and Martin Rodda, both of whom had served in America. Webb's military testimonials came from Generals Thomas Gage and Thomas Sterling, together with Colonel Isaac Barre (reputed author of the *Letters of Junius*), alongside all of whom he had fought in the Quebec campaign. He also secured a letter from Oliver De Lancey, the prominent New York loyalist, and from Joseph Galloway, the Maryland-born lawyer who was a member of the first Congress of 1774 but went over to the British in 1776, later publishing pamphlets attacking the conduct of the war by the Howes, pamphlets reprinted by John Wesley. The matter of compensation, nevertheless, dragged on for years.[45]

Webb had speedily re-established himself as a preacher. He was especially popular at Salisbury, where he seems to have had relatives.[46] One of the soldiers converted under his preaching became a pioneer

44. See the E. Boudinot correspondence in the New York Historical Society, New York City, April 7 to Aug. 5, 1778.

45. *WHS*, XXXIII, 157–9; MS letters of Webb to his son Charles, espec. Oct. 23, 1782, one n.d., and Aug. 12, 1793 (Methodist Archives, London).

46. Wesley, *Letters*, VII, 69; Wesley, *Journal*, VII, 295, 452.

of Methodist evangelism in the French-speaking island of Jersey.[47] Reminiscences of America, not all of them flattering, or even correct, punctuated his discourses. Once, when preaching in the New Room at Bristol, he accused the Americans not only of luxury but, what was worse, of Arminianism—by which he surely meant Arianism.[48]

In spite of some understandable lapses, however, Webb retained his love for America. He kept in touch with his American-born son Charles, and one of his letters to Charles shows that America had at the very least given him a taste for Indian corn. The father's own suppressed yearning for America came out vicariously in the longings of young Gilbert to join his stepbrother in their native land. Webb was obviously proud of young Gilbert's talent for arithmetic and his "good hand for book-keeping," as well as his complete trustworthiness, and was sure that he would prove a good clerk alongside Charles. Eventually in 1792, when he was about eighteen, Gilbert was fitted out by his parents and sent over with a consignment of carefully chosen goods to sell at a profit in America. In fact, he proved somewhat less religious and much more adventurous than his sober stepbrother Charles, and seems to have reacted violently against Charles's stuffy preaching.[49]

Little is known of Webb's only daughter, held back from schooling even when she was about ten because of the need for family economy. At that time Webb comforted himself with the thought expressed in a letter to Charles: "Your sister is very notable [whatever that may have meant!], and I hope will make a good woman." Her obituary in the *Methodist Magazine* shows that she developed into an intelligent, well-read, and charming young lady, though a little too gay for her parents' taste. At the age of nineteen she underwent an old-fashioned conversion, married a widower with two young sons, and nine months later died of convulsions and apoplexy in the last stages of pregnancy. This was on January 4, 1799. During her short period as young Mrs. Wright of Stourport she had become one of the shining lights of the Methodist society there.[50]

47. *WHS*, XXI, 83; *London Quarterly Review*, CLVI (July, 1951), 199–200.
48. *WHS*, XVIII, 126.
49. MS letters, Thomas Webb to Charles Webb, 1782–93, Methodist Archives, London; also one without date in Lovely Lane Museum, Baltimore; Wakeley, *Lost Chapters*, p. 153; Charles Webb to Gilbert Webb, Dec. 14, 1792, Library of Congress, Washington.
50. MS letter, Thomas Webb to Charles Webb, May 7, 1785, and Mary Gilbert to Gilbert Webb, Feb. 9, 1797, Library of Congress; cf. *Methodist Magazine*, 1799, p. 272.

Thomas Webb's financial affairs continued in disorder. A word from John Wesley to Lord North helped to secure for him an annual pension of £97 10s., but this was far from prosperity; he and Grace continued to look forward to those two golden events in the future, the settlement of his claims for compensation as a distressed loyalist, and the renewal of the remittances from Antigua. Meantime Webb kept warning Charles of his own imminent death. A sufferer from gout, he had felt himself beginning to "break up" in 1786, and he urged that Charles should take responsibility for his stepmother until the family ship came home.

LAST ROLL CALL

In fact Webb survived for another ten years, and during that period played a prominent part in the affairs of Bristol Methodism. He was the chief agent in building yet another Methodist chapel, on Portland Heights, Bristol, where on December 24, 1796, he was buried with all honors. The soldier preacher had answered his last roll call. For a century and three-quarters his body lay in a vault below the altar, the traditional green patch still over the eye lost in the service of King George, and a glory about the memory of his life given in the service of the King of Kings. It is altogether fitting that in May, 1972, with the closing of Portland Chapel, his remains (identified by that same green patch) were removed (together with those of his wife Grace) for interment at the New Room in Bristol, Britain's gateway to America in Wesley's day.[51]

His memorial tablet at Portland stated that he "founded the first Methodist Churches" in America. Contemporary engravings show him preaching in regimentals behind sword and Bible, and describe him as "Founder of the Methodist Societies in America."[52] Even a fellow-Englishman is constrained to admit, however, that this may claim too much, though it is somewhat better than the limited description under one American version of the engraving: "Capt. Thomas Webb, Pioneer Methodist Preacher in Brooklyn." One suspects that this had been colored by some local loyalty. A little fuller, though still not full enough, is the caption under the lithograph frontispiece to Lednum's *History of the Rise of Methodism in Amer-*

51. See *Methodist History*, X, No. 4 (July, 1972), 60–3.
52. Ibid., pp. 53–7.

ica (1859): "Captain Thomas Webb, who introduced Methodism into Pennsylvania, Delaware, and New Jersey." How in fact are we to summarize his ten years of pioneer evangelism in America, his widely spread activities in preaching and founding societies, his prominent share in building churches in New York, Philadelphia, and Baltimore, his zeal in securing reinforcements from England? Perhaps we cannot call him *the* founder of American Methodism, but he was certainly *a* founder, and—maybe we shall eventually hit upon a better term—the chief consolidator of early Methodism in America.

5. "COME OVER AND HELP US!"

As we have seen, during the colonial 1760's a grass-roots Methodism developed along the eastern seaboard of America, notably in the areas around Baltimore, Philadelphia, and New York. In part it was the result of a generation of seed-sowing by George Whitefield, and earlier by his tutor and senior colleague, John Wesley. A few small pockets of influence were characterized by genuine spiritual warmth, but also by a lack of theological sensitivity and of a tightly knit organization. A handful of British immigrants—mainly from Ireland—provided focal points of fellowship and growth. These small Methodist groups apparently had few links with any vigorous indigenous church life, and even ties with Methodism in their mother country seem to have been broken. Not until the Atlantic was effectively bridged by a persuasive appeal to Wesley did Methodism in America really begin to flourish.

THE WESLEYS AND AMERICA

For thirty years the Wesleys' continuing concern for America was channeled mainly through their younger colleague George Whitefield. Even though he came to differ keenly from them both in doctrine and practice they remained, as each maintained, "a threefold cord."[1] Whitefield raised the orphanage in Savannah planned by Charles Wesley; Whitefield followed up evangelical openings in the New England to which Charles had been invited; through Whitefield's journals and letters and personal conversation the two brothers vicariously experienced a gospel itinerancy in America similar to that which they themselves followed in the British Isles, though Whitefield was a preacher rather than an organizer, and at the end of a generation had little to show by way of societies and members.

Nor was Whitefield the Wesleys' only point of contact across the Atlantic during this lost generation of American Methodism. In 1738 John Wesley had been deeply moved by reading Jonathan Edwards'

Most of the material used here has appeared in two articles: (a) "Early American Methodism: A Key Document," *Methodist History*, III, No. 2 (Jan., 1965), 3–15, and (b) " 'Come over and help us!'—America to Wesley," *Christian Advocate*, March 18, 1971, pp. 13–14.

1. Charles Wesley, *Journal*, II, 178, 247.

Narrative of the Great Awakening in New England, and a few years later published his own abridged edition of it, as he did of Edwards' other works on the revival, and of his biography of the well known missionary to the Indians, David Brainerd.[2] When asked in 1745 whether he was interested in forming a prayer circle for evangelical ministers in England and Scotland Wesley urged that the clergy of America should also be invited to co-operate, mentioning specifically Edwards and Gilbert Tennent.[3]

During the following decade his thoughts frequently turned to America. In 1753 Gilbert Tennent visited England, along with the Reverend Samuel Davies of Hanover County, Virginia. They came to raise funds for the College of New Jersey, better known to us as Princeton. When Tennent and Davies called on the Wesley brothers the following year they were received sympathetically, and Wesley commended the project as "an admirable design, if it will bring Protestants of every denomination to bear with one another."[4] Wesley's friendship with Davies in particular flourished by correspondence until the latter's death in 1761. Wesley sent parcels of his own publications for distribution among Davies' parishioners: Davies described how some of the Black slaves to whom he gave Wesley's *Collection of Psalms and Hymns* occasionally spent the whole night singing them. Davies also passed on many of Wesley's tracts to neighboring clergy in Virginia for free distribution to poor people, especially Blacks.[5] For his part Wesley appreciated the writings of Samuel Davies, and printed an abridged edition of one of his sermons under the title of *The Good Soldier*.[6] Other publications by Wesley continued to sell in America.[7]

From 1755 to 1763 George Whitefield remained in the United Kingdom before making his sixth visit to America, which lasted from the summer of 1763 to that of 1765. In September, 1764, from Philadelphia, Whitefield wrote to Wesley hinting that he would welcome some of Wesley's itinerants to further the work in America, and con-

2. See Charles A. Rogers, "John Wesley and Jonathan Edwards."
3. Wesley, *Letters*, II, 33–4.
4. Wesley, *Journal*, IV, 101; Samuel Davies, *Diary*, p. 132.
5. Wesley, *Journal*, IV, 125–6, 149–50, 194–5.
6. Richard Green, *The Works of John and Charles Wesley: A Bibliography*, No. 178. Although Green did not know it, this was taken from Davies' *Religion and Patriotism the Constituents of a Good Soldier*, Philadelphia, 1755; reprinted in London and in Glasgow, 1756.
7. Pilkington, op. cit., p. 26.

tinued to make this plea after his return to England. Sympathetic though he was, Wesley suggested to Whitefield instead that some of his local preachers might be sufficient for the task.[8] Where Whitefield failed with Wesley an obscure layman succeeded. The organizing and invigorating of an embryo American Methodism along largely British lines resulted from the concern of one man above all others, and he is known to history almost solely through a letter appealing for Wesley's help.

AN ENGLISH EXILE

In September, 1767, this English Methodist layman, Thomas Taylor,[9] left London to set sail from Sir Francis Drake's Plymouth for America, reluctantly leaving behind his "dear wife and children."[10] The nature of his undertaking is not known, but he seems to have been facing a very lengthy exile, filled with anxiety about his family, yet quite unable to help them. During the voyage he underwent a deep religious experience, whose outcome he described thus: "I made a new covenant with the Lord, that I would go to the utmost parts of the earth, provided he would raise up a people with whom I might join in his praises. On the great deep I found a more earnest desire to be united with the people of God than ever before."[11] After "a very favourable passage of six weeks," on October 26 he arrived in New York. Going to recommended lodgings he asked his host whether there were any Methodists in the city, and was informed about "one Captain Webb, a strange sort of man, who lived on Long Island, and sometimes preached at one Embury's, at the rigging-house." In a few days he located Embury, discovered that he knew Wesley per-

8. See above, p. 26.

9. The letter which constitutes the raw material for this chapter is in fact signed only "T.T." The writer, however, identifies himself as one of the purchasers of land for the John Street Chapel in New York, and Taylor's is the only name that fits. The belief that he was an Irishman (see Wade Crawford Barclay, *Early American Methodism, 1769–1844*, I, 15) is probably due to confusion with Wesley's itinerant preacher of the same name, who spent much of his early ministry in Ireland, and was in fact there during the years 1768–70 when his namesake was in New York.

10. *A Letter, &c.*, no place, no printer, no date, 12mo., pp. 7, whose text is quoted throughout this chapter, with parenthetical references to the hypothetical text published by the present writer in *Methodist History*, III, No. 2 (Jan., 1965). The reference here is to *Letter*, p. 4 (p. 11).

11. Ibid., p. 4 (p. 11).

sonally, for a time "had been a helper in Ireland,"[12] and after a long silence had recently begun to preach in New York.[13] This seemed like an answer to Taylor's shipboard prayers. Heartily he threw in his lot with Embury and his group, which had been reinforced about nine months earlier by Webb.

Numbers and enthusiasm grew to the extent that the leading members (including Taylor) decided to rent a piece of land on which they might erect "a wooden tabernacle," but they were providentially led to a more permanent venture—the purchase of a house with a vacant lot adjoining, on which they might contemplate building a substantial preaching-house. For the time being they secured the property for themselves and their heirs, but Taylor pleaded that they should not retain it in their own names but hold it in trust for the Methodist people, as was the practice in England. Accordingly he wrote to John Wesley for legal advice, taking the occasion also to drop a hint about the need for financial help and to make a strong plea for leadership in this promising new field, asking Wesley to send out "an able, experienced preacher."

A KEY DOCUMENT

Taylor's letter, written to Wesley on April 11, 1768, less than six months after his arrival in New York, is one of the key documents of early American Methodism, by an observant and reliable witness.[14] It gives the earliest connected account of the rise of New York Methodism, and furnishes many details otherwise unknown, as well as confirming the general background of the familiar oral tradition about Barbara Heck and the game of cards that led her to prod Philip Embury into holding services in his own home. For this alone it would be of great importance, even if it held no unique significance as the means of bringing proven Methodist men and methods to America.

The letter itself, however, has long been shrouded in mystery. Until recently it was known only in two late copies, which differ considera-

12. Ibid., p. 3 (p. 11). In normal technical usage this would imply an itinerant preacher rather than a helper in a generic sense, such as a class-leader and local preacher. In that usage the word is frequently capitalized, but it does appear in lower case in the *Letter*, whose compositor used very few capitals. See Note 53, p. 41 above.

13. Ibid., p. 2 (pp. 9–10).

14. *Methodist History*, Jan., 1965, p. 8.

bly from each other. Most writers who have used it have quoted extracts only, as I propose to do here, for it is a lengthy document. Strangely enough, even those few who have purported to present the original document in its entirety have failed to do so. There are two main versions, which not only differ from but are independent of each other. The earlier version, printed in Charles Atmore's *Methodist Memorial* in 1802, preserved the original more accurately, but was seriously incomplete; the later version, published in the *Methodist Magazine* for October, 1823, was fuller, but suffered from numerous editorial revisions.[15] In January, 1965, I told the story of this letter, and tried to reconstruct the original document from these two later versions. I closed my introduction with these words: "I can only hope that one day my attempt to reproduce this key document will be rendered out of date by the discovery of the original."[16]

The original manuscript letter has not yet been discovered—and probably never will be. But something perhaps even more exciting *has* turned up. Searching for Wesley publications in Regent's Park College, Oxford (a Baptist institution), in an old volume of uncatalogued pamphlets I discovered a copy of the complete letter printed shortly after Wesley received it—printed undoubtedly on Wesley's authority, in an attempt to drum up recruits and financial support for the infant Methodism of America. It is an eight-page duodecimo pamphlet with no title page and the last page blank. The drop-title on page one reads simply, "A LETTER, &c." beneath a double row of printers' flowers similar to those used at the time by William Pine of Bristol, who probably printed this unique little item in the latter months of 1768.

This early printed letter in general substantiates the conclusion which I had reached earlier, namely that the fuller *Methodist Magazine* version had been touched up by a nineteenth-century editor, probably Nathan Bangs. Charles Atmore's version of 1802 was nearer to the original in substance as well as in time, though it was abridged. The contemporary document now discovered shows that there were about a dozen variants (all minor) in Atmore's version, apparently due to editing either by himself or by Wesley's preacher, Christopher Hopper, among whose papers Atmore found his copy. The only detail of real significance in which the 1823 version agreed with 1768 against

15. Ibid., pp. 4–8.   16. Ibid., pp. 8–9.

1802 was the description of the group of Embury's original companions in New York as "chiefly his own countrymen, Irish Germans." From the 1802 version the word "Germans" was omitted.

EARLY METHODISM IN NEW YORK

The first half of Taylor's letter is devoted to an account of the rise of Methodism in New York, the second to his appeal. He recounts the tradition that Whitefield's first two visits to America, in 1738, and from August, 1739, to March, 1741, were comparatively uneventful. His third visit, however, from August, 1744, to June, 1748, witnessed "a considerable shaking among the dry bones," when many "were savingly converted."[17] The impact was greatly increased during Whitefield's sixth visit, June, 1763, to July, 1765, "when his words were really as a hammer and as a fire."[18] Taylor summarizes what he had learned of the religious life of New York "eighteen months ago," i.e., about October, 1766, "when it pleased God to rouse up Mr. Embury to employ his talent (which for several years had been as it were hid in a napkin), by calling sinners to repentance, and exhorting believers to let their light shine before men."[19] Whitefield's visit had created a climate of spiritual sensitivity and expectancy: "Most part of the adults were stirred up, great numbers pricked to the heart, and by a judgment of charity several found peace and joy in believing. The consequence of this work was, the churches were crowded, and subscriptions raised for building new ones. Mr. Whitefield's example provoked most of the ministers to a much greater degree of earnestness. And by the multitudes of people, young and old, rich and poor, flocking to the churches, religion became an honourable profession. There was no outward cross to be taken up therein. Nay, a person who could not speak about the grace of God and the new birth was esteemed unfit for genteel company." Then came a spiritual slump. "Instead of pressing forward and growing in grace," as Whitefield had exhorted them, they "plead[ed] for the remains of sin, and the necessity of being in darkness"—in other words they insisted, "You can't change human nature"—and "esteemed their opinions as the very essentials of Christianity, and regarded not holiness either of heart or life."[20]

17. *Letter*, p. 1 (p. 9).
18. Ibid.

19. Ibid., p. 2 (p. 9).
20. Ibid.

It was to this condition that Embury strove to address himself: "He spoke at first only in his own house. A few were soon collected together, and joined in a little society; chiefly his own countrymen, Irish Germans. In about three months after, Brother White and Brother Sause from Dublin joined them. They then rented an empty room in their neighbourhood, which was in the most infamous street of the city, adjoining the barracks. For some time few thought it worth their while to hear. But God so ordered it by his providence that about fourteen months ago Captain Webb, barrack-master at Albany (who was converted about three years since at Bristol) found them out and preached in his regimentals. The novelty of a man preaching in a scarlet coat soon brought greater numbers to hear than the room could contain. But his doctrines were quite new to the hearers; for he told them point blank 'that all their knowledge and profession of religion was not worth a rush unless their sins were forgiven, and they had the witness of God's spirit with theirs that they were the children of God.' This strange doctrine, with some peculiarities in his person, made him soon be taken notice of, and obliged the little society to look out for a larger house to preach in. They soon found a place that had been built for a rigging-house, sixty feet in length and eighteen in breadth." [21]

Webb had moved from Albany to Long Island, to be near his wife's relations, and began effective preaching there, as well as making occasional visits to New York. In the meantime, "brother Embury was exhorting all who attended on Thursday evenings, and Sunday morning and evenings, at the rigging-house, to flee from the wrath to come." [22] It was as his hearers were becoming more numerous and serirous that Taylor arrived, to discover that Embury "had formed two classes, one of the men and another of the women, but had never met the society apart from the congregation." [23] The strange implication here is that Embury, the former class-leader, had organized the essential units of a British Methodist society, but either no longer arranged for them to have intimate spiritual fellowship as distinct groups, merely to assemble along with both members and non-members at a public preaching service, or—which is more likely—had not felt it a part of his pastoral function to meet with these groups "apart from the

21. Ibid., pp. 2–3 (pp. 9–10).   23. Ibid., p. 3 (p. 11).
22. Ibid., p. 3 (p. 10).

congregation." There is indeed more than a hint in Taylor's letter which is reminiscent of Barbara Heck—he does not feel that Embury is utilizing his full spiritual potential, even after he has begun to preach to his companions. He continues: "Mr. Embury has lately been more zealous than formerly; the consequence of which is that he is more lively in preaching; and his gifts as well as graces are much increased. Great numbers of serious people came to hear God's Word, as for their lives. And their numbers increased so fast that our house for this six weeks past would not contain half of the people."[24]

"We had some consultations how to remedy this inconvenience," Taylor writes, "and Mr. Embury proposed renting a lot of ground for twenty-one years, and to exert our utmost endeavours to collect as much money as to build a wooden tabernacle. A piece of ground was proposed; the ground rent was agreed for, and the lease was to be executed in a few days. We, however, in the mean time, had two several days for fasting and prayer for the direction of God, and his blessing on our proceedings—and Providence opened such a door as we had no expectation of. A young man, a sincere Christian, and constant hearer, though not joined in society, would not give anything towards this house, but offered ten pounds to buy a lot of ground, [and] went of his own accord to a lady who had two lots to sell, on one of which there is a house that rents for eighteen pounds per annum. He found the purchase money of the two lots was six hundred pounds, which she was willing should remain in the purchaser's hands on good security. We called once more upon God for his direction, and resolved to purchase the whole. There are eight of us who are joint purchasers, among whom Mr. Webb and Mr. Lupton are men of property. I was determined the house should be on the same footing as the Orphan House at Newcastle, and others in England; but as we were ignorant how to draw the deeds, we purchased for us and our heirs, until a copy of the writings from England was sent us, which we desire may be sent by the first opportunity."[25]

The young man who thus served as catalyst for a bold venture was apparently Joseph Forbes, a cordwainer, who deliberately kept in the background, though lending his name as security in persuading Mrs. Mary Barclay, widow of the Reverend Henry Barclay, second rector of Trinity Church, to sell the land without receiving the money. The

24. Ibid., p. 4 (p. 11). 25. Ibid., pp. 4–5 (pp. 11–12).

legal transactions are obscure, and several documents have disappeared, but undoubtedly Forbes played an important role in the purchase.[26]

APPEAL TO WESLEY

Having told his story, Thomas Taylor in effect appealed to Wesley for three things: legal advice, financial help, and qualified preachers. Assistance in settling the John Street Chapel on a trust deed similar to those in England was apparently delayed until a preacher could be found to bring over the "Large Minutes" of 1763, in which the model deed was printed. The preacher could also personally ensure that the procedure was carried out in the most approved manner. As a result of this slight delay, the New York property was not reconveyed to trustees until 1770. It closely followed Wesley's precedent, with some local variants, including the addition of New York to the list of three English cities where the Methodist annual conference was authorized to meet.

Taylor was diffident about asking Wesley for money, but there was no mistaking the implications of his description of the difficulties, the unexpected help, the makeshift financing, and the high rate of interest in New York: "Before we began to talk of building, the devil and his children were very peaceable; but since this affair took place many ministers have cursed us in the name of the Lord, and laboured with all their might to shut up their congregations from assisting us. But He that sitteth in heaven laugheth them to scorn. Many have broke through, and given their friendly assistance. We have collected above one hundred pounds more than our own contributions; and have reason to hope in the whole we shall have two hundred pounds. But the house will cost us four hundred pounds more, so that unless God is pleased to raise up friends we shall yet be at a loss. I believe Mr. Webb and Lupton will borrow or advance two hundred pounds rather than the building should not go forward; but the interest of money here is a great burden, which is seven per cent."[27]

Eventually he came right out with it, however: "Some of our brethren proposed writing to you for a collection in England: but I was averse to this, as I well knew our friends there are overburdened al-

26. *Methodist History*, Jan., 1965, pp. 12–13, n. 52.
27. *Letter*, p. 5 (pp. 13–14).

ready. Yet so far I would earnestly beg: if you would intimate our circumstances to particular persons of ability, perhaps God would open their hearts to assist this infant society, and contribute to the first preaching-house on the original Methodist plan in all America (excepting Mr. Whitefield's Orphan-House in Georgia). But I shall write no more on this head."[28]

It was surely as a means of fulfilling this request in particular that Wesley printed Thomas Taylor's letter for selective distribution. It seems likely that he gave or sent copies to many laymen of substance throughout Britain and Ireland, soliciting their sympathy and generosity. During the winter of 1768–9 a copy was also forwarded to each of his "Assistants," the itinerant preachers in charge of the forty circuits in the British Isles, around each of which a small group of preachers traveled in turn on a predetermined preaching and pastoral tour lasting a month or so. Wesley's instructions to one preacher, Robert Costerdine, have survived in a letter dated February 6, 1769: "If you read publicly on any Sunday that letter from New York, you may than receive what the hearers are willing to give."[29]

There is some mystery about the response to this appeal. Financial contributions seem to have been meager in the extreme—perhaps, as Taylor suggested, because the English Methodists were so hard pressed. Or it is possible that the money was in some way diverted from the New York building fund, though this seems unlikely. An important by-product of the letter, however, was probably that of stimulating volunteer immigrants, such as John Southwell, a merchant who in 1770 became one of the John Street trustees.[30] As we have seen, Thomas Ashton, later a pillar of the Ashgrove society, paid a double passage so that Robert Williams could accompany him.[31]

TOKENS OF BROTHERLY LOVE

At the Leeds Conference in August, 1769, Wesley urged the preachers assembled to go the extra mile "in token of our brotherly love" by themselves taking up a collection for their Methodist brethren in

28. Ibid., pp. 5–6 (p. 14). The parenthetical phrase was omitted from the 1802 version, perhaps because Atmore knew that in fact Whitefield's Orphan House was on a very different kind of trust deed from those of Wesley's preaching-houses.

29. Wesley, *Letters*, V, 126.

30. Ibid.; cf. *Methodist History*, Jan., 1965, p. 5.

31. See above, pp. 45–6.

America. This was "immediately done." Of the seventy pounds then subscribed, twenty went to pay the passage over for the two officially designated preachers. The remaining fifty eventually found its way into the current account at John Street rather than into the building fund itself—possibly in order to substantiate a proud claim that all the building money had been raised in America.[32]

The preachers themselves, however, remained the most important gift. Taylor had praised the pioneer efforts of Embury and Webb, but the climactic paragraph of his letter is this: "There is another point far more material, and in which I must importune your assistance not only in my own name, but in the name of the whole society. We want an able, experienced preacher; one who has both gifts and graces necessary for the work. God has not despised the day of small things. There is a real work begun in many hearts by the preaching of Mr. Webb and Mr. Embury: but although they are both useful, and their hearts in the work, they want many qualifications necessary for such an undertaking, where they have none to direct them. And the progress of the gospel here depends much on the qualifications of the preachers."[33] He asked for one qualified man only, even suggesting the name of Mr. John Helton.[34] He added: "If possible, we must have a man of wisdom, of sound faith, and a good disciplinarian—one whose heart and soul are in the work—and I doubt not but by the goodness of God such a flame would be soon kindled as would never stop until it reached the great South Sea."[35] He promised that if the cost of the preacher's passage could not be raised in England "we would sell our coats and shirts and pay it."[36]

Wesley had apparently presented the letter orally to his preachers when they met in conference at Bristol in August, 1768. Supplementing it was a note (probably from Thomas Webb) about "a few people in Maryland who had lately been awakened under the ministry of Robert Strawbridge," and who added their own "pressing call for help." He was not prepared to be rushed, however, nor to rush his preachers, in a matter of such importance. It was therefore "left to

32. See *Methodist History*, Jan., 1965, p. 6, and note 8.
33. *Letter*, p. 6 (p. 14).
34. Ibid., spelling the name "Hilton," which is occasionally used in the British *Minutes* (1775, 1776). After a few unsettled years, during several of which he was not stationed, he became a Quaker, and in 1778 published *Reasons for Quitting the Methodist Society: being a Defence of Barclay's Apology*.
35. Ibid.   36. Ibid., p. 7 (p. 14).

their consideration until the next yearly Conference." During the ensuing year Joseph Pilmore (for one) was "frequently under great exercise of mind respecting the dear Americans, and found a willingness to sacrifice everything for their sakes."[37]

Confirmation of the need, and of the best means of supplying it, came from another quarter. On October 14, 1768, Wesley dined with Dr. Carl Magnus von Wrangel, who had just returned from nine years as provost of the Swedish Lutheran churches on the Delaware, and (Wesley wrote) "strongly pleaded for our sending some of our preachers to help [the American Christians], multitudes of whom are as sheep without a shepherd."[38] Wesley continued to water the seed by occasional hints to individual preachers, especially when he passed along the printed copy of Taylor's letter. Thus on January 5, 1769, he wrote to Christopher Hopper: "If Joseph Cownley or you have a mind to step over to New York, I will not say you nay. I believe it would help your own health and help many precious souls."[39] He gave permission to one of his untried preachers, Robert Williams, to make the venture on his own without conference backing, provided he would be subject to the discipline of the appointed preachers when they arrived. It may well be that John King emigrated a few months later under similar circumstances, and his name (like that of Williams) appeared in the British stations for 1770 alongside those officially designated for circuit No. 50—"America."[40]

Still another challenge came from Thomas Bell, who had emigrated from England to America to ply his trade, apparently as a cabinet maker. On May 1, 1769, he wrote to one of Wesley's correspondents, George Cussons, a Methodist cabinet maker of Scarborough. He told of religious conditions in New York, of Embury, of Webb, and their colleagues, who had "built a large new house, which cost them six hundred pounds sterling." He himself had worked on it for six days, as well as donating a pound.[41] He reported that the Methodists were in general disfavor among the members of other denominations, and issued a plea which may well have reached Wesley's ears before the ensuing Conference: "In all the places of America where I have been there is as much need of the Methodist preachers as in any town

37. Pilmore, *Journal*, p. 15; cf. above, note 21, p. 59.
38. Wesley, *Journal*, V, 290; William Warren Sweet, *Methodism in American History*, p. 47.
39. Wesley, *Letters*, V, 123. 41. Seaman, op. cit., p. 433.
40. *Minutes* (English), I, 91.

of England. Mr. Wesley says the first message of the preachers is to the lost sheep of the Church of England. And are there none in America? They have strayed from England into the wild woods here, and they are running wild after this world. . . . And are not *these* lost sheep, and will none of the preachers come here? Where is Mr. Brownfield? Where is John Pawson? Where is Nicholas Manners? Are they living, and will they not come? No: they'll not come! But I shall never give over crying, 'O! my Saviour, send them, or some who are not ashamed of thy gospel, that they may go into the highways and hedges, and compel them to come in, that thy house may be filled.'' [42]

At the Conference which assembled at Leeds on August 3, 1769, Wesley finally issued the open challenge to which all this had been leading: "We have a pressing call from our brethren at New York (who have built a preaching-house) to come over and help them. Who is willing to go?" [43] Although several, including Pilmore, had almost certainly already resolved to volunteer, they diffidently remained silent. It seems certain that Wesley canvassed for two men rather than the one requested by Taylor, as he also did on subsequent occasions, looking for two men who could support each other spiritually, and work together amicably as senior and junior partner. John Pawson stated that "several of the brethren offered to go if I would go along with them." [44] On the following day the call was repeated. [45] This time the volunteers were forthcoming, and the *Minutes* record Wesley's choice: "Richard Boardman and Joseph Pilmore." [46] And so Taylor's letter secured experienced British leadership for American Methodism.

Thomas Taylor left the American scene within a few years. He went as he came, under circumstances about which we know almost nothing. His advocacy, however, had opened the door for the coming of the British preachers under whose guidance the infant Methodist societies were to weather many storms and become a powerful and

42. *Methodist Magazine*, London, 1807, pp. 45–6. Wesley had written to Cussons on Nov. 18, 1768. All three of Wesley's itinerants named by Bell had links with Yorkshire, and both Bell and Cussons probably knew them personally. At the 1769 Conference a group of preachers did in fact try to persuade Pawson to offer for America (see below, note 44).

43. *Minutes* (English), I, 86.

44. Jackson, *Early Methodist Preachers*, IV, 37.

45. Sweet, *Men of Zeal*, p. 91.

46. *Minutes* (English), I, 86.

influential American Christian community. We must be grateful that John Wesley did not merely file Taylor's letter, but gave it the widest currency in printed form, so that it might make its fullest impact. It was altogether fitting that the first American Methodist building thus to benefit from Wesley's advocacy should also be the first of the many to be named "Wesley Chapel."

Taylor's letter to Wesley closed thus:

> I most earnestly beg an interest in your prayers, and trust you and many of our brethren will not forget the church in this wilderness. I remain, with sincere esteem,
>
> Rev. and Dear Sir,
Your very affectionate Brother and Servant,
T.T.[47]

Neither Wesley nor his brethren forgot the struggling new church across the Atlantic. It is deeply satisfying after more than two centuries to be able to read an actual copy of the printed document which successfully enlisted the sympathy and adventurous dedication of Wesley's preachers with its appeal, "Come over and help us!"

47. *Letter*, p. 7 (p. 15).

6. WESLEY'S EARLY PREACHERS IN AMERICA

The scattered Methodist societies which arose in America during the 1760's owed their birth and initial sustenance not only to individuals but to a general movement of pietism and revival which had long been spreading over Europe and America, being known here as the Great Awakening. As we have seen, one of the chief carriers of the religious infection was a member of the Wesleys' Holy Club at Oxford, George Whitefield, and some American pockets of Methodist fellowship retained direct though tenuous links with his wide-ranging evangelism.[1] The individuals who formed the focal points of these pioneer Methodist societies, however, were for the most part local preachers who had emigrated from Britain for personal reasons—men of limited intellectual and administrative gifts, but eager to reproduce in as close a replica as possible the spiritual surroundings which they had regretfully left behind in their home country.

Both in Great Britain and in other countries Methodism has usually propagated itself by means of converted laymen, who from telling others of their own experience of salvation have graduated to preaching from a text, the exhorter thus becoming the preacher. At first these men were "local" preachers, exercising a "spare time" ministry in the area where they lived and worked. From their ranks emerged the specialists, the itinerant preachers—still laymen—who under Wesley's direction served various circuits, itinerating week by week within the circuits, and travelling year by year from one circuit to another, all the time supported financially by the Methodist people. A local preacher whose livelihood (or lack of it) took him to another area or country frequently gathered around himself a group of sympathizers and converts who met regularly for Christian fellowship—a Methodist society. This society the local preacher tried to oversee as best he could, but usually came to realize that this task demanded different talents and much more time than that of evangelical preach-

Published in its original form in *The Duke Divinity School Review*, XXXIV (1969), 143–62—an issue commemorating the bicentenary of the landing of Wesley's first itinerant preachers.

    1. See espec. pp. 30–2 above.

ing. He thereupon appealed to Wesley or to one of his itinerant preachers to supply the leadership, organization, and discipline necessary to keep alive the spiritual glow.

VOLUNTEERS FOR AMERICA

Already we have observed this happening in America. After emigrating from England to New York, Thomas Taylor discovered an infant Methodist society which had been raised by Philip Embury (an Irish local preacher) and strengthened by Captain Thomas Webb (an English local preacher). Unbeknown to him another local preacher (Robert Strawbridge) was raising other societies in Maryland, and Philadelphia also was becoming a Methodist center. Taylor (and almost certainly others) realized that expert help was highly desirable, and appealed to Wesley. Wesley in turn appealed to his preachers. Volunteers were forthcoming, of whom the first chosen were Richard Boardman and Joseph Pilmore.

Altogether from 1769 to 1774 Wesley sent over eight of his itinerants in matched pairs, with one each time as the recognized leader. All were young men in their early thirties except for the two chosen in 1771, Francis Asbury and Richard Wright—Asbury was only twenty-six and Wright apparently younger still. Following them in 1773 were two very experienced men, Thomas Rankin and George Shadford, chosen to face increasing problems. In 1774 came two men with lesser experience, James Dempster and Martin Rodda. After the successful Revolution Wesley sent two more, preachers with many more years and itinerant experience to their credit than any of their predecessors, and ordained to boot, in order to salvage whatever might remain of Methodist traditions and discipline in the liberated colonies. To a greater or lesser degree each of these ten men helped to impress Wesley's ideas upon American Methodism, though the key period for this process was the first decade, and the key figure the man who remained behind when his loyalist brethren left for England, Francis Asbury.

One important element in American Methodist progress during the 1770's was the struggle for power between the pioneer local preachers and their absent leader, operating through these itinerant preachers despatched with delegated authority to guide the fortunes of the new societies. Regarded in another way this was a struggle also between a tendency to somewhat formless revivalism and organized churchmanship. It is true that the immigrant local preachers, notably Robert Strawbridge in Maryland, warmed enthusiastically to the growing community of converts looking to them for leadership, and strove to organize them into a self-sufficient church complete with ministry and sacraments. It is also true on the other hand that neither Wesley nor his itinerants despised emotional evangelism. Nevertheless on the issue of revivalism versus church order there existed a clear line of demarcation between the immigrants and Wesley.

Out of the resulting tension, and to some extent arising from it, was forged a vigorous new denomination, tautly disciplined and closely organized, yet at the same time flexible enough to grasp every evangelical opportunity presented by the American frontier. Upon the expanding frontier, therefore, Methodism proved a formidable rival to the Baptists, about whom Asbury made the comment: "Like ghosts they haunt us from place to place."[2]

BOARDMAN AND PILMORE

Before leaving London the first two British itinerants, Boardman and Pilmore, sought and received additional advice and blessing not only from Charles Wesley but also from that veteran missionary George Whitefield, whom John Wesley had asked to keep an eye on them when he embarked on what proved to be his last visit to America.[3] Both in organizing the societies and in tempering the eager outcroppings of undisciplined emotionalism they were far more successful than has sometimes been acknowledged, either by their contemporaries or by some later historians. After a very stormy passage they disembarked at Gloucester Point, New Jersey, on October 21, 1769, and were surprised to discover in nearby Philadelphia another Methodist society, which was already receiving the friendly succor of Captain Webb and of Robert Williams.

Boardman, who was the senior by a few months and had served for six years as an itinerant (at least four as an Assistant) against Pilmore's three (none as Assistant), was now Wesley's Assistant in charge of Methodism throughout the American continent—Circuit No. 50 in the British *Minutes* for the following year. After discussion he decided that the two of them must divide forces; leaving his junior col-

2. Asbury, *Journal*, I, 176.
3. Pilmore, *Journal*, pp. 17–18; Wesley, *Letters*, V, 184.

league to organize the work in Philadelphia, he went on to their original destination of New York.

Pilmore proved himself fully adequate to this first major responsibility. He attended worship at St. Paul's Church and secured the cooperation of the local Anglican clergyman, the Reverend William Stringer; he preached in the open air; he introduced the good British Methodist practice of a preaching service at 5.00 A.M. before people went off to their work; he publicly read and explained Wesley's *Nature, Design, and General Rules of the United Societies*, of which a new edition (making at least nineteen thus far) had just been published. Soon he was introducing prayer meetings and the love-feast, visiting the local prisoners (and preaching a charity sermon for them), attempting a preaching itinerary in the rural areas, and helping to secure Old St. George's as a permanent building for the parent society in Philadelphia, which he settled upon the type of trust officially recommended by Wesley.[4] Once established in Old St. George's Pilmore publicly nailed his Methodist colors to the mast, so that his hearers would all know what he as Wesley's agent stood for:

1. That the Methodist society was never designed to make a separation from the Church of England, or be looked upon as a church.

2. That it was at first and is still intended for the benefit of all those of every denomination who, being truly convinced of sin and the danger they are exposed to, earnestly desire to flee from the wrath to come.

3. That any person who is so convinced, and desires admittance into the society, will readily be received as a *probationer*.

4. That those who walk according to the oracles of God, and thereby give proof [of] their sincerity, will readily be admitted into full connection with the Methodists.

5. That if any person or persons in the society walk *disorderly*, and transgress the holy laws of God, we will admonish him of his error; we will strive to restore him in the spirit of meekness; we will bear with him for a time; but if he remain incorrigible and impenitent, we must then of necessity inform him, he is no longer a member of the society. . . .[5]

4. Pilmore, *Journal*, pp. 24–9.
5. Ibid., p. 29. This is largely a summary of Wesley's *General Rules*.

After five months Pilmore claimed: "In Philadelphia there are now one hundred and eighty-two in society to whom I have given tickets, and they meet in class, and attend to all the discipline of the Methodists as well as the people in London or Bristol." That same entry was preceded by a prophetic note: "If we had but more preachers—men of faith and prayer who would preach Christ Jesus the Lord—'tis probable the American Methodists would soon equal, if not exceed, the Europeans."[6]

Meantime Boardman was tracing a similar path in the New York area, though (one suspects) with not quite the vigor and finesse displayed by Pilmore, to whom it was left later to introduce the love-feast to the New York society and (more important) to straighten out the legal tangles over the new building there.[7] Like Pilmore, Boardman seems to have made limited preaching itineraries around his headquarters, and to have been genuinely concerned about the rural areas. His first letter to Wesley reported: "There appears such a willingness in the Americans to hear the word as I never saw before. They have no preaching in some parts of the back settlements. I doubt not but an effectual door will be opened among them."[8]

From the outset both Boardman and Pilmore were impressed with the response of Blacks to Methodist preaching and fellowship. Indeed the English preachers in general, especially upon their first contact with Blacks, whether slaves or indentured servants, responded much as did John Wesley at first to the Indians, seeing them as romantic representatives of the noble savage popularized by Jean-Jacques Rousseau. Certainly they seem to have become more emotionally involved than their American brethren by the uninhibited tears, the exuberant faith, of the Africans, and a favorite phrase—"the poor Negroes"— surely reflected tender compassion rather than a factual description of their obvious poverty. Boardman wrote to Wesley, in his first letter to him from New York: "The number of Blacks that attend the preaching affects me much. One of them came to tell me she could neither eat nor sleep because her master would not suffer her to come to hear the word. She wept exceedingly, saying, 'I told my master I would do

6. Ibid., p. 40. Robert Williams seems already to have printed class-tickets, and issued them to the members in New York; see Wakeley, *Lost Chapters*, pp. 195, 414–15, 424 (for his description of them as love-feast tickets see p. 135 below).

7. Wakeley, op. cit., pp. 199–206; see also my notes on the legal problem in *Methodist History*, III, No. 2 (Jan., 1965), 12–13.

8. *Arminian Magazine*, VII (1784), 164.

more work than ever I used to do, if he would but let me come. . . .' "⁹
At about the same time Pilmore was noting in Philadelphia, "many
of the poor Africans are obedient to the faith."¹⁰ At a love-feast in
Philadelphia in September, 1770, he stated that "even the poor Negroes came forth, and bore a noble testimony for God our Saviour."¹¹
His experiences in New York were similar to those of Boardman: "A
few days ago the Lord was pleased to manifest his love to a poor Black.
Her mistress has persecuted her very much because she came to the
Methodist Church, but she thought it was better to be 'beaten for
hearing the word of God here than to burn in Hell to all eternity.' We
have about twenty Black women that meet in one Class, and I think
upon the whole they are as happy as any Class we have got."¹² Like
Boardman before him, and Asbury and Coke after him, Pilmore
showed genuine compassion for Blacks, and maintained a fierce anger
for the oppression which they encountered, reproducing in his Journal
a letter from a slave who was prevented from attending class-meetings
and a watchnight service.¹³

Boardman and Pilmore, however, suffered from the common human
failing of not being able to do everything at the same time. To this
was apparently added the complication that the man in charge, Boardman, was somewhat less able and forceful than his junior colleague,
and was also living under the shadow of the recent death of his wife
and young daughter.¹⁴ Nor was Pilmore inclined to undermine the

9. Ibid. Barbara Heck's Black servant Betty had been one of the founding members
of the New York society (Bibbins, op. cit., p. 102), and Thomas Webb numbered Negroes
among his first converts both in Long Island (see above, p. 57) and in New York, the best
known among the latter being Peter Williams, who worked out his freedom as sexton
there, and became one of the founders of the African Methodist Episcopal Zion Church
(Wakeley, Lost Chapters, pp. 438–79; HAM, I, 609–10).

10. Pilmore, Journal, p. 26.
11. Ibid., p. 58.
12. Methodist History, X, No. 3 (April, 1972), 56–7. Although the letter is undated,
it was almost certainly written about the end of November, 1770, a date supported by
careful comparison of the references to Matachin, Whitemarsh, Williams, and Webb,
with the entries under those names in Pilmore's Journal.
13. Pilmore, Journal, p. 107; cf. pp. 96, 131, 137, 179. For Asbury, see Journal, I, 9–10,
43, 56, 57; III, 15. "Black Harry" Hosier, an impressive though illiterate Black preacher,
first appears in Asbury's Journal in 1781 (I, 403; cf. p. 362), though it is just possible that
he was the Negro of whom Asbury wrote to his parents in 1773 that he "will be fit to
send to England soon, to preach" (III, 15). Hosier accompanied several of the regular
itinerants on their travels, including Bishop Thomas Coke (Methodist History, vol. X,
No. 1 [Oct., 1971], 19–22). For Coke's comments on Hosier and his passionate champion-
ship of the Blacks, see Thomas Coke, Extracts of the Journals, pp. 46–9, 61–75.
14. Lockwood, op. cit., p. 39.

authority of Boardman and take over the reins for himself. In spite of their eagerness to preach the gospel in the "back settlements," New York and Philadelphia clearly constituted key areas upon which initially they must concentrate. Successfully they introduced or reinforced most of the features appropriate to large city societies, and pleaded with Wesley for more trained helpers. Pilmore wrote on May 5, 1770: "Brother Boardman and I are chiefly confined to the cities, and therefore cannot at present go much into the country, as we have more work upon our hands than we are able to perform. There is work enough for two preachers in each place, and if two of our brethren would come over I believe it would be attended with a great blessing, for then we could visit the places adjacent to the cities."[15] A further dream was confided to a fellow lay itinerant in England, and might well have disturbed Wesley if it reached his eyes: "The chief difficulty we labour under is want of ordination, and I believe we shall be obliged to procure it by some means or other. It is not in America as it is in England, for there is no church that is one Established more than another. All sects have equal authority with the Church of England."[16]

REINFORCEMENTS NEEDED

There seems little doubt that appeals for help reached Wesley from both Boardman and Pilmore not only because of the magnitude of the opportunity but also because it was difficult to maintain the traditional Methodist discipline in view of the increasing independence of the local preachers. Embury in New York (until he left for Ashgrove in 1770), and Webb as preacher-at-large and pastor in his own Long Island estate, were apparently content with their lot. Robert Williams was more ambitious. He was in any case a little more than a local preacher, though a little less than a regular itinerant. As a tireless evangelist and colporteur he seems to have acted as a free lance, and his not uncommendable activities in publishing Methodist literature were eventually regarded as an overstepping of his powers. Williams had arrived a few weeks before Pilmore and Boardman. Some months later came John King. He had never served as an itinerant in England,

---

15. *Arminian Magazine*, VII (1784), 224.
16. *Methodist History*, X, No. 3 (April, 1972), 57. Cf. note 12 above.

but as a local preacher Wesley regarded him as "stubborn" and "headstrong," and he gained a reputation for "screaming" while he preached. In view of his lack of credentials Pilmore allowed him to serve some of the country societies only, and even then with extreme reluctance.[17] In his 1770 *Minutes* Wesley did indeed append the names of both Williams and King to those of Pilmore and Boardman (in that order) on the American circuit, but they were dropped from the *Minutes* of 1771, almost certainly because of complaints from the regular itinerants.

Yet so overwhelmed did Boardman and Pilmore find themselves by the problems and opportunities of New York and Philadelphia that they left Webb and Williams and King almost unsupervised. When Pilmore heard Williams preach a few times in Philadelphia he admired his sincerity, but noted that his limited gifts were only likely to prove useful among "the country people, who are in general like sheep without shepherds."[18] Unfortunately Williams was preacher rather than pastor, so that the country people still remained largely without a shepherd, as did those in the other cities. Williams had preached in Baltimore before Pilmore, as probably had King, but not until Pilmore's visit in June, 1772, were the *General Rules* expounded there, and a society organized.[19] Similarly Williams had preached in Norfolk, Virginia, but it was left to Pilmore to organize the first Methodist societies in Portsmouth and Norfolk in November, 1772.[20] Pilmore's extended journey into the South, however, during which he accomplished such consolidation, was not possible until Wesley had answered the call for reinforcements. Nor until that time does any serious attention seem to have been paid to supervising the increasingly independent evangelism of the Southern pioneer, Robert Strawbridge. For some years he had been very effective in forming societies, building meeting houses, and inspiring his converts themselves to exhort; he had even begun to baptize and (apparently) to administer the Lord's Supper to his followers. Although Boardman may have attempted a preaching foray into Maryland, neither he nor Pilmore undertook any serious supervision of Strawbridge's work. Pilmore

17. Wesley, *Letters*, VI, 166–7; Pilmore, *Journal*, p. 58.
18. Pilmore, *Journal*, p. 25.
19. Ibid., pp. 138–40.
20. Ibid., p. 162. This was four months after he had begun preaching in the area. Cf. Sweet, *Virginia Methodism*, pp. 49–51, 53–7.

heard him preach "a plain, useful discourse" during a rare visit to Philadelphia in January, 1770.[21] So far, so good. But he returned South to be a law unto himself. Success naturally fed his self-confidence if not his self-esteem, and every year of his continued independence made the deferred but inevitable power struggle likely to be the more severe.

Wesley's mail contained not only appeals from Boardman and Pilmore but complaints about them. From the outset Pilmore had resisted Boardman's demands that they should change places three or four times a year, visualizing himself as what he eventually became, an evangelical parish clergyman with settled headquarters—though in his zeal to "do more good in the itinerant way" he did indeed refuse the possibility of ordination and a living in the West Indies.[22] Under the warmth of American generosity, both with praise and with money, even Boardman came to share Pilmore's desire to spend most of his time as the pastor of a large society, with occasional preaching excursions into the country.

For whatever reason help was clearly needed in America. But Wesley's efforts to recruit more preachers during 1770 failed. Pilmore sadly notes, "I find by Mr. Wesley's letter that none were willing to come; so it is very uncertain whether ever we shall have an opportunity of returning to old England or no."[23] John Wesley, now well into his sixties, began to wonder whether this was not a providential summons for his own return. In February, 1770, he wrote to Lady Maxwell: "I have some thoughts of going to America, but the way is not yet plain. I wait till Providence shall speak more clearly on one side or the other."[24] In writing to Whitefield of this possible return he said: "My age is no objection at all; for I bless God my health is not barely as good but abundantly better in several respects than when I was five-and-twenty."[25] In December, 1770, faced with the failure of his efforts to recruit preachers, he was a little more positive: "If I live till spring, and should have a clear, pressing call, I am ready to embark for America."[26] The picture changed, however, and at the following

21. Pilmore, *Journal*, p. 37.
22. Ibid., p. 62; Lockwood, op. cit., pp. 125, 199–211; Wakeley, *Lost Chapters*, pp. 211–18.
23. *Methodist History*, X, No. 3 (April, 1972), 56. Cf. note 12 above for date.
24. Wesley, *Letters*, V, 182; cf. pp. 168, 177, 267, 273, 303.
25. Ibid., V, 183.
26. Ibid., V, 212.

Conference five preachers volunteered for America. Two were chosen, both young men, apparently better designed to supplement rather than to supplant the labors of their predecessors, complaints or no. Richard Wright, who had been admitted on trial only the previous year, and even then not given a regular station, proved a broken reed, though during the two and a half years that he remained he did a little good. His head, also, seems to have been turned by American generosity and flattery.[27] The senior of the pair, Francis Asbury, was only twenty-six years old, and had had only four years' experience in country circuits, even then not as an Assistant. The choice did not seem unduly promising.

FRANCIS ASBURY

Asbury, nevertheless, whether so commissioned by Wesley or not, believed himself capable of doing a better job than his two seniors, and was prepared to shake things up, cost what it might. Less than a week after joining Boardman in New York, he noted in his *Journal*: "I remain in New York, though unsatisfied with our being both in town together. I have not yet the thing which I seek—a circulation of preachers, to avoid partiality and popularity. However, I am fixed to the Methodist plan, and do what I do faithfully, as to God. I expect trouble is at hand. This I expected when I left England."[28] Two days later came a similar complaint: "I judge we are to be shut up in the cities this winter. My brethren seem unwilling to leave the cities, but I think I shall show them the way. I am in trouble, and more trouble is at hand, for I am determined to make a stand against all partiality. . . . I am come over with an upright intention, and through the grace of God I will make it appear: and I am determined that no man shall bias me with soft words and fair speeches. . . ."[29]

The following spring Asbury's mind was somewhat eased by Boardman's plan that the two younger men should take over New York and Philadelphia for three months, while Boardman himself visited the Boston area and Pilmore toured Virginia.[30] Asbury was greatly disturbed, however, when he reached Philadelphia for the first time

27. Asbury, *Journal*, I, 37, 116.
28. Ibid., I, 10.
29. Ibid.; cf. p. 16.
30. See Wakeley, *Lost Chapters*, pp. 203–4, for notes on Boardman's introduction of Methodism into New England ahead of Jesse Lee.

since his arrival there four months earlier, to find society discipline (as he thought) unduly relaxed, especially in the matter of strangers being given unlimited access to the private gatherings of the society. He found the same kind of thing when he took a tour of duty in New York, and put forward an agenda of sixteen points "for the better ordering of the spiritual and temporal affairs of the society." In this tightening of discipline he was supported by a letter from Wesley, and much strengthened on October 10 by a further letter appointing him Assistant in place of Boardman.[31] Already he had heard a whisper which seemed to imply that his senior colleagues were being recalled to England, and he had clearly added his own to other complaints about them.[32] Boardman took the news of Asbury's promotion over him with good grace, but Pilmore felt that he had been betrayed, and "went weeping away."[33]

As a matter of fact Asbury's added responsibility was for a short time only, and he must surely have known it. At the Leeds Conference in August, 1772, Thomas Webb had stirred the assembly with an appeal for still more preachers for America, and there appears to have been no lack of volunteers. For almost two years Wesley had been pleading with Thomas Rankin, one of his most experienced men, to help straighten the tangled American skein. Webb's appeal was just sufficient to tip the scales in America's favor, even though Rankin was wise enough to make allowances for Webb's "lively imagination."[34] Rankin, a man of thirty-five who had been an itinerant preacher for eleven years, at least seven of them as an Assistant, had even spent the year 1770–1 on the London circuit—when Wesley earmarked him for America. He chose as his companion George Shadford, who was a year younger, had begun his ministry as Rankin's junior colleague in Cornwall, and had now itinerated for four years, the latter two as Assistant.

It was arranged that the two men should each take charge of an English circuit until the spring, when they would return to America with Webb. They sailed on Good Friday, April 9, 1773, accompanied by Webb's new bride and another English local preacher, Joseph Yerbury—his name is spelled in several different ways. Webb had persuaded Yerbury to try his hand at the American itinerancy, but the

31. Asbury, *Journal*, I, 41, 46; both letters have disappeared.
32. Ibid., I, 39, 41, 45.
33. Ibid., I, 48; cf. Pilmore, *Journal*, pp. 134, 206.
34. Jackson, *Early Methodist Preachers*, V, 183–4.

young man found that he was not cut out for the task and returned to England with Richard Wright.[35] The party arrived in Philadelphia on June 1, 1773.

THOMAS RANKIN

Rankin, of course, being appointed "General Assistant" by Wesley, immediately took over responsibility from Asbury, and Asbury seems to have been genuinely happy to give place to such an obviously experienced disciplinarian.[36] Even Pilmore and Boardman seemed to turn over a new leaf, though by December both had determined to return to England.[37] Although somewhat austere and even domineering in character, contrasting greatly with Shadford's warmth and spiritual informality, on the whole Rankin merited Asbury's gratitude. Asbury was cautious, however. In such a pioneering situation it was still frequently necessary for him to make his own working decisions, but he was very careful to add the proviso—"unless Mr. Rankin has given orders to the contrary."[38] As General Assistant Rankin in effect exercised an episcopal role, stationing the other preachers in their circuits, but limiting himself to none.[39]

Within six weeks of his arrival Thomas Rankin had summoned the preachers to America's first General Conference, designed to set the tone for a more tightly organized connection. By this the authority of Wesley and the British Conference was explicitly extended to America, and their doctrine and discipline as contained in the British *Minutes* was accepted as the American norm. Any preacher who proved disloyal to the *Minutes* was no longer to be regarded as in connection with Wesley. Wesley's writings were to be reprinted only with his consent or that of his authorized itinerant representatives; Williams, who had erred at this point, was warned that he might sell what he had, but must reprint no more without explicit permission. No preacher was to administer the sacraments. The printed rule on this point was inflexible, but Asbury's manuscript account shows

35. Ibid., V, 185, and Thomas Rankin, MS Journal for June 5, 1774.
36. Asbury, *Journal*, I, 82.
37. Rankin, MS journal, Aug. 29, Dec. 2, 1773.
38. Asbury, *Journal*, III, 19.
39. *Minutes* (American, 1795), pp. 14–15 (1775); see also the much fuller manuscript minutes kept by Philip Gatch, copied from the *Western Christian Advocate* of May 19 and 26, 1837, by the Baltimore Conference Methodist Historical Society, 1964, pp. 2–3; cf. Asbury, *Journal*, I, 246.

that an exception was made in the case of Strawbridge, who had been doing it for years, a practice winked at by Boardman and Pilmore, so that even Asbury had felt "obliged to connive . . . for the sake of peace."[40] Strawbridge, however, was only to administer "under the particular direction of the Assistant." To Asbury was allotted the task of bringing Strawbridge to good old-fashioned Methodist wisdom. At the Maryland Quarterly Meeting on August 2, Asbury reports: "I read a part of our *Minutes,* to see if brother Strawbridge would conform; but he appeared to be inflexible. He would not administer the ordinances under our direction at all. Many things were said on the subject; and a few of the people took part with him." A firm beginning had at last been made, however, and at least Strawbridge now knew that in Wesley's eyes he was clearly a renegade, only able to continue his defiance at the cost of a schism, which in a few years almost took place.

The names of Williams and King (as mentioned above) had been dropped from the British *Minutes* in 1771, clearly because these two were regarded by Wesley simply as local preachers assisting the regular itinerants. Nor were their names reinstated until 1773—there had just been time for an assurance to reach England that these two, at any rate, were prepared to toe the connectional line. The name of Strawbridge never appeared in the British *Minutes,* and in 1774 was dropped from the American *Minutes* (in which it appeared in 1773), and dropped surely as an implied threat to his precarious status. In 1775 he was once more stationed, but then dropped completely. The reason is clearly illustrated in Asbury's *Journal* for August 27, 1775, describing a Virginia Quarterly Meeting: "Mr. Strawbridge discovered his independent principles, in objecting to our discipline. He appears to want no preachers: he can do as well or better than they." For better or worse the government of the Methodist societies *as a connection* was to remain firmly under the control of Wesley's official itinerant preachers and those who were loyal to them.

By the time of the first American Conference in 1773 there had begun a trickle of British and native local preachers into the full-time itinerancy. The 1773 *Minutes* list ten preachers stationed in six circuits. Of these men four were British itinerants— Rankin, Shadford, Asbury, and Wright. Five were British immigrants, all apparently local preachers in their homeland—King, Strawbridge, Yerbury, Wil-

40. *Minutes* (American, 1795), pp. 5–6 (1773); Asbury, *Journal,* I, 60, 85.

liams, and Abraham Whitworth. One only was a native American—
William Watters, a promising young man of twenty-one, a product of
Baltimore, Maryland, though brought into the ministry by Williams
rather than by Strawbridge.[41] Within a few years the four British-
trained itinerants were reduced to one, and the American-raised
greatly multiplied. By the standards of their most competent leaders,
Rankin and Asbury, however, the native preachers left much to be
desired. During an extended journey into the South in 1772 Pilmore
had noted—and if Rankin or Asbury ever read these words they would
have said, "Amen!": "God has undoubtedly begun a good work in
these parts by the ministry of Messrs. John King, and Robert Williams, and Robert Strawbridge, but there is much danger from those
who follow a heated imagination rather than the pure illumination
of the Spirit and the directions of the Word of God. Wherever I go
I find it necessary to bear my testimony against all wildness, shouting,
and confusion in the worship of God, and at the same time to feed and
preserve the sacred fire—which is certainly kindled in many hearts of
this country."[42] Eight years later a sympathetic evangelical clergyman
confessed his fears to the great friend of the Methodists, the Rev. Devereux Jarratt of Bath parish, Dinwiddie County, Virginia: "The
Methodists . . . countenance so many illiterate creatures void of all
prudence and discretion that I have no expectation of any good and
lasting effects from their misguided zeal." Jarratt's reply showed that
he was in general agreement, though he pointed out: "Surely [Wes-
ley's] preachers from Europe are not such lame hands as those among
us."[43]

Small wonder that there was erosion in the ranks of the American
Methodist itinerancy. It is impossible to secure adequate information
about many of the preachers, not even the date and place of their
birth, or whether they were immigrants or American-born. Between
1773 and 1778, however, the American *Minutes* record the names of
over 60 men, quite apart from the British itinerants. Of these only
28 remained in 1778—including 10 admitted on trial that very year!
A few were very young, like William Duke, who was accepted into
the itinerancy when he was sixteen. Many left to get married, or the
better to support a wife and family. In some instances a lack of apti-
tude was clearly demonstrated; others became "worn out," still others

41. Watters, op. cit., pp. 18–30. 43. Asbury, *Journal*, III, 24–5.
42. Pilmore, *Journal*, p. 138.

simply weary. One of the technical terms contributed by American Methodism was applied to the men thus lost to the itinerancy—they "located." Some of them became men of substance whose homes were thrown open as preaching centers, such as Colonel John Beck; others helped to raise important churches, as did William Moore, one of the founders of Lovely Lane Chapel, Baltimore. Upon the tough and courageous residue was soon to descend the destiny of staffing and steering a new denomination, fortunately under the supervising eye of Francis Asbury.

Rankin's second American Conference, held in May, 1774, continued the work begun in the first. His journal recorded: "We proceeded in all things on the same plan as in England, which our Minutes will declare."[44] Traveling south from the Conference, he noted: "I met all the societies as I rode along, and found many truly alive to God. Nevertheless, I saw the necessity of enforcing our discipline strongly wherever I came. I found a degree of slackness in this respect in almost every society. I am more and more convinced that unless the whole plan of our discipline is closely attended to we can never see that work, nor the fruit of our labours, as we would desire."[45] The British Conference that year sent replacements for Pilmore and Boardman, who had returned in January—James Dempster, an itinerant of ten years' standing, eight of them as an Assistant, and Martin Rodda, who had been an itinerant intermittently for seven years, the last as Dempster's colleague in Cornwall.

THE WAR YEARS

The new men came at a difficult period. Such was the anti-British atmosphere that within a year Rankin wrote telling Asbury that both Rodda and Dempster were returning to England, and he with them. In his reply Asbury apparently stated his opinion that to desert the Americans would be "an eternal dishonour to the Methodists," and shamed them into remaining for at least the time being.[46] For the time being they all stayed, and worked faithfully, and seemed to be giving special attention to training the American preachers who

44. Jackson, *Early Methodist Preachers*, V, 200.
45. Rankin, MS Journal, July 29, 1774.
46. Asbury, *Journal*, I, 161, 163.

would soon be taking over the reins.[47] As a partial symbol of this loyalty the British *Minutes* for 1775 not only listed six American preachers in the stations for circuit "51, America," but officially noted their admission to the Methodist itinerancy.[48] The declared policy of the British preachers in America was to remain neutral in political matters, and some of them were avowed pacifists. Yet their sympathies were naturally with the mother country. Martin Rodda apparently gave them a bad reputation by injudicious loyalist propaganda, but in his favor it should be noted that he shared with Rankin some of the credit for bringing Freeborn Garrettson into the American ministry.[49]

In 1776 James Dempster left the itinerant work, though for a time he seems to have served the Methodist cause in beleaguered New York.[50] In September, 1777, Rankin and Rodda set out for England, though in fact they were not able to sail until the following spring. In March, 1778, Shadford also gave up the work, leaving Asbury, in spite of attempted persuasion and admitted nostalgia, alone.[51]

In view of this eventuality there had been tearful farewells, and the careful consideration of emergency arrangements, at the Conference of 1777, which had been preceded by a preparatory caucus. Question 11 (not reproduced in the printed *Minutes*) was one of the most significant in its acknowledgment of the past and its looking towards the future: "Q.11. Can anything be done in order to lay a foundation for a future union, supposing the old preachers should be, by the times, constrained to return to Great Britain? Would it not be well for all who are willing to sign some articles of agreement, and strictly adhere to the same till other preachers are sent by Mr. Wesley and the brethren in conference?" The twenty preachers pres-

47. Asbury at least was concerned about this. On an earlier occasion he had chided Williams for what he felt was faulty doctrine, and it seems fairly certain that he similarly passed on his opinions about their preaching technique to other rising preachers such as Samuel Spragg, who spoiled a good sermon with "a few pompous, swelling words," and Richard Webster, whose language contained "some little inaccuracies." See his *Journal*, I, 97, 188, 195–6.

48. *Minutes* (English), I, 116, 118. The men were William Duke, John Wade, Daniel Ruff, Edward Dromgoole (in fact a native of Ireland), Isaac Hollings, and Richard Webster.

49. Freeborn Garrettson, *The Experience and Travels of Mr. Freeborn Garrettson*, pp. 44–7, 82.

50. Barclay, op. cit., I, 44, 375 (n. 194).

51. Asbury, *Journal*, I, 228, 234–5, 243, 259, 263–9.

ent resolved: "We will do it."[52] Their document (to which in fact twenty-five signatures were appended) was almost word for word a copy of that signed by the preachers in the British Conferences of 1769, 1773, 1774, and 1775, pledging allegiance to their evangelical task and to the doctrines and discipline of Methodism as set forth in the *Minutes*.[53] The American version went on to add a fourth point: "To choose a committee of Assistants to transact the business that is now done by the General Assistant and the old preachers who came from Britain."[54] The committee consisted of three native Americans —Daniel Ruff, William Watters, and Philip Gatch—together with two British immigrants who had fully thrown in their lot with America— Edward Dromgoole and William Glendenning.[55] Whatever the duration or the fortunes of the war, the preachers in conference were convinced that British Methodism must remain their model, and that if at all possible they must remain under Wesley's wing. The deep emotions of the leave-taking were undoubtedly caused not merely by sentimental attachments but by a catastrophic sense of the loss of spiritual guidance entailed by the break. Asbury's *Journal* noted: "When the time of parting came, many wept as if they had lost their first-born sons. They appeared to be in the deepest distress, thinking, as I suppose, they should not see the faces of the English preachers any more. This was such a parting as I never saw before."[56] Perhaps we should view the occasion also through the eyes of one of those same native preachers, William Watters: "I never saw so affecting a scene at the parting of the preachers before. Our hearts were knit together as the hearts of David and Jonathan, and we were obliged to use great violence to our feelings in tearing ourselves asunder. This was the last time I ever saw my very worthy friends and fathers, Rankin and Shadford."[57]

The last two years had seen an even greater swing to the South in the expansion of Methodism. During 1775–6 a wildfire revival had spread through much of Virginia, spilling over into North Carolina, so that by this time two-thirds of the American Methodists lived with-

52. Gatch, MS Minutes (1777).
53. *Minutes* (English), I, 88, 110, 116, 121.
54. Gatch, MS Minutes (1777); cf. Watters, op. cit., pp. 73–4.
55. Ibid.
56. Asbury, *Journal*, I, 239.
57. Watters, op. cit., p. 57.

in the orbit of the evangelical clergyman, the Reverend Devereux Jarratt.[58] Jarratt had co-operated heartily with Robert Williams and his colleagues because he was assured that like their founder they "were true members of the Church of England," whose "design was to build up and not to divide the church."[59] George Shadford sponsored a petition to the General Convention at Williamsburg to dissociate the Methodists from the Baptists, pointing out that they were "not Dissenters, but a Religious Society in communion with the Church of England."[60] Like many of Wesley's Anglican colleagues, Jarratt even agreed to attend the deliberations of the Methodists' Conference.[61] Williams himself died before the revival reached its climax, but his task was eagerly taken up by Shadford, and (somewhat less eagerly) by Rankin.[62]

The Virginia revival added to the dimensions of Methodist opportunity, but also of the difficulty, especially as the Episcopal clergy who were theoretically needed to administer the sacraments to Methodists were in increasingly short supply—or in increasingly hotter water with liberty-minded Americans. After lengthy discussion of the problem the members of the 1777 Conference unanimously agreed not themselves to begin administering, but "to lay it over for the determination of the next Conference."[63] When that Conference came round Asbury had prudently but sadly gone into semi-retirement in Delaware until his way should open up for a fuller itinerancy—though at least he had remained in America to do what little he could. Upon the committee, therefore, was thrown the responsibility of guiding affairs at the Leesburg Conference. Watters reports: "Having no old preachers with us, we were as orphans bereft of our spiritual parents, and though young and unexperienced to transact the business of conference, yet the Lord looked graciously upon us, and had the uppermost seats in all our hearts, and of course in our meeting. As the consideration of our administering the ordinances [was] at the last conference laid over till this, it of course came on and found many advocates. It was with considerable difficulty that a large majority was

58. Lee, *Short History*, pp. 51–9; Gewehr, op. cit., pp. 138–66.
59. Devereux Jarratt, *The Life of the Reverend Devereux Jarratt*, p. 108.
60. Sweet, *Virginia Methodism*, pp. 76–7.
61. Asbury, *Journal*, I, 178.
62. Gewehr, op. cit., pp. 147–57; Lee, *Short History*, pp. 57–8.
63. Watters, op. cit., p. 57.

prevailed on to lay it over again, till the next conference, hoping that we should by then be able to see our way more clear in so important a change." [64]

For the 1779 Conference a preparatory meeting was held at Judge Thomas White's in Delaware, mainly for the convenience of Asbury, whose headquarters this was. William Watters came in the hope of persuading Asbury to attend the regular Conference planned to meet in Fluvanna, Virginia, but without success. Asbury and those of the Northern circuits felt it unwise to court danger to their cause by going into Virginia, and Watters was deputed to carry their greetings and opinions. When the more numerous Southern brethren met at the appointed time they were inclined to regard this preliminary gathering as a conspiracy to defeat their position on the sacramental issue, and accordingly refused to endorse the Northern proposition that, in succession to Rankin, Asbury should be regarded as "General Assistant in America." Claiming that "the Episcopal Establishment is now dissolved, and therefore in almost all our circuits the members are without the ordinances," they appointed a presbytery of three preachers to ordain themselves and the others in order that they might duly administer the sacraments. Interestingly enough, this same group which thus made a daring ecclesiastical innovation was extremely conservative in other ways, reinforcing the authority of the Assistant in each circuit, and insisting that the local preachers and exhorters should not get out of line. That lesson at least they had well learned from the British itinerants, and the ordination proposals were considered as carefully and prayerfully as even John Wesley could have wished—though he could hardly have agreed with the conclusions reached. [65]

Watters' chief reason for attending both conferences was his fear that if steps were taken to administer the sacraments "an entire division" might result. [66] Others also were anxious to prevent this. In 1780 Northern preachers again held a separate Conference, which on this occasion was attended not only by Watters but by two of the ordaining presbytery of the south, Philip Gatch and Reuben Ellis. Asbury and his colleagues were adamant that only the complete cessation of administration of the sacraments could prevent a schism be-

64. Ibid., pp. 68–9.
65. Gatch, MS Minutes (1779), pp. 9–11; cf. Watters, op. cit., pp. 73–4.
66. Watters, op. cit., pp. 71–2.

tween the Northern and Southern Methodists. Asbury, Garrettson, and Watters were asked to attend the Southern Conference to present this point of view. The ultimatum in fact seemed to harden the issue. And then suddenly the matter was resolved by Asbury's suggestion that his brethren should simply suspend administration for one year. This first delay led to others, and matters stood in pretty much the same position when the war ended in 1783. Asbury and others urged upon Wesley that it was now up to him to help them out of their dilemma.

WHATCOAT AND VASEY

It was at this stage, after a decade's enforced delay, that Wesley sent over his last pair of itinerants, Richard Whatcoat and Thomas Vasey. Each was older than any of his predecessors. Vasey had been born in the same year as Asbury, and was now nearing forty, having been an itinerant for nine years. Whatcoat was forty-eight, and had been an itinerant for sixteen years, and frequently an Assistant. He was regarded by Wesley as an admirable successor to Asbury as General Assistant, and eventually like him was in fact elevated to the American Methodist episcopacy. These men were the first exemplars of the precious gift of Holy Orders so long impatiently awaited by American Methodism, and they assisted Dr. Thomas Coke in ordaining Asbury. Through these years of waiting, however, Asbury had grown steadily in stature among his American colleagues, as they had in his eyes (helped partly by the training which he strove to furnish), so that when the time came he refused vicarious ordination from Wesley's hands alone, but sought and received the mandate of the American itinerants. Thus was born a church which had been strangely preserved to make the best of two worlds, the old and the new, the episcopal and the presbyterian, of ordered worship and revival meeting, of city and frontier.

In a sense, however, Asbury's ordination and the official setting up of the Methodist Episcopal Church in 1784 were only the icing on the cake. The main task had been accomplished by those eight pioneer preachers rather than by their two belated successors. It is true, as William Warren Sweet has pointed out, that the departure of the British itinerants to leave the work in the hands of native preachers can hardly be regretted; it was one of the better by-products of the sad conflict between a repressive mother country and a vigorous, virile, colony. It is doubtful, however, whether their return home should be described as an "unmixed blessing."[67] It was certainly not so regarded by the native preachers themselves. Another important point must be made. Although American Methodism had not been unduly hurt by the withdrawal of the British preachers, especially as they regretfully left Asbury behind, it would have been immeasurably hurt had they never come. They came with a purpose; they fulfilled that purpose, and they left, albeit sooner than either Wesley or they had intended, and under far different circumstances from those that any of them would have wished.

They had fulfilled their purpose. The first decade of the Methodist Societies in America constituted the period of securing church order, the second that of securing Holy Orders. Had the American Methodists been without the oversight of Wesley's delegates in either quest Methodism would not have developed along the same lines that it did, and one suspects that it might have evaporated into a formless and dwindling revivalist sect. Not that the actual Methodist discipline in all its details so earnestly inculcated by Boardman and Pilmore and their later colleagues was all that important in itself. A living organism needs periodically to discard its tissue that it may be renewed, needs also to adapt itself to differing environments. Many of the prominent features of early Methodism, both in Britain and America, became outmoded, notably the early morning services, the love-feasts, the class-tickets (at least in America), and even the class-meeting itself. The chief value of the work and witness of the early British itinerants was that they helped to ensure that the scattered American Methodist societies did indeed learn to function as part of a living organism, a connectional unity, instead of developing at random. The Methodist Episcopal Church, for all its seeming dissociation from Wesley's British Methodist societies, was in fact their vigorous extension into a new area and a new era, and owed a great debt to those agents of his who struggled against prejudice and persecution to help set it on its feet.

67. Sweet, *Religion on the American Frontier*, IV, 36.

7. FRANCIS ASBURY—JOHN WESLEY'S EPISCOPAL APPRENTICE

On Wednesday September 4, 1771, Francis Asbury, who had celebrated his twenty-sixth birthday only two weeks earlier, embarked for America at the tiny port of Pill near Bristol, opening a new chapter in his own life and that of the Christian Church. After a week he was sufficiently recovered from the devastations of seasickness to set down in his freshly begun *Journal* a few revealing thoughts: "Whither am I going? To the New World. What to do? To gain honour? No, if I know my own heart. To get money? No. I am going to live to God, and to bring others so to do. . . . The people God owns in England are the Methodists. The doctrines they preach, and the discipline they enforce are, I believe, the purest of any people now in the world. . . . If God does not acknowledge me in America, I will soon return to England."[1]

There is not the slightest doubt that Asbury did indeed sail for America not out of discontent, not urged on by a restless wanderlust, not beckoned by ambition or wealth, but primarily as an evangelist—"to live to God, and to bring others so to do." Yet unlike many evangelists he was no free lance, no emotional tub-thumper. To him both doctrine and discipline were essential to his primary task: he sought to introduce men not only to conversion but to Christian fellowship, to church and sacrament. And he was convinced that the best way to do this was by the proved methods of Methodism. God had used Wesley and his preachers greatly in England; if Asbury were not used to similar good purpose in America, he was resolved to return home. England was not merely his birthplace; it was his training-ground for evangelism. John Wesley was not only a great leader who had recognized young Frank's potential; he was his tutor in evangelism and churchmanship. Asbury was not simply one of Wesley's preachers who was permitted to leave the homeland for an overseas venture, but one whose total Methodist experience was to be focused on making that venture fruitful, even to the point of founding a new church

Delivered at the Francis Asbury Bicentennial Celebration, Lake Junaluska, N.C., Sept. 4, 1971.
  1. Asbury, *Journal*, I, 4–5.

and becoming its leading bishop. He was John Wesley's episcopal apprentice.

The first one-third of Asbury's life therefore deserves closer study than the youthful background of many immigrants. English Methodism under John Wesley not only formed the backdrop against which Asbury's gifts matured, but was woven into the fabric of his thought and ecclesiastical practice. Although eventually he rebelled against the control of American Methodism by the distant and aging hand of Wesley, that hand had been effectively at work guiding his own early training, until he reached the stage when in order to fulfil Wesley's spiritual ideals he felt compelled to shake off Wesley's restraints.

CHILDHOOD AND YOUTH

Asbury's early formative years were spent among a cluster of small Staffordshire towns and villages on the western fringes of Birmingham, rapidly earning for themselves the name of the "Black Country" because of industries associated with coal, iron, and eventually steel. Methodism gained a strong footing in the area, as it did in most of the underchurched regions most subject to the worst turmoils of the Industrial Revolution. This in spite of vigorous persecution, of which the Wednesbury riots of 1743 merely constitute the best known example—the same kind of thing continued sporadically for a generation. The Methodists adjusted so well to their rough environment, however, that at Bradley they even persuaded the local ironmaster to build them an iron pulpit, which still survives.[2] Most of the villages have been swallowed up by the towns, and even the towns are now indistinguishable from the metropolitan sprawl of Birmingham.[3]

Owing so much to his own marvelous mother, Susanna Wesley, the founder of Methodism constantly urged the importance of religion in the home, and for Methodists Christianity was never a thing of Sunday and the parish church only. Young Francis Asbury was blessed in coming to such a home, poor in material things, but rich in the spiritual atmosphere created and maintained by his mother. He was born in Handsworth near Birmingham on August 20 or 21, 1745,

2. Frank Baker, *The Methodist Pilgrim in England*, p. 77; *WHS*, IV, 200.
3. See W. C. Sheldon, "The Landmarks of Bishop Asbury's Childhood and Youth," pp. 97–103.

two years after the anti-Methodist riots at Wednesbury—about four miles from his birthplace—had left bitter memories of shattered homes, looted furnishings and shopgoods, bruised and broken bodies, miscarriage and rape. Asbury must have been shown some of the hacked pieces of furniture preserved for a century and more as souvenirs by the courageous Methodists and their descendants.

Joseph Asbury, his father, was "employed as a farmer and gardener by the two richest families in the parish," the Wyrleys of Hamstead Hall and the Goughs of Perry Hall.[4] Unfortunately he was unthrifty, as well as careless about religion, which threw a heavier burden on his wife Elizabeth, a descendant of an "ancient and respectable" Welsh family named Rogers. Elizabeth Asbury was about thirty years old when baby Francis was born, her husband a little older. Their only other child, baptized Sarah on May 3, 1743, died soon after her fifth birthday, and was buried in Handsworth parish churchyard on May 28, 1748. Francis Asbury speaks of his "lovely sister," but being not yet three when she died he could hardly remember her well. Nevertheless he owed much to her, for her death threw his mother upon the resources of religion. A family tradition tells of a vision before his birth in which it was revealed to Elizabeth Asbury that her child would be a boy, and that he would become a great religious leader. She devoted herself wholeheartedly to the realization of that dream. If Susanna Wesley was "the Mother of Methodism," then Elizabeth Asbury may lay claim to being "the Mother of American Methodism." Her constant reading of religious books exercised a strange fascination over young Francis, and in later years he retained a vivid picture of her standing "by a large window poring over a book for hours together."[5]

This would surely be in the cottage on Newton Road in the parish of Great Barr, to which the family moved when Asbury was still a young child. His actual birthplace (near the present railway station) at Hamstead was long ago sacrificed to modern progress. His childhood home, however, so much more important in his development,

4. Asbury, *Journal*, I, 720. This is from Asbury's longest autobiographical account of his youth, inserted under the date July 19, 1792 (pp. 720-2); another is inserted in his journal for July 18, 1774 (I, 123-5), and another brief summary on Aug. 24, 1794 (II, 43). Cf. also, for some youthful memories, Robert J. Bull, "John Wesley Bond's Reminiscences of Francis Asbury," pp. 3-33. Because of imperfect recollection these (and still other) accounts are difficult to reconcile with each other in some details, though they agree in outline. Cf. *WHS*, XII, 99-100.

5. Ibid., I, 720.

still stands, a small green oasis in Birmingham's concrete desert, lifted above the noisy bustle of the arterial road beside which it rests. While still very young Francis was sent to school, apparently at Snails Green, his parents paying a shilling a week for his tuition. By the time he was six he could read his Bible, and "greatly delighted in the historical part of it." Such a student was he that he "would pry into the Bible by twinkling firelight," though rebuked by his mother: "Frank, you will spoil your eyes!" It was one of the joys of this other Frank who now writes to sit in that same ingle-nook in 1970, as two hundred American Methodists made pilgrimage to the restored cottage with its simple furnishing, and tried to visualize that serious young boy whom his playmates aptly nicknamed "Methodist parson."[6]

Adolescence was not kind to the young boy. An abortive spiritual conflict when he was twelve was combined with cruel beatings at school, so that his father reluctantly removed him from that place of terror when he was about thirteen. For a few months he became a servant "in one of the wealthiest and most ungodly families" in the parish, where his early religious tendencies and training were almost stifled. From this he was rescued at the age of thirteen and a half by being bound apprentice in a godly home where he "was treated more like a son or an equal than an apprentice." For generations there has been speculation about the trade which he thus learnt, which he terms only "a branch of business." In 1874 F. W. Briggs, in his *Bishop Asbury*, put forward as a fact his attractive theory that Asbury was apprenticed to a Methodist blacksmith, father of the iron-founder Henry Foxall, who became a wealthy benefactor of American Methodism, building the first Foundery Methodist Episcopal Church in Washington, D.C. In default of hard evidence this theory filled the vacuum, and has been repeated so many times that it has almost come to be accepted as proven fact. British local historians, however, now point to much earlier documentary evidence claiming that Asbury was bound apprentice to John Griffin, whose trade was "chape filing," i.e., making fittings for sword scabbards, belt buckles, bucket handles, and similar hardware.[7]

6. Ibid., I, 720–1.

7. J. M. Day, brochure for the official reopening of the Asbury Cottage, Newton Road, Great Barr, Nov. 27, 1957, p. 7, quoting a manuscript of the local historian, Joseph Reeves, dated 1834. (See also *Methodist History*, XI, No. 1 [Oct., 1972], 44.) This would add more point to one of Asbury's enquiries in 1802, in a letter to John Rogers of Walsall: "Is she that was Widow Griffin now living, and in what circumstances? And

For some years the Asbury home had been a center for religious gatherings.[8] When Francis was about fourteen he gained a new spiritual impetus from one of their religious visitors (not a Methodist) whom Mrs. Asbury persuaded to take the boy under his wing. He forsook the ministrations of the "blind priest" (as Asbury calls him) at Great Barr parish church for the evangelical preaching sponsored by the Earl of Dartmouth at All Saints' Church, West Bromwich. He began to delve into sermon literature, especially the writings of George Whitefield and John Cennick, which so gripped his interest that he wanted to know more about Methodism. Once again his mother served him well. She advised him to go over to Wednesbury, the focal point of Methodist witness and persecution, still under threat from the Wolverhampton mob, who were adept at destroying Methodist preaching-houses.[9] The devout enthusiasm of the worshipers, their warmhearted singing of hymns, their extempore prayers and preaching, impressed him greatly. He became a regular visitor. Here he heard many of the Methodist leaders, including the saintly John Fletcher, who in 1760 became vicar of Madeley in Shropshire, about twenty-five miles to the northwest.[10] He would surely have been present when John Wesley preached in the new chapel at Wednesbury, a plain, square building seating 350, on March 4, 1760.[11] During the summer of that year Alexander Mather came to the Staffordshire Circuit—the ex-baker preacher whom thirty years later Wesley was to ordain as superintendent for the British Methodists after his death. Under Mather's fervent appeals Asbury experienced a new sense of divine forgiveness, possibly during one of the prayer meetings maintained by Mrs. Mather. A few months later, as he prayed with a companion in his father's old barn, he "experienced a marvelous display of the grace of God, which some might think was full sanctification." He was about sixteen.[12]

---

in what station? Be pleased to write me if she has religion" (*Journal*, III, 243). For Foxall, see *Wesleyan Methodist Magazine*, 1824, pp. 505–8, and Homer L. Calkin, "Henry Foxall," pp. 36–49. F. W. Briggs, *Bishop Asbury*, pp. 10–12, makes Foxall almost an adolescent contemporary of Asbury, whereas he was born thirteen years later—his dates are 1758–1823. Foxall's journal apparently mentioned no early links with Asbury himself, but only with his mother.

8. Asbury, *Journal*, III, 144; cf. *WHS*, XXII, 123.
9. Jackson, *Early Methodist Preachers*, II, 181–3.
10. Asbury, *Journal*, I, 124.
11. Wesley, *Journal*, IV, 367.
12. Asbury, *Journal*, I, 125; cf. Jackson, *Early Methodist Preachers*, II, 179–81.

BEGINNINGS IN CHRISTIAN WITNESS

Francis Asbury's first efforts at witnessing to his faith were made under his mother's guidance. Every two weeks she conducted a devotional meeting for women, and took her son with her to read the Bible and announce the hymns. Francis records with a glint of humor —he was not *entirely* devoid of that saving grace: "After I had been thus employed as a clerk for some time, the good sisters thought Frank might venture a word of exhortation. So, after reading, I would venture to expound and paraphrase a little on the portion read."[13] Soon he began to conduct meetings at home, and also in the house of his great friend Edward Hand, of Sutton Coldfield. So impressed was Alexander Mather with the reports of the young man's gifts that while he was still only seventeen he was appointed leader of the first Society Class at West Bromwich Heath.[14]

This was, of course, a class for Christian fellowship rather than for teaching. Most of the twenty members were young men of about his own age, including James Mayo, James Bayley, Thomas Russell, and Thomas and Jabez Ault. They clung together at the weekends. Some of them would walk over to Wednesbury every Sunday morning for the 5:00 A.M. Methodist preaching service, then on to All Saints at West Bromwich for the morning and afternoon Anglican worship, returning to Wednesbury for the Methodist evening service. They were loyal churchmen and loyal Methodists at the same time. The first meeting-place of Asbury's first little flock was in the home of Joseph Heywood. But in 1764 Bayley and Russell bought an unfinished building facing the Common, twenty-four feet square, and completed it, so that they had their own "Society room."[15] Here services were held on Sundays at 8:00 A.M.—as if there weren't enough Sunday services for them!—the men sitting on one side of the central pillar and the women on the other, according to Wesley's instructions. To this room would come occasionally another of the fruits of Alexander Mather's Staffordshire ministry, Richard Whatcoat, nine years Asbury's senior, a class-leader and local preacher of Wednesbury, who was to become a brother bishop with him in America.[16]

13. J. B. Wakeley, *The Heroes of Methodism*, p. 24.
14. H. H. Prince, *The Romance of Early Methodism in and around West Bromwich and Wednesbury*, pp. 47, 84, etc.
15. Ibid., pp. 55–6.
16. Jackson, *Early Methodist Preachers*, V, 312–15; cf. Phoebus, *Whatcoat*, pp. 9–13.

When Asbury was eighteen he himself received official status as a local preacher. His first public service was conducted at Manwoods cottage on the estate of the Earl of Dartmouth—the same Lord Dartmouth (1731–1801) who during the first few years of Asbury's American ministry was Colonial Secretary (1772–5), greatly troubled by the restless spirit of independence in the American colonies. Lord Dartmouth was a regular worshiper at the little Methodist chapel in Wednesbury, where he surely would have met young Francis Asbury; when in the chapel he encouraged his tenants, who were accustomed to addressing him as "My Lord," to call him simply "Brother Dartmouth." Standing behind a chair in Manwoods cottage as a young man of about eighteen Francis Asbury began a preaching career of over fifty years, which was to knit together the largest branch of the Methodist family in the world. Let us not overglamorize the lowly beginnings of this craftsman preacher, however. An English local preacher was neither "fish, nor fowl, nor good red herring"—a mere stopgap, untrained, unlicensed, unorganized, unremunerated, and too often unappreciated. Asbury himself thus sums up the labors of the following two or three years: "Behold me now a local preacher! The humble and willing servant of any and every preacher that called on me by night or by day; being ready with hasty steps to go far and wide to do good, visiting Derbyshire, Staffordshire, Warwickshire, Worcestershire, and indeed almost every place within my reach, for the sake of precious souls; preaching generally three, four, and five times a week, and at the same time pursuing my calling."[17]

What in those days he lacked in culture he made up in zeal, and an old Methodist at Shottle remembered him preaching in a farmhouse there as "a youth not quite out of his 'teens, with a voice like the roaring of a lion"![18] Even then he was showing a spirit of marked independence, and a letter is preserved in which the Assistant or superintendent preacher in charge of the circuit, William Orpe, felt constrained to remind the young local preacher that he was expected loyally to fulfill his appointments.[19] This does not imply slackness, however. On most weekdays he would be up at 4:00 A.M. in order to finish work so as to be able to attend Methodist gatherings four or

---

When preaching his funeral sermon Asbury said that he had known Whatcoat since he (Asbury) was fourteen (ibid., p. 104).

17. Asbury, *Journal*, I, 722.
18. *WHS*, XVI, 76.

19. Asbury, *Journal*, III, 10.

five miles distant, from which he sometimes did not return until midnight—walking both ways. On Sundays he would "hold meetings" at
three or four different places—again traveling on foot.[20]

ITINERANT PREACHER

During the closing weeks of 1766 the twenty-one-year-old Asbury
was called upon to supply the appointments of this same William
Orpe, who was besieged by complex problems both within and without the circuit, and shortly afterwards left the itinerancy altogether.[21]
This experience proved so successful that at the ensuing Conference
Asbury was "admitted on trial" as an itinerant preacher, and appointed
to the Bedfordshire circuit as "Helper" to James Glassbrook.

Glassbrook merits more than a passing mention, for he played an
important part in initiating Asbury into the challenges, the satisfac-
tions, and the frustrations of the regular Methodist itinerancy, which
he himself left in a few years for the Presbyterian ministry. He had
been Wesley's traveling-companion on several occasions, and would
have much to tell Asbury, from the time when he was left behind on
the Liverpool quay while Wesley and the rest of the party set sail
hurriedly for Ireland, to the occasion when an Irish magistrate broke
his staff on Glassbrook's arm in revenge for protecting Wesley from
a mob which the magistrate himself had led. He would describe his
first coming to Bedfordshire in 1766, the death there of his young
wife, Wesley's funeral sermon for her, and his tours around the circuit
with Wesley, during one of which he must have pleaded for an energetic companion to help him build up the circuit, which included
parts of several neighboring counties and most of Northamptonshire.
Doubtless Glassbrook remembered young Asbury, as a vigorous local
preacher in Staffordshire when he had served there from 1765–6, and
may well have asked for him specifically. The two men got on well
together, and it was a great joy to Asbury in later years to meet Glassbrook again as a Presbyterian minister in New York, exclaiming, "The
Lord be with him and bless him!"[22]

20. *Methodist History*, IV, No. 1 (Oct., 1965), 25.
21. Asbury, *Journal*, III, 543. Orpe actually continued to fulfill many of the major
circuit responsibilities, such as attempting to settle problems connected with Methodist
property in Wednesbury and Darlaston, as is shown by a series of letters to him preserved by his descendants, transcripts of which are in my possession.
22. Ibid., I, 540.

As an itinerant Asbury really itinerated, from town to village, from village to town, for a circuit of two or three hundred miles, preaching to groups large and small; visiting families both Methodist and non-Methodist; trying to organize new societies—and to settle disputes in established ones; gratefully accepting whatever hospitality was offered, which varied from the occasional Epicurean to the normal Spartan; and hardly ever sleeping in the same bed (along with numerous tiny companions) for two successive nights. A valuable training-ground indeed for the American wilderness!

The 1768 Conference at Bristol received Asbury into "Full Connexion," and according to resolutions passed by the preceding Conference he should have been present on this occasion, though his earliest major biographer, F. W. Briggs (with what justification we do not know) claims that his first and last appearance at an English Conference was in 1771.[23] He was stationed that year in Colchester, or Essex, in sole charge of this one-man circuit, though he was not listed among the official list of Assistants. He did not stay long in Colchester, however. Like it or not, he was an itinerant preacher, not only *within* the circuits, but *among* them, and must go where he was sent, and when he was sent, by John Wesley, sometimes with the advice of his senior itinerants, sometimes without it, and occasionally against it. And so after a month or two Asbury was lifted out of Essex and sent to Wiltshire, to serve under his former colleague in the Staffordshire Circuit, Nicholas Manners. On October 26 that year he wrote to his parents his earliest letter to survive, assuring them that although he "had no choice" in his appointment he was "very well contented," that he was "in health and strength," and that at least his "bread and water" were sure. He confessed to a sense of unworthiness for his great task, but reassured his parents that this was the fulfilment of their own religious training of him: "I wonder sometimes how anyone will sit to hear me, but the Lord covers my weakness with his power. . . . I trust you will be easy and more quiet. As for me, I know what I am called to. It is to give up all, and to have my hands and heart in the work, yea, the nearest and dearest friends. . . . Let others condemn me as being without natural affection, as being stubborn, disobedient to parents, or say what they please. . . . I love my parents and friends, but I love my God better and his service. . . . And

23. Briggs, *Asbury*, p. 21. Asbury also hoped to go to Conference in 1770; see his *Journal*, III, 8.

tho' I have given up all, I do not repent, for I have found all."[24]

At the 1769 Conference Wesley sent Asbury once more to the Bedfordshire Circuit, under the superintendency of "that amiable man, Richard Henderson," who later retired from the itinerancy to establish a well-conducted private asylum at Bristol. Asbury's own statement, that he was "appointed Assistant in Northamptonshire," implies that he was chiefly responsible for the work in that county, though both men would itinerate around the whole of both counties, Henderson with his headquarters in Bedford, Asbury with his in Towcester, Northants.[25] Although never officially listed by Wesley as an Assistant in the British work, Asbury certainly knew from personal experience the problems and occasional rewards of that administrative burden.

Towards the end of the Conference year, on July 20, 1770, he wrote to his parents: "I do not expect to stay here another year. Where I shall go I cannot tell." In those days it was very rare for any preacher, especially a junior preacher, to be appointed to a circuit for more than one year at a time, or for him to have any idea where in fact he would be sent; and Asbury had already spent two terms in Bedfordshire, though with a year intervening. Is more implied here, however, than a statement of this obvious fact? Was America already in his mind? It is fairly certain that he had read a copy of Thomas Taylor's letter appealing for help in America, which Wesley had printed and circulated to the Assistants,[26] even though he may not have been present at the 1769 Conference and among those who then volunteered. Asbury's July 1770 letter to his parents contains other hints that he was unsettled as to his most fruitful field of service. He wrote: "Sometimes I please myself that I shall go hence and leave these parts"— and he may well have had in mind leaving England rather than leaving Bedfordshire.[27] At this time Wesley was seeking reinforcements for Boardman and Pilmore, though it seemed unsuccessfully.[28]

In fact at the 1770 Conference Asbury was appointed once more to the South Wiltshire or Salisbury Circuit, his place in Bedfordshire being taken by his old friend Richard Whatcoat. Visions of a wider field of labor now opened out more clearly before him. For six months

24. Asbury, *Journal*, III, 3–4.

25. Ibid., I, 125, III, 6–8.

26. See above, chap. 5, espec. pp. 79–82.

27. Asbury, *Journal*, III, 8.

28. Wesley may well have made an appeal at the 1770 Conference, as well as approaching preachers privately in advance. See pp. 91–2.

he had "strong intimations" of a divine call to work overseas.[29] It is just possible that the decision slowly crystallizing in his mind was aided by his mother's desire to disentangle him from a sentimental attachment of which there are hints—the one gossamer thread of "romance" in his life. Many women certainly found both him and the glamour of his calling strangely attractive—witness the "four affectionate sisters" who wrote to his mother from Basingstoke in the Salisbury Circuit in August, 1771, protesting about his going to America without bidding them goodbye, and asking to be kept in touch with him.[30]

At the Bristol Conference in 1771 the challenge—and the opportunity—came: "Our brethren in America call aloud for help," said Wesley, "Who are willing to go over and help them?" Asbury offered himself, and rejoiced that out of the five volunteers he was one of the two chosen. Within a month he was preaching his last sermon on English soil—a leavetaking message to parents and friends most of whom he was never to see again. His text was Psalm 61, verse 2: "From the end of the earth will I cry unto thee." It cost him much to leave home and kindred, as is witnessed by his affectionate letters and sacrificial remittances home: but the call of God was not to be denied.

APPRENTICESHIP COMPLETED

The springs of Asbury's evangelism—his eager desire "to live to God, and to bring others to do so"—were there from his early years, fed by the example and training of his mother. The proven methods of evangelism he had now learnt at the feet of John Wesley, to some extent directly in face to face meetings, to a much larger extent indirectly, through Wesley's ambassadors—his people, his preachers, his sermons, his books, his letters. Asbury's personal links with Wesley seem to have been relatively few, though Wesley did pay fairly regular annual visits to most circuits, so that almost every year from the opening of the Wednesbury chapel in 1760, when he was fourteen and a Methodist novice, Asbury had had fairly easy opportunities of hearing Wesley preach. (It is possible that in some of his later years as an itinerant preacher his own circuit responsibilities may have prevented

29. Asbury, *Journal*, I, 3.
30. Ibid., III, 9–10. For the possible romance, see his reference to Nancy Brookes, ibid., III, 4, though this is by no means unambiguous; but cf. also III, 36, where "what once befell me in England" in the context of a discussion of marriage may well imply a broken romance.

their paths from crossing, though this appears unlikely.) No comment upon any of these undoubted contacts, however, appears to have survived from the pen of either man. A few letters almost certainly passed between them during Asbury's English years, but again none have survived. Indeed the earliest extant examples of their correspondence during his American years is one from Asbury in 1780 and from Wesley in 1783.[31] The studious Asbury, however, had steeped himself in Wesley's writings, and thoughtfully pondered the commentary offered upon those writings by his itinerant colleagues and the Methodist people. His apprenticeship to his metalworking craft had been completed during six and a half years with Mr. Griffin; his apprenticeship to his life's work also was completed during his years in England. When he came to America he speedily showed himself the master craftsman, equipped with a thorough understanding of Wesley's doctrine and discipline, an understanding nurtured by extensive reading, and tried out in the rough and tumble of English circuit life.

During the voyage, once over the worst of his seasickness, he spent much time in study, and all the books which he lists were written or edited by Wesley—with the one exception of the Bible. In this he was continuing the practice which he had begun as a young man, when he "became possessed of Mr. Wesley's writings, and for some years almost laid aside all other books but the Bible, and applied himself exceeding closely in reading every book that Mr. Wesley had written. . . ."[32]

For most of the other Britishers who wielded a major influence upon early American Methodism—John Wesley, George Whitefield, Thomas Webb, Thomas Taylor, Thomas Rankin, Thomas Coke; with Robert Strawbridge, Robert Williams, and Philip Embury as exceptions to the general rule—the Atlantic was little but an extended and uncomfortable hiatus between home and a period or periods of missionary activity in America. For Francis Asbury, however, it was the boundary separating conclusively the two segments of his life: the first one-third a faithful apprenticeship to Wesley, the second two-thirds a fruitful prosecution of his life's task. Yet the apprenticeship was certainly of inestimable influence, probably of inestimable worth.

31. Ibid., I, 450, III, 24; Wesley, *Letters*, VII, 190–1, and cf. VI, 13, in which Wesley asks one of the women leaders in Salisbury to "encourage Mr. Asbury" to "exhort believers . . . to press after *full* salvation as receivable *now*, and that by simple *faith*"; this letter should be dated 1771, not 1773.
    32. Asbury, *Journal*, I, 7; III, 533.

Without it Asbury could never have learned Wesley's spirit and methods; without these American Methodism could hardly have developed as it did—might never have developed at all. Asbury embarked at Pill as Wesley's apprentice; seven and a half weeks later he landed for the first and last time on American soil as the potential master craftsman of American Methodism.

8. FRANCIS ASBURY—MASTER CRAFTSMAN OF AMERICAN METHODISM

From the moment that he set foot on American soil in 1771, at the age of twenty-six, Francis Asbury saw himself as called to fulfil a great destiny, though it turned out to be far greater than he imagined. The American Methodists became to him wife and children, over whom he yearned, for whom he dreamed and sacrificed, but whom he was determined to subject to loving discipline for their eternal good. In all this he followed Wesley's examples, Wesley's rules, and always Wesley's spirit—though on occasion he forsook Wesley's explicit instructions the better to fulfil Wesley's long-range purposes. Nor did he count John Wesley—however much he might respect and love him —as his conscience and final arbiter in every problem. The situation confronting him presented not only many similarities to that in England, but many differences. He must come to terms with new circumstances, and devise his own answers—or rather discover God's answers. If Wesley's methods worked, as in many cases they did, well and good. If something different were needed, something different must be found. But whether he was following Wesley's blueprints, devising some adaptation of them, or boldly venturing upon some new experiment, the end product was the important thing: he was here in America, he maintained, "to live to God, and to bring others so to do."[1] The task was far more important than the tradition, far more important than the man himself—though in fact he proved admirably fitted for the task.

MASTER CRAFTSMAN

Asbury was a master craftsman. He had learned much about Methodism from Wesley, from his itinerants, from his people—from their mistakes as well as from their triumphs. He was convinced that Methodism had the answer to the religious problems of this vast New

Delivered in summary at the Francis Asbury Bicentennial Celebrations of the Baltimore Annual Conference, October 29, 1972.

1. Asbury, *Journal*, I, 4–5.

World, a new world no longer amenable to the ordered ways of the Established Church as he had known them in England, and as they were somewhat lamely functioning in America, with decreasing efficiency, during the generation preceding the Revolution. Indeed Methodism itself, in spite of Wesley's protests to the contrary, was a kind of revolution against the establishment. In America there was a danger that if true religion were not completely overshadowed by the urgent physical demands of a pioneering life it would become fragmented into a thousand varieties of noisy, novelty-seeking sects. *Some* kind of unifying order was surely needed in order to avoid sterility on the one hand and spiritual chaos on the other. The methods of Methodism offered one answer, perhaps the best answer, for the new situation.

Asbury had asked God to guide him as he approached this venture in the New World, though at the time he could not possibly envisage its eventual dimensions. "If God does not acknowledge me in America," he had vowed, "I will soon return to England."[2] A few years sufficed to convince him that America was indeed where God needed him. Even when the fratricidal agonies of the Revolution prevented him from exercising an open ministry except at too high a cost, not only to himself, but to his fellow-Methodists, unlike his English colleagues he still remained firmly convinced that this was where he was needed, and that this therefore was where he must stay.[3]

Indeed because of the Revolution he was needed all the more. For who else was now available to pull this Methodist people into a semblance of readiness for spiritual combat? True, there were dedicated and talented native preachers, but they still needed guidance—this much had been clearly demonstrated. And they were not only prepared to accept his guidance, but eagerly sought it—this also had been demonstrated. It seemed likely, indeed, that this was the only British guidance which they would accept, for had he not proved himself as one with them when others had left? He was the only capable leader experienced in the administration of British Methodism to throw in his lot with them. He must forge Methodism as a powerful sword in the hand of the Lord. He must craft this weapon to the glory of God,

2. Ibid.

3. James Dempster was the only other regular itinerant who remained. He retired because of illness, upon recovering became a Presbyterian minister in New York, and was the father of John Dempster (1794–1863), missionary and educator, who founded what later became Garrett Theological Seminary. (See Barclay, op. cit., I, 44, 347, 375.)

fitted to God's hand, a superb instrument of which neither John Griffin nor John Wesley nor his Master himself could ever be ashamed.

There is no doubt that in all this his English Methodist training was of immense importance. We must not forget, however, his apprenticeship as a chape filer to John Griffin, even though here we must be on our guard against high flights of fancy. Surely one can imagine Griffin saying to his young apprentice, however, as had been said a million times before and was to be said a million times later: "If a job's worth doing, it's worth doing well!" It is not fanciful to picture the master craftsman insisting on the last detail of patient perseverance in fashioning the metal fittings for a sword handle or its scabbard, or the less romantic parts of belt buckle or bucket, so that they should be both functional, durable, and graceful. Craftsmanship was a matter of pride in those days, and the master was paid to impart his craft—if necessary to beat it into the apprentice. During six arduous years Asbury learned his worldly skills in this school, and would rise at four in the morning so that his tasks would be completed to his master's satisfaction before he took time off for his Methodist meetings in the evening. Into his life's work of fashioning American Methodism into a superb spiritual instrument he infused the same care, the same assiduity, the same long hours. As often as not he continued to rise at four in the morning; he sweated, and ached, and groaned, and occasionally grumbled—but he made a good job of it.

RELIGIOUS PRAGMATIST

Whatever aided this supreme task he welcomed, and molded it to his purposes. Whatever did not immediately prove suitable might be twisted about in various experimental positions, but if then it didn't work it was discarded. Like his ecclesiastical master, John Wesley, Asbury was a religious pragmatist. Like Wesley he honored the past ages of the church, especially the apostolic era. But no practices instituted by the church alone were sacrosanct. He was an ecclesiastical Darwinist: he believed in the survival of the fittest. Even his doctrine of the ministry was functional: you were a minister because you were used by God, and only so long as you were used by God. Holy hands laid on you might confer the acknowledgment and blessing of church leaders upon the demonstrated activity of the Holy Spirit within you, but they did not *convey* the Holy Spirit, thus bringing about a change in your spiritual character.[4] Only the forms of worship, the styles of preaching and pastoral practice, the methods of administration, which continued to function efficiently were (in his view) worth preserving. The value of keeping in touch with the past was in order to deal with the present and prepare for the future. Liturgical worship, for instance, had certainly sustained an important role in the universal church; therefore the Book of Common Prayer, as modified for the Church of England, and again modified by Wesley for his overseas Methodists, *ought* to be of value. In Asbury's opinion, however, this was not one of the fundamental necessities of religion on the expanding frontier, and could therefore become subsidiary to the love-feast and the camp meeting—provided that "holy noise" did not degenerate into pandemonium, and that these spiritual "happenings" were under the oversight of one of the regular preachers.[5] The same was true about social concerns. However important, they were not *primary*. Thus the complete emancipation of Black slaves (about which Asbury felt just as strongly as Wesley) proved such a disruptive issue that it seemed likely to hinder the major task of building up the church. This goal, therefore, was regretfully modified, and left for fulfilment by a later generation.[6]

4. See William R. Cannon, "The Meaning of the Ministry in Methodism," pp. 3–19, espec. pp. 17–19.

5. Cf. L. C. Rudolph, *Francis Asbury*, pp. 115–21. Wesley's *Sunday Service of the Methodists*, of course, was a late development, not drilled into Asbury during his English apprenticeship, and was therefore the more readily neglected. See Lee, *Short History*, p. 107: "At this time the prayer book, as revised by Mr. Wesley, was introduced among us . . . But some of the preachers who had been long accustomed to pray extempore were unwilling to adopt this new plan. Being fully satisfied that they could pray better and with more devotion while their eyes were shut than they could with their eyes open. After a few years the prayer book was laid aside, and has never been used since in public worship." Cf. *HAM*, I, 422, 424, and Paul S. Sanders, "The Sacraments in Early American Methodism," pp. 355–71.

6. Cf. David H. Bradley, "Francis Asbury and the Development of African Churches in America," pp. 3–29. Unfortunately the modern edition of Asbury's *Journal* follows an expurgated text which sadly disguises his deep sympathy with the slaves. Some of the deleted passages (for Feb. 23, March 27, and April 23, 1779) follow: "I have lately been impressed with a deep concern for bringing about the freedom of slaves in America, and feel resolved to do what I can to promote it. If God in His providence hath detained me in this country to be instrumental in so merciful and great an undertaking, I hope He will give me wisdom and courage sufficient, and enable me to give Him all the glory. I am strongly persuaded that if the Methodists will not yield on this point and emancipate their slaves, God will depart from them . . . I have just finished my feeble performance against slavery; if our conference should come into the measure, I trust it will be one of the means toward generally expelling the practice from our Society. How would my heart rejoice if my detention in these parts should afford me leisure in any measure in so desirable a work . . . I was employed according [to] the desire of the con-

The one essential thing for Asbury was "living to God." This meant that every Methodist was expected, not only to pass through a conversion experience and to remain spiritually alert, but to maintain higher than average standards of morality, stewardship, and discipline. In spite of his whole-hearted endorsement of the kind of frontier revivalism seen at its most typical in camp meetings, Asbury had no use for emotionalism running riot. His approving phrase describing a series of gatherings in 1814 is revealing: "Order, spirituality, in all our Conferences!"[7] "Order" was necessary not only to restrain but to maintain "spirituality." It was therefore important that those whom God called to preach the gospel and shepherd his people should be carefully trained, and that by a constant itinerancy they should be kept alive to the varying needs of the people from whom they had sprung. To ensure an efficient itinerancy it was essential that the preachers should be tightly ordered and firmly disciplined—though the specific rules and administrative practices to which they must respond and which they in turn would enforce should be flexible enough for variation in face of constantly changing circumstances. To ensure a disciplined people, an adequate ministry, and a smoothly running itinerant organization, it was essential in Asbury's view to have an acknowledged leader or leaders—an apostolate, an episcopacy. Not only must the bishop, however, demonstrate administrative ability, and be accorded genuine authority to accompany his God-given charisma: he must himself be prevented from losing touch with the grassroots problems of people and preachers; therefore he also must be kept on the move. Asbury believed just as firmly in an itinerant episcopacy as in an itinerant ministry in general. All this was how he had seen it work in Wesley's Methodism. This was how it was to work with Asbury's Methodism. Yet all to the glory of God, never to the glory of John or Francis.

This pragmatic churchmanship of Asbury's was not developed piecemeal after he set foot on American soil, but was already a co-ordinated, semi-automatic approach to his task. Most of the specific methods he used came readily to him as conditioned reflexes from his British training. Unlike Wesley's churchmanship, which clearly

ference in preparing a circular letter, to promote the emancipation of slaves, and to be read in our Societies." See *Methodist History*, IX, No. 2 (Jan., 1971), 34–6. See also W. Harrison Daniel, "The Methodist Episcopal Church and the Negro in the Early National Period," pp. 40–53.

7. *Methodist History*, II, No. 3 (April, 1964), 59.

changed through the decades, Asbury's remained almost static throughout nearly half a century in America, needing only minor on-the-spot adjustments from time to time, and tireless application. That is not to say, of course, that there were no ecclesiastical crises in his ministry, but only that those crises did not bring to birth any new concepts, but simply forced into temporary prominence one or other of the elements already present in his thought and practice. Like Wesley's *Journal* and *Letters*, the more interesting reading in Asbury's *Journal* and *Letters* tends to be in the earlier pages; the remainder is little more than a steady unfolding of what we have already seen, lit up by the occasional purple passage, the especially interesting illustration of a familiar principle, yet all integrated into the powerful cumulative effect of a life lived on an unusually high plateau of Christian dedication—a constant source of inspiration to many but (it must be confessed) a trifle boring to others because of the constant reappearance of the same characters and situations with only a slight variation of costumes and lines.

WESLEY'S ASSISTANT

Asbury had been in New York hardly a week before he was trying to implement Wesley's insistence upon an itinerant rather than a settled ministry—much to the dismay of Richard Boardman and Joseph Pilmore, who were inclined to develop pastorates in the cities. To his *Journal* he confided: "I am fixed to the Methodist plan, and do what I do faithfully, as to God. . . . My brethren seem unwilling to leave the cities, but I think I shall show them the way. I am in trouble, and more trouble is at hand, for I am determined to make a stand against all partiality. I have nothing to seek but the glory of God; nothing to fear but his displeasure. . . . I am determined that no man shall bias me with soft words and fair speeches."[8]

Both Boardman and Pilmore were six or seven years older than Asbury, but he knew his Wesley better, and was much nearer to Wesley's dreams for the American venture. What he wrote in the first extant letter home to his parents put the matter succinctly: "I am under Mr. Wesley's direction; and as he is a father and friend, I hope I shall never turn my back on him." It seems likely that Wesley had in fact primed him to tighten up Methodist discipline by discreetly remind-

8. Asbury, *Journal*, I, 10.

ing his senior colleagues that this was an important part of their responsibilities. They were having trouble in exercising control over the activities of the local preachers who had arisen in America or had arrived as free-lance volunteers from Britain. Even in the cities Asbury discovered what he considered laxity in society discipline, and put forward a sixteen-point plan of reform. In all this he was firmly supported by Wesley, from whom on October 10, 1772, he received a letter appointing him Assistant in charge of all the American work—even that of superintending his older colleagues.

This was in the first instance for a short time only, as we have already seen, and Asbury seems to have been genuinely happy to have handed over the reins to a far more experienced British preacher in Thomas Rankin.[9] Points of friction developed, however, and eventually each man saw the other through dark-tinted spectacles, and their estrangement prompted Rankin to drive a wedge between Wesley and Asbury—which unfortunately he was the better able to do after he returned to England during the Revolutionary War.[10] Even in this short time, however, Asbury had made his mark. Pilmore, for one, considered Asbury far too much of a disciplinarian, although this was from his later standpoint of preferring a settled to an itinerant ministry.[11] Rankin was, if anything, even more of a martinet than Asbury. Indeed Asbury could hardly have tolerated him at all had he not been so firm in enforcing Wesley's discipline. Rankin, however, seems to have displayed altogether too much of the sophisticated Englishman condescending to set the natives straight.[12]

RECRUITING PREACHERS

Asbury himself, far more than any other of his British colleagues, realized both the need for native preachers, and their potential. He actively recruited for them at conferences. At the 1782 Conference,

9. See pp. 93–5 above.

10. See Albea Godbold, "Francis Asbury and His Difficulties with John Wesley and Thomas Rankin," pp. 3–19.

11. Pilmore, *Journal*, p. 134.

12. Cf. William Duke, MS Journal (transcribed by the Reverend Edwin Schell from the original in the Diocesan Library, The Peabody Institute, Baltimore), for Dec. 4, 1775: "Mr. R[ankin], as his manner is, spoke exceeding rough to me upon some occasion, so that I could hardly bear it, and as soon as we got on the road I opened my mind to him. He satisfied me that his design was good."

having asked Jesse Lee if he were willing to take a circuit, he encouraged the young man by calling out to a group of preachers nearby, "I am going to enlist Brother Lee!" When one of these took up the military metaphor, asking "What bounty do you give?" Asbury answered, "Grace here, and glory hereafter, will be given if he is faithful."[13] The call of Ezekiel Cooper in November, 1784, to supply the newly formed Caroline circuit in place of the appointed preacher, who had died, is probably typical. Cooper had served for a year as a classleader, and had also begun to accompany the circuit preacher on his rounds, diffidently speaking at his request on occasion. After the quarterly meeting at Barratt's Chapel Asbury asked the preachers to nominate any "young speaker in the circuit that would travel," and Cooper was mentioned. He was called in. Later Cooper reminded Asbury of what happened: "I began to make some excuse, from the short time I had been speaking at all, that probably I should stay at home and improve my gifts more before I ventured to take a circuit. But this you paid no attention to, and would have me to go and try my gifts. At length I consented, in conformity to your judgment and the advice of some others of our brethren the preachers, to set out and make trial of the itinerant life."[14]

Asbury did try to check the credentials of these young men in a searching but kindly way, so as to eliminate any obvious misfits. Thomas Ware tells how he ventured on some public testimonies about his Christian experience, which convinced others—but not Ware himself—that he was called to preach. In an emergency he had even supplied for a sick itinerant for a week. Asbury heard about this from Caleb Pedicord, who vouched for the young man's worth. In August, 1782, Ware was summoned to meet Asbury in New Mills (i.e., Pemberton), New Jersey. Asbury took his hand, saying, "This, I suppose, is brother Ware, or shall I say, Pedicord the younger?" Ware admitted that Pedicord was indeed his spiritual father. "Sit down," said Asbury, "I have somewhat to say unto thee." He then asked a series of questions: "Have all men since the fall been possessed of free will?"—"Can man turn himself, and live?"—"Are all men accountable to God?"—"On what do you found the doctrine of universal accountabili-

13. Leroy M. Lee, *Life and Times of the Rev. Jesse Lee*, p. 105. In fact Lee hesitated, and did not become a regular itinerant until the following year.

14. Lester B. Scherer, *Ezekiel Cooper, 1763–1847*, pp. 13–16.

ty?" Apparently finding the answers satisfactory he looked at Ware sternly and said, "What is this I hear of you? It is said you have disturbed the peaceful inhabitants of [Mount] Holly, by rudely entering into a house where a large number of young people were assembled for innocent amusement, . . . and proceeding to address them in such a way that some became alarmed and withdrew, and the rest soon followed." Ware attempted to explain and defend his conduct, though admitting that his zeal might have carried him too far. Asbury continued, "Was it not bold and adventurous for so young a Methodist to fill, for a whole week, without license or consultation, the appointments of such a preacher as George Mair?" Ware felt sure that he was now in serious trouble, claimed that this was a despairing measure because of Mair's illness, and stated that he wished that Asbury's informant would first have informed him of his errors. The mask of sternness broke—Asbury did not completely lack a sense of humour—and the young man found himself clasped in Asbury's arms, with the affectionate words, "You are altogether mistaken, my son. It was your friend Pedicord who told me of your pious deeds, and advised that you should be sent to Dover circuit."[15]

Asbury knew that some of these young men were indeed ill prepared. But they were desperately needed. And he frequently marveled how such poor tools could be so greatly used: "The Lord hath done great things for these people, notwithstanding the weakness of the instruments, and some little irregularities."[16] In 1773 he pointed out to his parents in England that being stationed in Maryland he was "in the greatest part of the work," where they had "many country-born preachers and exhorters."[17] They exercised him greatly. On August 25 that year he licensed two exhorters; on the twenty-eighth he met Philip Ebert, who had begun to itinerate, but of whose fitness Asbury doubted; on the twenty-ninth Daniel Ruff broached the subject of his own call to the ministry while he and Asbury slept in the same bed, which shook under them because of Ruff's agitation; on September 1 he lamented: "I was in company with Brother Whitworth [who was expelled the following year] and Brother Strawbridge, . . . but was much distressed on account of so few preachers well qualified for

15. *Sketches of the Life and Travels of Rev. Thomas Ware, Written by Himself*, pp. 70–8. Asbury does not mention the interview, but this is the only date that fits the circumstances. The editors' note on p. 70 is incorrect.
16. Asbury, *Journal*, I, 50.
17. Ibid., III, 18.

the work, and so many who are forward to preach without due qualifications." [18]

Both in those early years and throughout his life Asbury sought to
help these young men reach their potential by sympathetic counsel—
which could turn to austere discipline if they refused all help—upon
self-improvement by reading, upon preaching and pastoral practice,
upon administration. He himself loyally followed Wesley's advice
about setting aside a long morning for study, and urged it strongly
upon his American colleagues. From Wesley's *Minutes* this advice was
incorporated in the American *Discipline*.[19] In the absence of any regular training facilities for preachers, Asbury became a one-man seminary
faculty. We note entries in his *Journal* about "some little inaccuracies" in the language of Richard Webster, and "a few pompous,
swelling words" which spoiled an otherwise good sermon by Samuel
Spragg.[20] We must surely assume his helpful suggestions to remedy
these deficiencies, as those of Isaac Rollins, of whom Asbury said:
"His exhortation was coarse and loud enough, though with some
depth. I gave him a little advice, which he seemed willing to take."[21]
At the same time there was some justification for Nathan Bangs's observation that Asbury was perhaps not sufficiently concerned about
ministerial education, for he was convinced that when all was said
and done it was not impossible for God to work his will through a
poorly constructed and lamely delivered exhortation, provided it
came from a converted heart.[22]

As a preacher Asbury himself was moving, but not brilliant. All
his sermons (usually brief) began with the Bible and ended with its
application to the spiritual life of his hearers. His simple, terse sentences were often striking, occasionally punctuated by bursts of eloquence. His approach was varied, but always carefully planned. As
Bishop Tipple has said, Asbury did not strive for effects but for results.[23] And these he richly secured, in conversions, in the feeding of
the souls of people and preachers alike, in a genuine lifting of the

18. Ibid., I, 91–2.
19. John J. Tigert, *A Constitutional History of American Episcopal Methodism*, p. 562.
20. Asbury, *Journal*, I, 188, 195–6.
21. Ibid., I, 61.
22. Cf. ibid., III, 487–8; William B. Sprague, *Annals of the American Methodist Pulpit*, p. 24.
23. Ezra Squier Tipple, *Francis Asbury, the Prophet of the Long Road*, p. 239;
Sprague, *Annals*, pp. 18–19, 21–2, 27–8; cf. *Methodist History*, IV, No. 1 (Oct., 1965),
19–21.

spirit. And this frequently in settings which would throw most of us wildly off target—"in the widow Bynton's backroom," "in a tavern," "under an arbor near the church," "in a tobacco-house," "in a close log house, without so much as a window to give us air," "in a paper mill," "in an orchard," "upon the banks of the Banister River," "in a log pen open at the top, bottom, and sides," "underneath the court-house within the arches," "in a log cabin, scarcely fit for a stable," "be-hind the barracks, to a number of soldiers and others," "at the gal-lows, to a vast multitude," and "from a wagon, at the execution of the prisoners."[24]

SUPERINTENDENT OF AMERICAN METHODISM

We have already seen how Asbury held the fort on behalf of Wes-ley's principles during the war, and barely managed to prevent a schism over the action of four Southern preachers who ordained each other in order to secure the administration of the sacraments. This he did by seeking delay, pending an appeal to Wesley.[25] During these troubled years and the even more perplexing ones which followed he provided the key Anglo-American link. He became even more sympa-thetic to American aspirations, yet throughout remained determined to preserve as firm an attachment as was possible to the parent Method-ism. To the end of his life he apparently never renounced his British citizenship.[26] Small wonder that when communications were restored after the war Wesley wrote to Edward Dromgoole in Virginia: "I am persuaded Bro: Asbury is raised up to preserve order among you, and to do just what I should do myself, if it pleased God to bring me to America."[27] Small wonder that Wesley's first letter to the American preachers in general after the signing of the Peace of Paris in Septem-ber, 1783, was sent to Asbury, naming him as the "General Assistant" superintending the whole work of Methodism in America, and plead-ing, "Let all of you be determined to abide by the Methodist doctrine and discipline published in the four volumes of *Sermons* and the *Notes upon the New Testament,* together with the large *Minutes* of the

24. Tipple, *Asbury,* pp. 214–16.
25. See above, pp. 101–3; cf. *HAM,* I, 177–80.
26. Tipple, *Asbury,* pp. 313–14.
27. Sweet, *Religion on the American Frontier,* IV, 12–16. (The *Minutes,* both Ameri-can and English, use the spelling "Drumgoole.")

Conference."[28] This task also Asbury proceeded to carry out, in the spirit of Wesley's churchmanship, if not according to the exact letter of Wesley's instructions. So confident was Wesley in Asbury that he appointed him to fill the first vacancy arising in the "legal hundred" —the select body of preachers in whom by law the British Conference was incorporated—even though he was never again to set foot on British soil.[29]

In 1784 Asbury accepted vicarious ordination from Wesley's hands, not only as deacon and elder, but as "superintendent," with delegated authority over the whole Methodist enterprise in America. Eager as Asbury was to secure an ordained ministry, however, he knew the American situation far better than Wesley could ever hope to do, and at one blow demonstrated his conviction that spiritual unity with British Methodism need not rest upon administrative subordination, not even to an apostolic man such as John Wesley. Rather than accept ordination by virtue of Wesley's appointment of him as general superintendent he sought (and readily secured) election to that position by his colleagues, thus enunciating a democratic principle far in advance of Wesley's firm belief in authoritarian rule. In spite of his profound respect for Wesley, he also disapproved the "binding minute" accepted by the majority of his colleagues at the Christmas Conference, by which they acknowledged themselves "ready, in matters belonging to church government, to obey [Mr. Wesley's] commands."[30] As Asbury wrote later to a British friend: "My real sentiments are union but no subordination; connexion but no subjection."[31] Or as with a somewhat sardonic twist he told George Shadford: "Mr. Wesley and I are like Caesar and Pompey: he will bear no equal, and I will bear no superior."[32]

It is understandable that relations between them became somewhat strained, especially with the American translation of "superintendent" into "bishop." In his *Sunday Service of the Methodists in North America* (1784) Wesley deliberately altered the terms used in

28. Lee, *Short History*, pp. 85–6; cf. Asbury, *Journal*, I, 450.
29. *WHS*, IV, 38; XIII, 15–16.
30. Tigert, op. cit., p. 534; Asbury, *Journal*, II, 106; III, 545–6. Perhaps it should be pointed out that in seeking election Asbury was on fairly safe ground. His colleagues at the 1782 Conference had in a similar manner unanimously endorsed Wesley's choice of him as General Assistant for the American work. See *Minutes* (American, 1795), p. 55.
31. Asbury, *Journal*, III, 63.
32. Ibid., III, 75.

the Book of Common Prayer—"bishop," and "consecration." These smacked of a lordly hierarchy, of sterile pomp and ceremony, of wealth. Wesley wanted none of these for his missionary church either in America or elsewhere, but a leader who was a true pastor of the pastors. Therefore he had vicariously "ordained" Asbury a "superintendent." As an ordained presbyter himself he was transmitting presbyterial orders to Asbury and others. He recognized Asbury as "the elder brother of the American Methodists," but claimed that he himself was "under God the father of the whole family."[33] In that capacity, therefore, as the "essential minister" of Methodism, he was also investing Asbury (and likewise Coke) with delegated responsibility and authority as "superintendents."[34]

Nor was the ordination itself unimportant to Asbury, though it was far from all-important. Twenty years later, realizing that behind the occasional open challenges to his authority lay much private criticism—in this also he was one with Wesley!—he thus assessed the sources of that disputed authority: "I will tell the world what I rest my authority upon: 1. Divine authority. 2. Seniority in America. 3. The election of the General Conference. 4. My ordination by Thomas Coke, William Philip Otterbein, German Presbyterian minister, Richard Whatcoat, and Thomas Vasey. 5. Because the signs of an apostle have been seen in me."[35] There is little doubt that in this issue Asbury was representing Wesley's genuine and deep concern for American Methodism far better than Wesley himself realized, and perhaps hardly deserved Wesley's rebuke: "How can you, how dare you, suffer yourself to be called 'bishop'? I shudder, I start at the very thought! Men may call me a knave or a fool, and I am content. But they shall never by my consent call me bishop!"[36] This was in 1788. The use of the term seems to have developed only gradually, and in his later years Asbury himself was not too happy about it.[37] Nor does he seem to have attempted any reproof for the many who still called him plain "Mr. Asbury."[38] Whether superintendent or bishop, how-

---

33. Wesley, *Letters*, VIII, 91.

34. See Baker, *John Wesley*, pp. 263–71.

35. Asbury, *Journal*, II, 469–70. This statement seems to answer affirmatively the question raised in my *John Wesley* (pp. 395–6) as to whether Asbury was ordained by "an unusual college of four."

36. Wesley, *Letters*, VIII, 91.

37. Baker, *John Wesley*, p. 271; Asbury, *Journal*, III, 378.

38. Cf. the contemporary documents presented in Sweet, *Religion on the American Frontier*, IV, 135, 141, 149, 165, 178, 185, 230. In only two of the seven instances (1807–8)

ever, Francis Asbury had warmed his hands and his heart at Wesley's evangelical fire, he had filled his mind with Wesley's pragmatic churchmanship; now he took over Wesley's apostolic status for the American people.

Asbury was now officially one of the "superintendents" of American Methodism, but he was not the only one, nor—as yet—the chief one. The formulation of the polity of the new church was chiefly the work of Thomas Coke, with his three British colleagues assisting. Asbury, although at first taken aback by the idea of an episcopal constitution, gradually came to accept it.[39] As Bishop Tigert pointed out, Asbury's main contribution had been his insistence that a General Conference should be called to approve both the ordinations and the proposed new constitution.[40] It was not for him sufficient that John Wesley had sent a carefully integrated plan by the hands of a trusted clerical emissary. The preachers themselves must decide whether a distinctly new church should be formed, and what should be its polity. And if Wesley was to remain their spiritual head it should be by resolution rather than by assumption. All this was worked out at the Christmas Conference, and written into the first American *Discipline*.[41] American Methodism came of age by Asbury's insistence upon an enabling conference. During the following years he seems to have been mainly responsible for rearranging these same constitutional regulations into a more logical form, so that the 1787 and later *Disciplines* appear on the surface very different from the first, although in fact the basic assumptions and British derivation remain the same.[42]

ASBURY'S AUTHORITY THREATENED

Not that Asbury sought to abolish rule by authority, insisting that every issue should be settled by vote. Both by Wesley's desire and by

is he called "Bishop Asbury," in the others (1787–1809), "Mr. Asbury" or "Brother Asbury."

39. See pp. 150–3 below; cf. John Vickers, *Thomas Coke, Apostle of Methodism*, pp. 81–3.

40. Tigert, op. cit., pp. 191–4.

41. Ibid., pp. 533–602.

42. Asbury, *Journal*, I, 499, 510. Although Asbury seems to have furnished the initiative and guidelines, Dickins (stationed at the time in the Bertie Circuit, North Carolina), seems to have undertaken some editing and the scribal labors; it is barely possible that he was in fact included in the "we" of the entry for November, 1785. See also David Sherman, *History of the Revisions of the Discipline of the Methodist Episcopal Church*, pp. 86–9.

the mandate of the American preachers he himself was now in the driving seat, and he resolved to exercise his power to good purpose. There is no doubt that authority suited him. He was a capable organizer and a tireless worker. But he was never very good at delegating responsibility. He believed not only that "If a job's worth doing, it's worth doing well," but that "If you want a thing well done, do it yourself." (Like Wesley, Asbury was fond of quoting proverbs.) He was perhaps unduly anxious lest some of his colleagues might by their inexperience or overenthusiasm damage or hinder his beloved Methodism. He did make one significant effort to share control with others, however, although it was misunderstood, and backfired. During the last years of his life Wesley had gathered around him a council of senior preachers in London, who served to keep the wheels of Methodism oiled, acting as an executive body on Wesley's behalf between Conferences. In 1789 Asbury persuaded the American Conference similarly to appoint an executive Council, and it seems at least possible that the idea came from England, though it was differently constituted and met a very different situation. Because of the huge distances it was impracticable for all American preachers to come to one conference, so they met sectionally, with Asbury traveling from one session to another with the same agenda; before an issue was settled each group had to agree. At first there were three sessions, one in the Carolinas, one in Virginia, and the other in Maryland. In 1788 there were six, in 1789 eleven, in 1790 fourteen, in 1792 seventeen. In order to secure a common mind with greater efficiency Asbury suggested a Council consisting of the two bishops (when Coke was available) together with the presiding elders (or their substitutes) from at least nine districts. The idea had some merit, especially that of avoiding great expense and disruption of local activities. In the scheme as it was presented, however, there were serious flaws, and some preachers saw it as a stratagem whereby Asbury intended to secure a stranglehold on Methodism by means of a group of yes-men whom he appointed. After meeting on two occasions only it was thrown overboard in favor of a delegated quadrennial General Conference—a scheme favored by Coke, as well as by James O'Kelly and Jesse Lee, from whom apparently came the original idea.[43] The first such General Conference met in 1792.

43. Lee, *Short History*, pp. 149–59; *HAM*, I, 429–31, 433–5; Tigert, op. cit., pp. 243–54, 257–8, 263–5.

Asbury's authority, therefore, by no means went unchallenged, but it was generally accepted with a good grace because of the way in which it was exercised—in general, Wesley's way. In the year of Wesley's death, however, and in each of the two following years, serious disputes threatened both Asbury's authority as bishop and other important aspects of Methodist polity. The first two led to schisms, the third was healed. It is instructive to see his position in these emergencies.

William Hammet,[44] an Irishman who had kissed the Blarney stone, was ordained by Wesley in 1786 in order that he might serve in Newfoundland. He was driven with storm-swept Coke to the West Indies, and remained a missionary there until 1791, when he went with Coke to recuperate in Charleston, S.C. He so impressed the Methodists there that they decided they were going to have him as their minister. Asbury (present in Charleston, as was Coke, for a Conference) confided to his *Journal*: "I am somewhat distressed at the uneasiness of our people, who claim a right to choose their own preachers—a thing quite new amongst Methodists. None but Mr. Hammet will do for them. We shall see how it will end."[45] Subsequent events give reason for us to believe that the last phrase held something of a threat. Asbury was resolved to preserve Methodism as a genuine connection, not as a mere affiliation of independent congregations choosing their own preachers. For the time being he appeared to raise no public objection, and did indeed appoint Hammet to Charleston, but only as junior to another elder, Reuben Ellis, who had been ordained a year earlier. This brought about a split in the church, and Hammet formed the first schismatic Methodist denomination, though he claimed that (unlike Asbury, who was too autocratic) he was being true to Wesley and his principles, therefore naming his group the Primitive Methodist Church. This fizzled out after his death in 1803.[46]

The case of James O'Kelly is much better known. Here was another Irishman, far more gifted, and with more spiritual graces, than Hammet. But he could not tolerate what he called the "ecclesiastical mon-

44. His name has usually been spelled "Hammett," though other variants exist; in manuscript letters at Duke University, however, his son Benjamin uses only one *t*, as did Hammet himself in his published *Impartial Statement of the Known Inconsistencies of the Reverend Dr. Coke*.

45. Asbury, *Journal*, I, 668.

46. D. A. Reily, "William Hammett," pp. 30–43; *HAM*, I, 617–22; *WHS*, XXVIII, 99–101; Jerry O'Neil Cook, "The First Schism of American Methodism."

archy" of Englishmen, and in 1787 successfully blocked Wesley's appointment of Whatcoat as a "superintendent."[47] Especially he challenged Asbury's right to assign preachers to their stations, whether by himself or abetted by an aristocracy of presiding elders, as in Asbury's Council, adopted in 1789. O'Kelly continued to snipe at Asbury's power, and in 1792 appealed from the bishop's autocratic decision to the judgment of his peers, meeting in the first General Conference—but was not prepared to accept the verdict when it went against himself. He walked out of that 1792 General Conference to form a new church, reorganized in 1801 as The Christian Church, which later merged with the Congregationalists; within recent years this merger has in turn become one constituent of The United Church of Christ.[48]

Until his death Asbury continued to press his twin concerns of the need for an authoritative episcopacy in order to secure a constantly itinerating ministry. Illuminating on this point is his attitude towards a possible union with the Germans of the United Brethren, and possibly other denominations, for whom he felt genuine affection, Philip William Otterbein being in many respects a close friend although much older.[49] Asbury maintained that they possessed good men and adequate financial resources, but were hindered from real success by antiquated methods, by the independence of their preachers, and by the lack of a "master-spirit to rise up and organize and lead them." He was convinced that under no circumstances could a spiritual reformation be perpetuated without "a well-directed itinerancy." This it was, rather than the use of the German language in American work and worship, which damped his enthusiasm for a union with the United Brethren which would have radically altered the patterns of both their history and that of Methodism.[50]

Asbury was not merely concerned with protecting his own prerogatives for the sake of personal prestige, however, but because he believed—even though mistakenly on occasion—that since he consistently exercised his authority to the glory of God it must always

47. Charles Franklin Kilgore, *The James O'Kelly Schism in the Methodist Episcopal Church*, pp. 10–13; Asbury, *Journal*, III, 51–3.
48. Kilgore, op. cit., pp. 12–34; Frederick A. Norwood, "James O'Kelly—Methodist Maverick," pp. 14–28, a slightly fuller version of which is in *HAM*, I, 440–52.
49. Cf. Paul H. Eller, "Francis Asbury and Philip William Otterbein," pp. 3–13.
50. See Paul Blankenship, "Bishop Asbury and the Germans," pp. 5–13, espec. p. 10.

turn out for the good of man. He was equally strict where no question of episcopal authority was involved, but simply a matter of Methodist administration at a lower level. He was convinced that if Methodism was to maintain its spiritual glow it must safeguard the standards of pastoral discipline at the local level, and to this end he was even prepared to do battle with one of his most capable lieutenants. In order to maintain true spiritual fellowship what might seem elaborate precautions were taken to protect the confidential nature of private society meetings, so that hearts could be opened, advice or admonition offered, without embarrassment or social danger. To this end the first *Discipline* of 1785 repeated as its eleventh rule a provision of Wesley's *Minutes*: "At every other meeting of the society in every place, let no stranger be admitted. At other times they may; but the same person not above twice or thrice. In order to this, see that all in every place show their tickets before they come in." (The twelfth rule, not present in Wesley's *Minutes*, but added by the American Conference of 1773, made a similar provision for love-feasts, whence the class or membership tickets later came to be known as "love-feast tickets."[51]) In order to "prevent improper persons from insinuating into the Society" the sixteenth rule made provision for would-be members to be presented with a copy of Wesley's *General Rules* the first time they met in class, after three or four visits to be given a note authorizing fuller participation, and to be issued a ticket only after recommendation "by a Leader with whom they have met at least two months on trial."[52]

The obvious assumption—not spelled out in the *Discipline*—was that the class-meetings which formed the component units of the society were to be fenced in a similar way to the fellowship meetings of the complete society. In 1793, however, Ezekiel Cooper drew Asbury's attention to the fact that in Lynn, near Boston, where the redoubtable pioneer Jesse Lee had formed the first Massachusetts society in 1791, Lee was now allowing anyone who wished to attend society classes for as long as a year without becoming members. Although other factors were involved, including Lee's strong belief in a settled Methodist ministry for New England, his laxity in society discipline seemed to form the major reason why at the following Conference Asbury replaced him with Cooper. At first Lee refused to go on a mission to Maine, as Asbury directed. Asbury compromised by listing Lee for

51. Asbury, *Journal*, I, 85; Wakeley, *Lost Chapters*, pp. 412–25.
52. Tigert, op. cit., pp. 536–7, 545–6.

both places, with titular authority only in Lynn. Lee hung on so long in Lynn, however, that there was an altercation between him and Cooper, and Cooper informed Asbury that he wished to resign. After long delays Lee did in fact leave for Maine, where he proved eminently successful, and eventually became reconciled to both Cooper and Asbury.[53] This little known chapter in the life of Jesse Lee illustrates not only his own rugged independence, but the trials of a bishop, especially one like Asbury, so deeply concerned for the daily welfare of grass-roots Methodism.

THE HALLMARK OF APOSTOLICITY

Some men, like Hammet and O'Kelly, reacted to the status popularly accorded to them as preachers by being unable to accept any superior, even a revered bishop. The majority of the preachers, however, were prepared to respect an authority which bore the hallmark of apostolicity. This they found in Asbury. He called them to self-discipline—but first (like Wesley) he himself regularly rose at 4:00 A.M., spent long hours in prayer and Bible study, lived frugally, fasted every Friday, missed meals to keep appointments, and always counted people as more important than his own pleasure or pain.[54] He called them to pastoral service and itinerant preaching—but first he himself gave far more than he could afford in money and effort. During his last two years, crippled with rheumatism, wheezing with asthma, weakened by pleurisy, he refused to give up his traveling, so that the Reverend John Wesley Bond accompanied him, carrying him in his arms like a little child. Bond tried to hold Asbury back, but to no avail, for he would reply: "It has never been my practice to say to the younger preachers, 'Go, boys,' but 'Come.' I have ever set an example of industry and punctuality, and if ever the young men should neglect their appointments it must not be by our example." Bond carried him into the church at Richmond, Virginia, on March 24, 1816, where at the age of seventy he preached what was to be his last sermon, exactly

53. *Methodist History*, VI, No. 4 (July, 1968), 44–6; cf. Scherer, *Ezekiel Cooper*, pp. 81–5, basically the same story by the same writer.

54. Robert J. Bull, "Lewis Myers' Reminiscences of Francis Asbury," pp. 5–10. So successful was Asbury in inculcating early rising that when Thomas Coke arrived in 1784 he confessed that Freeborn Garrettson "makes me quite ashamed, for he invariably rises at four in the morning, and not only he, but several others of the preachers; and now, blushing, I brought back my alarm to four o'clock." (Thomas Coke, *Extracts of the Journals of the Rev. Dr. Coke's Five Visits to America*, p. 15.)

a week before he died. He sat on a table to deliver his message, and it was not only his frequent pauses for breath which caused the sermon to last almost an hour. He had many spiritual things to impart to his beloved Methodists.[55]

When Asbury, therefore, summoned his preachers to forsake the comforts of homelife, to endure constant and toilsome travel, they went, they suffered. For they knew that his ministerial labors claimed him so completely that he had never found time to "purchase land, to build himself a house, or even to marry a wife."[56] They knew that he was in labors more abundant than they. They knew that he was ready to be called a fool for Christ's sake, counting episcopal service far more important than episcopal dignity. They responded to his call, not always gladly, not always without a murmur, but they responded—to a leader whom they trusted, whom they respected, for whom they felt a reverent awe if seldom a deep personal affection. A number even realized the secret depths of his devotion to them, as testified to by John Wesley Bond: "O, how often have I heard him in the dead hour of the night, when from the violence of his cough he was unable to lie down, and nearly gasping for breath, yet spending that breath in whispers of prayer for the work of God in general, and particularly for those engaged in carrying it on. His active mind was almost incessantly running from Conference to Conference, and through the different districts, circuits, and stations, calling the different preachers by name, and commending them to the protection of God. . . ."[57] Such men saw about him the apostolic glow which we have learned to describe as "charisma," and fell under his spell. Henry Boehm, who heard him preach fifteen hundred sermons, testified, "He seemed born to sway others."[58] In 1787 the preachers deliberately rebuffed Wesley rather than risk losing Asbury.[59] When in 1800 he tried to resign because of serious illness he was persuaded to continue, with another bishop elected to ease his burden. He meant too much to them; they could not let him go.[60]

---

55. *Methodist History*, IV, No. 3 (April, 1966), 12–13.
56. Ibid., p. 16; cf. Ware, *Life*, pp. 182–3.
57. *Methodist History*, IV, No. 3 (April, 1966), pp. 12–13; cf. the testimony of David M. Reese: "I have heard it said that he prayed for every one of the travelling preachers by name, twice every day, and for each circuit all over the connection." (Sprague, *Annals*, p. 20.)
58. Tipple, *Asbury*, pp. 237–8, 303.
59. Tigert, op. cit., p. 234.
60. Lee, *Short History*, pp. 264–7.

MR. METHODISM

Asbury gave not only direction but cohesion to the whole body of Methodists—an army which grew steadily under his leadership, from 5,000 in 1776 to 15,000 in 1786 and 214,000 at his death in 1816. In 1776 they occupied a handful of seaboard states between New York City and North Carolina: by 1816 Methodists had spread into the entire settled part of the nation east of the Alleghenies, and also—keeping pace with the frontier pioneers—up to the next great divide of the Mississippi River, and even beyond into Missouri and Arkansas.[61] Preventing religious fragmentation under such conditions was enormously difficult, but Asbury more than anyone else accomplished it. On August 10, 1787, Thomas Coke wrote from England a letter addressed simply, "The Revd. Bishop Asbury, North America."[62] The fact that it was delivered testifies not only to his fame but to his all-ranging itinerancy. His was no leadership from headquarters, but from the field, in personal touch with the living problems and opportunities as they arose. Even when expansion, coupled with his own failing health, necessitated the election of new bishops, of Whatcoat in 1800 and of McKendree in 1808—both of whom, like Asbury, remained single to keep up with their task—Asbury continued to maintain his itinerancy over all the settled parts of the United States.[63] His rugged face, with its large mouth and prominent nose, which seemed unprepossessing until you were arrested by the glint in his blue eyes, became familiar throughout the American scene. Sometimes, it is true, he was not recognized, because people were looking for someone more imposing than this wiry-looking man with 150 pounds packed tightly onto his 5′ 9″ frame, dressed in dingy black (replacing the grey of his middle years) topped off with a low-crowned broad-brimmed black hat from which escaped flowing white locks.[64] As in England under Wesley, so in America under Asbury, Methodism became a true "Connexion,"

---

61. Cf. Barclay, op. cit., I, 140–57; Sweet, *Religion on the American Frontier*, IV, 51–65.

62. At Drew University; cf. Tipple, *Asbury*, pp. 155, 158.

63. Cf. Sweet, *Religion on the American Frontier*, IV, 65. Between quadrennial General Conferences "every bishop was expected to have made the complete round of the entire church." From April, 1815, to his death in March, 1816, Asbury traveled through Maryland, Delaware, Pennsylvania, New Jersey, New York, Massachusetts, New Hampshire, West Virginia, Ohio, Kentucky, Tennessee, North Carolina, South Carolina, and Virginia.

64. Henry Boehm, quoted in Tipple, *Asbury*, pp. 302–3.

every part linked with every other part, not only by a chain of office and command, a series of committees and conferences and traveling preachers, but by the tireless itinerancy of one man, their father in God, Francis Asbury.

Asbury's *apologia pro vita sua* was contained in "A Valedictory Address" to Bishop William McKendree, dated August 5, 1813. In this he used two important adjectives to describe Methodism as he envisioned it: "apostolical" and "missionary." He claimed that contrary to popular opinion it was still possible for Methodism to retain "such doctrines, such discipline, such convictions, such conversions, such witnesses of sanctification, and such holy men," as "in former apostolical days." But only if they remained a missionary church, if their preachers, bishops and elders alike, itinerated, as did Paul, Timothy, and Titus, thus maintaining "the traveling apostolic order and ministry that is found in our very constitution." [65]

As he neared the end of his course, and was within grasp of the prize of his high calling in Christ Jesus, Francis Asbury did as St. Paul had done—asked his colleagues to indulge him in a little foolish boasting.[66] (The passage is lengthy, but little known, and illustrates several aspects of Asbury's apostolic ministry): "I . . . am now in the forty-fifth year of my mission in this country, during which time I have laboured extensively. Sixty times I have crossed the wide range of the Allegheny mountains, in going and returning to and from the western country; and often before there was even a bridle path to point the way, or a house to shelter us; and when Indian depredation was committed before and behind and on either side of me. Twenty-nine visits I have made to North and South Carolina, and various parts of Georgia; and frequently when their rude pole-bridges would be floating by the waters that at times inundate the lowlands of that country, so that sometimes I had to wade and lead my horse along the best way I could. And there it was I caught such colds as have fastened like a vulture on my lungs ever since. And by frequent exposure to bad weather, and having to sleep in pole-cabins, where there was nothing between the logs to keep out the wind, I have had such attacks of the rheumatism that my feet and legs have been so swollen that I was unable to walk, and would have to be carried and sit on my horse; where, not being able to keep my feet in the stirrups, I had to let them

65. Asbury, *Journal*, III, 475–92, espec. pp. 475–6, 491–2.
66. Cf. 2 Cor. 11:16–30.

hang. And in this painful condition I have travelled hundreds of
miles preaching the gospel. And from these repeated swellings, and
the severe pains acompanying them, the use of my limbs [was so
taken] from me that I have not been able to stand to preach a sermon
for seven years, but have had to rest myself against a table or stool.
Besides all my labours and sufferings in other parts of this newly
settled country. But what of all this? True, it is not forgotten before
God. Yet I can trust in nothing I have ever done or suffered. I stand
alone in the righteousness of Christ. I stand in the justifying and in
the sanctifying righteousness of Jesus Christ. And, Glory to God!
I feel as great a verity in the doctrine I have preached as ever I did
in my life. It is the doctrine of the Scriptures; it is the doctrine of
God." [67]

In his later years Asbury spoke of Wesley as an "apostolic man." [68]
He himself had become American Methodism's "apostolic man."
Largely through his insistence, the doctrinal standards of the Methodist Episcopal Church remained those of Wesley. The patterns of
worship and society life, allowing for the differences of setting, continued recognizably similar. Asbury's evangelical warmth kept
Methodism in touch with the common people, and his insistence upon
the itinerant principle equipped the church to move with the extend-
ing frontier. The organization of the church as a whole was firmly
patterned upon Wesley's Methodism. [69]

John Wesley had cherished great dreams about the future of
American Methodism, greater than has often been recognized. Nevertheless he was mistaken in believing that from England he could effectively bring those dreams to realization, and that his plan for doing
so must necessarily be the best. He had chosen well in 1771, however,
when he despatched Francis Asbury as his ambassador to America,
nor did he mistake when in 1784 he sought Asbury's ordination as
the apostolic man of American Methodism. Asbury had not only

67. *Methodist History*, IV, No. 1 (Oct., 1965), 26; cf. p. 27, where he similarly "gave
some account of his own labours and sufferings" while preaching in New York City, possibly on June 18, 1815, ending, "My strength is almost gone"; and then gathering fresh
energy, to cry, "But *glory* to *God!* My heart's not *gone;—*my *faith;—*my *love* to God's not
gone!" The words "ran through the congregation like electricity," bringing tears to
most eyes, and an echoing "Glory to God!" from most lips. (Spelling and punctuation
modernized.)

68. Asbury, *Journal*, III, 546, 549.

69. Cf. the assessment of early Methodist success in Sydney E. Ahlstrom, *A Religious
History of the American People*, pp. 437–9.

eagerly learned the methods of British Methodism, but had drunk deeply into the very spirit of John Wesley. With his finger closely on the pulse of the new nation he was able to accomplish what Wesley himself could only dream of doing, and what by purely British methods could never have been done—he brought about a healthy transplant of British Methodism into American soil.

9. DR. THOMAS COKE—THE FIRST METHODIST BISHOP

At 10:00 A.M. on September 18, 1784, Dr. Thomas Coke and two preacher companions upon whose heads John Wesley had laid ordaining hands set sail from Bristol for New York, embarked on a voyage to form a new church in America, supposedly according to an authoritarian plan laid down by Wesley, but in the final result embodying an important democratic modification brought about by the insistence of Francis Asbury. Because of Asbury, also, Coke's ardent courtship of American Methodism was rejected, at least after the initial successes of his first visit. For good reasons, of course. Indeed even in Britain any cause enthusiastically espoused by Thomas Coke was under suspicion from most of his colleagues as "another of the little doctor's harebrained schemes," partly because a man of higher ecclesiastical status who leaped suddenly into Wesley's favor was bound to incur some jealousy from those of the itinerant preachers who had any remnants of sin clinging to them, partly because of his undoubtedly mercurial character. He was here today and gone tomorrow. In his dealings with American Methodist preachers he was equally unfortunate. Somehow later Americans have never warmed to him, and he has been given a bad press in volumes on American Methodist history. Only two American biographies of him have been written, a slight work by F. E. Upham in 1910, and the one real effort to atone, in 1923, by Bishop Warren A. Candler, who rightly claimed that Coke had usually been ranked "far below his real worth."[1] Yet like him or not, errors or not, overshadowed by Asbury or not, justice should be done to his undoubted importance in the history of early Methodism in America. He was the transmitter from Wesley of American ministerial orders, he was the chief formulator of the original *Discipline*, he was a pioneer in several aspects of social concern, and the effective promoter of government by a quadrennial General Conference. Had he had his own way he would have transformed Methodism into a church rather than a society at a much earlier stage in its history,

1. Warren A. Candler, *Life of Thomas Coke*, p. iii. Over one-third of almost four hundred pages is devoted to Coke's work in America.

and he himself might have remained here permanently as one of Methodism's joint fathers-in-God.

Altogether Coke spent just under three years in the United States, stretching over nine visits made during twenty years. After the first epoch-making visit of 1784-5 he came every two years; with the introduction of the quadrennial General Conference in 1792 he came every four years only, for the sessions of that conference, until 1804. In that, the year of his last visit, he came early, offering himself for full episcopal service alongside Asbury, but left rebuffed. All but two of his nine visits were for two to four months only. His first ebullient tour of 1784-5 lasted seven months, and a similar period was occupied by his last nostalgic itinerary, when he realized that he was not going to be allowed to assist in making his dreams for American Methodism come true. During the ten years left to him he remained relatively stationary in the British Isles until his final missionary voyage took him to the east instead of once more to the west.

Thomas Coke's influence upon the development of American Methodism was significant, and could have been much more significant but for the greatness—and the stubbornness—of Francis Asbury. There was genuine affection between the two men, true respect for each other's capabilities. But Coke was a man bubbling over with bright ideas for all kinds of missionary ventures in which he wanted to get other people so involved that henceforth they could carry on with only an occasional supervisory visit from him as general director. Asbury was deeply convinced that American Methodism needed not so much ideas as action on the spot—not a promoter but a pastor-preacher. He therefore resisted all Coke's attempts to continue as a religious executive, and tried to divert his energies into the role of visiting evangelist, prepared to support him as an administrative bishop only if he fulfilled that task as a full-time resident, full-time preaching, full-time itinerant bishop. For him it was that, or resign. When eventually Coke surrendered and seemed prepared to undertake that kind of ministry, Asbury still mistrusted his volatile nature—though not his sincerity—and remained unenthusiastic. It is probable that the motives of both men were somewhat mixed and unclear to themselves, and that the terms "ambitious" and "wholly dedicated to the glory of God" could be applied equally—and truthfully—to both men. Asbury urgently needed episcopal help; he would certainly have preferred the help of someone who would remain subsidiary to him in authority; yet above all Asbury was convinced that the work would only make genuine progress under a bishop *like* himself rather than of the kind that Coke apparently desired to be. Coke's contribution, therefore, remained less than it might have been, and was concentrated especially during his earlier visits to America. Indeed during his first seven months' tour of America—upon which we shall here concentrate—he accomplished sufficient in the way of Methodist beginnings to have brought most men fame if accomplished during a lifetime.

WESLEY'S AMBASSADOR

Six weeks after Coke left Bristol Wesley wrote to Asbury asserting his confidence in the doctor: "I hope you will . . . find him a man after your own heart, seeking neither profit, pleasure, nor honour, but simply to save the souls for whom Christ has died, and to promote his kingdom upon earth."[2] A few days later, on November 3, Coke arrived in New York after a storm-tossed voyage, during which he had read Augustine's *Confessions* for devotion, Virgil's *Georgics* for culture, the lives of Francis Xavier and David Brainerd for missionary inspiration, and the 556 pages of Bishop Benjamin Hoadly's "treatises on conformity and episcopacy" in order to underpin his and Wesley's ecclesiastical authority for ordaining preachers and constituting a new church.[3] From New York he traveled south to meet Asbury, discussing with John Dickins and others along the way "Mr. Wesley's Plan," which seemed to be well received.[4] And so to Barratt's Chapel, where "a plain, robust man" came up to him in the pulpit after the sermon and kissed him—Asbury, as he correctly surmised. They took an immediate liking to each other, in spite of their many dissimilarities, and in spite of Asbury's strong reservations about the suggested new plan of church government.

Thomas Coke, indeed, with all his faults, was a very likable man. He was a good mixer, generous with praise[5] and forgiveness as well

2. *HAM*, I, 211.

3. Coke *Journals*, 1793, pp. 7–13.

4. Ibid, pp. 13–16.

5. Cf. his public tribute to Asbury: "In the presence of brother Asbury I feel myself a child. He is, in my estimation, the most apostolic man I ever saw, except Mr. Wesley." (Ware, *Life*, p. 108.)

as with money, an optimist who really enjoyed life,[6] cultured and witty, with a warm and kindly sense of humor. He could on occasion tongue-lash a man or a group of men, and then apologize so sincerely that they realized that his irritability and impetuous temper had gained the better of him, but that his bark was worse than his bite.[7] He would sometimes jump to conclusions, sometimes forget important administrative details. As Wesley told Adam Clarke, "The doctor is often too hasty; he does not maturely consider all circumstances."[8] His delicate complexion and courtly ways, combined with a gentle musical voice (which with typical Welsh *hwyl* could rise almost to a scream when his preaching became fervent) were mismatched with a dumpy figure—he was only 5′ 1″ tall, two inches shorter than John Wesley[9]—but those like Thomas Ware who at first thought him effeminate were soon captivated by his unaffected charm.[10]

Before they met, Asbury had taken the precaution of gathering a group of preachers together "to form a council." These men unanimously agreed with him that "the design of organizing the Methodists into an independent episcopal church" was too important a decision for anyone except a general conference,[11] and "therefore sent off Freeborn Garrettson like an arrow . . . to gather all the preachers together at Baltimore on Christmas Eve."[12]

Undoubtedly this conference idea caught Coke a little off guard. The reaction of John Dickins, the preacher in charge at New York, was what he had expected from most of them: Dickins highly approved Wesley's plan, was sure that Asbury would agree to it, and urged Coke to make it public, because in any case "Mr. Wesley has determined the point, and therefore it is not to be investigated, but complied with." It seemed that Dickins was happier with an absentee autocracy than Asbury and the rest![13] Here was Asbury refusing to

6. Cf. ibid., p. 115: "Never did I see any person who seemed to enjoy himself better than he did, while thousands pressed to him to have their children dedicated to the Lord by baptism and to receive themselves the holy supper at his hands."

7. The Reverend Alfred Griffith relates such an incident at a Conference, probably the General Conference of 1796 (Sprague, *Annals*, p. 70).

8. Wesley, *Letters*, VIII, 101; cf. his forgetting to prepare Joseph Cownley's letters of orders, ibid., VIII, 98.

9. [Jonathan Crowther], *The Life of the Rev. Thomas Coke . . . Written by a Person who was long and intimately acquainted with the Doctor*, pp. 511–12.

10. Ware, *Life*, p. 109.

11. Asbury, *Journal*, I, 471–2.

12. Coke, *Journals*, 1793, p. 16.

13. Ibid., p. 13. Not enough research has been done to recover the original text of

be satisfied with Wesley's fiat; first he calls a council; now he demands a general conference—and gets his way! Assuredly there was good reason for Coke's initial assessment of Asbury: "He has so much wisdom and consideration, so much meekness and love; and under all this, though hardly to be perceived, so much command and authority."[14] And so instead of stubbornly—and stupidly—insisting that this was a matter strictly between him and Asbury, as the joint superintendents appointed by Wesley, Coke wisely yielded to Asbury's instincts, and agreed to assist at the birth of the first independent new church in America.

The two men did agree, however, that guidance for the conference was essential, and arranged to meet a week in advance at Perry Hall, the mansion of Mr. Harry Dorsey Gough, about twelve miles from Baltimore, in order to "mature everything for the conference."[15] To this meeting Coke came reinforced by experience—if somewhat weary in body—from the eight-hundred-mile preaching tour of backwoods Methodism which Asbury had mapped out for him at their first meeting.[16] Also coming to Perry Hall, and sitting in on the pre-Conference sessions, were the other two men recently arrived from England, Whatcoat and Vasey.[17] They discussed the method of presenting Wesley's plan for the new church, prepared a brief agenda, and together worked through the 1780 edition of Wesley's large *Minutes*, a summary of British Methodist regulations which had gradually accumulated over forty years of experience and experimentation.[18]

The four men would undoubtedly discuss at length the question which was troubling Asbury so greatly, as it had at first troubled Coke. It was relatively easy to justify Wesley's ordination of Whatcoat and Vasey as elders, and their assistance in ordaining other elders: this

Coke's first American journal with any certainty. Clearly this passage was revised either for American or for English consumption, for when it was published in *The Arminian Magazine* (Vol. I, Philadelphia, 1789, p. 242) the passage about not being investigated but complied with read: "Mr. Wesley has determined the point, though Mr. Asbury is most respectfully to be consulted in respect to every part of the execution of it." Cf. Vickers, *Coke*, p. 79n.

14. Coke, *Journals*, 1793, p. 16.

15. Ibid., p. 22; Asbury, *Journal*, I, 473–4.

16. Coke, *Journals*, 1793, pp. 16–22; Asbury, *Journal*, I, 472.

17. Not, as has sometimes been supposed, William Black, an Englishman who had emigrated to Nova Scotia in 1775 and had become the mainstay of Methodism there. He did indeed ride to Perry Hall with Coke, and also attended the sessions of the Conference itself, but during the interval he was engaged in a brief preaching tour. See Jackson, *Early Methodist Preachers*, V, 284.

18. Phoebus, *Whatcoat*, p. 21.

was simply the presbyterial ordination of presbyters. But what right had a presbyter such as Wesley (or Coke) to ordain a *bishop*? In spite of Hoadly and the precedent of the Alexandrian Church, very little, apart from dire ecclesiastical need. Coke had consented only after long hesitation. The deciding factor was that Wesley was undoubtedly already exercising the functions of a scriptural *episcopos*—he was the "essential minister," the "apostolic man," the father in God of the Methodists, and as such he surely had power to confer upon others whatever God-given authority over them he himself possessed. And Wesley certainly saw that authority as stretching to the whole body of Methodists, in the West Indies, in the United States, in Canada, as well as in the British Isles.[19] Coke persuaded Asbury that this might indeed be the best course to follow under the peculiar circumstances of postwar American Methodism. He also sought to persuade preachers and people along similar lines when he preached at Asbury's ordination as superintendent on December 27, 1784.[20]

Although finally Asbury insisted that his superintendency must depend upon election by his peers rather than upon Wesley's appointment alone, his vicarious ordination by Coke undoubtedly underpinned his authority and his own sense of decorum. He could never look upon Coke as his father in God—Coke was, after all, two years his junior!—but he accepted Coke as his episcopal elder brother, the first to be ordained by Wesley, in order that a similar ordination might be passed on to him. Whenever in later months and years they issued joint proclamations, prepared joint publications or jointly signed documents—even the address congratulating George Washington on being elected the first President of the United States in 1789[21]—"Thomas Coke," though chronologically and alphabetically later, always preceded "Francis Asbury." When they both preached from the same pulpit Coke always preached first.[22] As a matter of course Coke presided at the sessions of the Christmas Conference, just as it was a matter of course for both to recognize in John Wesley their principal link with the Church of England, from which most of the preachers

19. Baker, *John Wesley*, pp. 262–70.
20. Thomas Coke, *The Substance of a Sermon preached . . . at the Ordination of the Rev. Francis Asbury to the Office of a Superintendent*, pp. 7–9; cf. Vickers, *Coke*, pp. 88–90.
21. Asbury, *Journal*, III, 70–1; *The Arminian Magazine*, Philadelphia, I (1789) 284–5; *HAM*, I, 247–51; Vickers, *Coke*, pp. 126–9.
22. Warren Thomas Smith, "Thomas Coke: the Early Years, 1747–1785" (unpublished manuscript), p. 397.

had sprung either directly or at one or two removes, and upon whose clerical orders, sacraments, public worship, doctrine, and discipline the new church was to be based, though with modifications both great and small, mostly derived from the practices of the British Methodist societies, but some from the special circumstances of American Methodism.

THE CHRISTMAS CONFERENCE

The first and major order of business for the first day of the Christmas Conference was the presentation by Coke of Wesley's well known letter of September 10, 1784, "To Dr. Coke, Mr. Asbury, and our brethren in North America." This (wrote Thomas Ware) was "read, analysed, and cordially approved."[23] The "analysis" probably consisted of Coke's verbal account of Wesley's intentions, as revealed both by an exegetical commentary upon the letter itself and by his personal knowledge of Wesley's mind. Wesley had originally drawn up "a little sketch" of his proposals, but this has disappeared.[24] Whether from a manuscript or from memory, however, Coke outlined for the preachers Wesley's scheme for a new independent church. Approval of the letter and Coke's interpretation of what in general was involved implied not only that the preachers applauded Wesley's acknowledgment of American disentanglement "both from the state and the English hierarchy," but that they accepted his statement, "I have accordingly appointed Dr. Coke and Mr. Francis Asbury to be joint superintendents over our brethren in North America." Indeed it seems likely that the "cordial approval" of this document after "analysis" was generally construed as the unanimous election of Coke and Asbury as superintendents, though there may have been a separate vote on this. In any case, when the preachers reassembled on Monday, December 27, the proceedings of Friday, December 24, were recapitulated and unanimously confirmed.[25]

23. Ware, *Life*, pp. 105–6.
24. Baker, *John Wesley*, pp. 241–2, 253–4.
25. See *HAM*, I, 202–3, 213–15; Asbury, *Journal*, I, 474. The varied nature of their sessions tends to confirm the view that the first action was a kind of omnibus resolution approving Wesley's letter and Coke's interpretation of it. This may account for O'Kelly's insistence that Asbury was never in fact elected (see Kilgore, *O'Kelly Schism*, pp. 8–9, and Vickers, *Coke*, pp. 87–8). The MS journal of Thomas Haskins—a critical observer—is the most specific, and shows that the first question before the Conference was, "Whether we should have the ordinance administered among us, and we should be erected into an

Also included in the implications of this omnibus resolution was acceptance of the *Sunday Service of the Methodists in North America: with other occasional services*. Wesley's language here, however, was much less authoritarian. He had "appointed" Coke and Asbury: he merely "advised" the preachers in general to use the *Sunday Service* on the Lord's Day. In practice the liturgical orders for public worship were seldom used except in the handful of cities, and it is probable that even the orders for baptism and the Lord's Supper were frequently set aside in favor of extemporary services.[26] The forms for the ordination of deacons, elders, and superintendents, however, almost certainly continued in regular use from the outset. Nor can it be too much emphasized that Wesley's provision of these latter forms in the *Sunday Service*—they were frequently omitted from the Book of Common Prayer as unnecessary for the regular worshiper—set the stage for the formation of American Methodism into an episcopal church. A further important element accepted with this opening resolution was the credal statement contained in Wesley's revision of the Thirty-nine Articles of the Church of England. These formed a quite distinct entity, a century older than the Book of Common Prayer, though often bound up with it. Again the American Methodists accepted with only minor revision what Wesley had provided for them, and what Coke urged upon them. Did he say, we wonder, that Wesley was doing for American Methodists what he had not done for the British Methodists, because they remained members of the Church of England—providing a new Liturgy, new Articles of Religion, a new ministry, all freshly minted for American Methodism, yet all fashioned from the tested patterns of the Church of England, "the best constituted national church in the world"?[27]

Thomas Coke was the promoter par excellence of the *Sunday Service*. He had introduced some minor alterations into Wesley's copy for the first edition of 1784,[28] and seems to have been given carte

independent church—unanimously carried in the affirmative." This settled, they went on to matters of detail: the polity and title, ministerial orders, and the powers of a superintendent (see Sweet, *Men of Zeal*, p. 173).

26. *HAM*, I, 313–15. Undoubtedly many would sympathize with the regulation about baptism approved by the controversial Fluvanna Conference of 1779: "Q.25. What ceremony shall be used in the administration? A. Let it be according to our Lord's command, Matt. 18:19, short and extempore." (See Sweet, *Virginia Methodism*, p. 82.) See also note 5, p. 121 above.

27. *To Dr. Coke, Mr. Asbury, and our Brethren in North-America*, circular letter, 4 pp., dated "Bristol, Sept. 10, 1784" (see Baker, *Union Catalogue*, No. 376A).

28. Baker, *John Wesley*, pp. 252–5.

blanche in seeing through the press the editions of 1786,[29] 1788,[30] and
1790;[31] we can also assume that he was responsible for the edition of
1792. It was doubtless Coke's enthusiasm that kept these editions
rolling into America. They were all printed in England, each just
before Coke set sail upon another voyage to the United States. Even
a generous enthusiast such as Coke, however, would hardly have been
responsible for five editions of a 300-page book in eight years unless
those books were proving of value. In 1792 the forms still in regular
use were in fact revised and incorporated into the *Discipline*, so that
henceforth they were published in America, and were no longer de-
pendent upon Coke. Jesse Lee's comment about "the prayer book" being speedily "laid aside"[32] is only half true. The liturgical "Sunday
service," with its readings, collects, and Psalter, was assuredly dropped
—if indeed in most places it was ever adopted.[33] The "other occasional
services," however—Lord's Supper, Baptism, Matrimony, Burial, together with the three forms for Ordination, and the Articles of Religion—remained vigorously alive, first separately, then as incorporated in the *Discipline*. Two indeed have come into almost universal
currency in the hymnal, so that in spite of the changes in content and
doctrinal approach wrought by the years we still retain a part of
Wesley's original *Sunday Service*, and have even learned to appreciate the liturgical use of the Psalter so despised by our forebears.

A BLUEPRINT FOR THE NEW CHURCH

The name of the new church was apparently not Coke's idea—and
certainly not Wesley's, although not out of line with his general plan
—but that of John Dickins.[34] Its constitution, however, owed more to
him than to any man except Wesley. It is unlikely that Coke came
fortified with many printed copies of the 1780 large *Minutes* for
preachers to mark up and use in debate, for he expected no such con-

29. Vickers, *Coke*, p. 88n.
30. See British Museum, Add. MSS. 48809, folio 62, for Strahan's account with Coke.
31. See letter of Coke to Mr. Holmes of Salisbury, Oct. 12, 1790: "If you want prayer
books, be pleased to write to Mr. Tyler Tailer, . . . and to settle for them with him or
me." (Methodist Archives, London.)
32. Lee, *Short History*, p. 107.
33. Thomas Haskins loyally tried to use the morning service, but made the comment, "Although this is most excellent in itself, yet I scarcely think it will be of much
use among us as a people. But it is agreeable to our newly adopted plan." (Sweet, *Men
of Zeal*, p. 174.)
34. Ware, *Life*, p. 106.

ference as Asbury had requested. But the four British preachers at least had copies available, as surely did some of the others. There seems little doubt that Coke acted as both presiding officer and secretary, guiding the lengthy debate on the constitution, and preparing the *Minutes . . . , composing a Form of Discipline*, which he eventually saw through the press in Philadelphia.[35] From Tuesday, December 28, until Friday, December 31, 1784, with intervals for electing and ordaining the preachers, most of the time was taken up in going through the seventy-seven questions of the 1780 *Minutes*, revising, omitting, adding, along the lines already agreed at Perry Hall, until they had completed the eighty-one questions of the scissors-and-paste *Discipline*.

No less than three-quarters of the 1785 *Discipline* was a direct transcript from the 1780 *Minutes*, with only minor omissions and modifications, and a few additions made necessary by the different situation in America. There were only three major innovations. The first was an agreement designed to secure "the future union of the Methodists": "During the life of the Rev. Mr. Wesley we acknowledge ourselves his sons in the gospel, ready in matters belonging to church government to obey his commands. And we do engage after his death to do everything that we judge consistent with the cause of religion in America and the political interests of these States to preserve and promote our union with the Methodists in Europe."[36] ("Europe," incidentally, was the euphemism already current among American Methodists by which they avoided mentioning any link with "England" or "Britain," which might be deemed unpatriotic—though it was a very un-English manner of speaking, and Coke must have found it somewhat difficult to swallow.)[37] This overenthusiastic minute binding the Americans to Wesley's rule was urged by Coke;

35. Neither Wesley's *Minutes* nor the American *Discipline* made any provision for electing a secretary for the Conference, though this was provided for in Britain by Wesley's Deed of Declaration of 1784, which came into effect upon his death in 1791. Whether there should be a separate secretary or not remained the prerogative of the presiding officer, though in fact Wesley appointed Coke as the secretary of the British Conferences from 1784 onwards—indeed he was either secretary or President of the British Conference for every year except four between 1784 and 1814, when he left on his last voyage. (William Peirce, *The Ecclesiastical Principles and Polity of the Wesleyan Methodists*, p. 414; *WHS*, XXXVIII (May, 1972), 118–19; Tigert, op. cit., pp. 580–4; Sherman, op. cit., pp. 143–53.)

36. Tigert, op. cit., p. 534.

37. Cf. *Minutes* (American, 1795), pp. 5 (1773) and 62 (1783), where "European" first occurs.

Asbury, though disagreeing with it, did not raise a public protest, no more than he joined the outcry when it was repealed in 1787, after Coke tried to force Wesley's decision that Richard Whatcoat should be ordained an additional superintendent.[38] Unlike the first innovation, the second was a lasting success—the provision for a threefold ordering of the ministry, which the *Discipline* carefully indicated was based on the underlying assumptions of the *Sunday Service*.[39] The third was another failure, though a failure with some elements of glory in it—the rules aimed at the complete emancipation of Black slaves, rules which caused such a furore that within a year they were modified.[40] Coke was an even more ardent abolitionist than Asbury, and probably the author of the petition for emancipation in Virginia, somewhat lukewarmly received by George Washington in 1785.[41] He found himself in serious trouble because he supported the minute threatening excommunication for Methodist slaveholders, and because of his constant preaching against slavery in general, though like Asbury he came to realize that in this he was guilty not only of taking foolhardy risks but of tactical blunders.[42]

The preparation of a blueprint for a new church must necessarily be a complex task, and the *Discipline* of the Methodist Episcopal Church had been drawn up and debated under great pressure of time. Clearly it was far from perfect, but it was completed, a nuclear polity linking the constitution to British Methodism just as firmly as the *Sunday Service* tied the American Methodists to the Church of England. Asbury was rightly dissatisfied with the ordering of the questions and answers—a conference procedure itself taken over in 1773 from British Methodism—though not in general with their substance. He was responsible for rearranging the material into a more appropriate order, which after editing by John Dickins received the approval of Coke and the three annual Conferences held in 1787, and

38. Asbury, *Journal*, II, 106; III, 545–6.
39. Tigert, op. cit., pp. 534–5.
40. Ibid., pp. 554–6; cf. *Minutes* (American, 1795), p. 83 (1785).
41. See Richard K. MacMaster, "Liberty or Property? The Methodists' Petition for Emancipation in Virginia, 1785," pp. 44–55.
42. Vickers, *Coke*, pp. 94–8; Candler, *Coke*, pp. 77–82. Cf. Donald G. Mathews, *Slavery and Methodism*, pp. 5–12. Mathews is incorrect, however, in stating that the prohibition against slavery in the *General Rules* came from Wesley. It was added in the American editions only, and first appears appended to the *Discipline* of 1788; this revised edition of the rules is signed, "Thomas Coke, Francis Asbury, May 28, 1787."

thus became the basis of the standard *Discipline*.[43] Other rearrangements major and minor have taken place over the years. Throughout all, however, the basic themes have remained similar, though with a progressively multiplying accretion of purely American legislation.

CHRISTIAN CONCERNS

At that founding Conference it was Thomas Coke who first directed the feet of American Methodists into the paths of missionary concern for those outside their own country. Before coming to America he had published one of the first missionary manifestoes, *A Plan of the Society for the Establishment of Missions among the Heathens.*[44] His voyage reading had included the lives of Francis Xavier and David Brainerd.[45] At the Conference he chiefly seems to have been responsible for establishing the Nova Scotia Mission, and succeeded in securing money as well as men to second the work of William Black, who had come from Nova Scotia to plead for help. Coke continued successfully to beg money for the new church's first missionary venture during the weeks following, thus helping Freeborn Garrettson and James Cromwell on their pioneer way.[46]

The Christmas Conference also served to display another side of Coke's many-faceted enthusiasm—his zeal for education. As early as 1779 Asbury had discussed with Dr. Samuel Magaw, the friendly Anglican rector of Christ Church, Dover, Delaware, the project of "erecting a Kingswood School in America," and in June, 1780, a subscription list for it was begun.[47] By 1782 the site in Abingdon had been selected.[48] Coke's arrival brought fresh fuel to a dwindling flame. Whoever first mentioned the project at their initial meeting, Coke entered in his *Journal*: "He and I have agreed to use our joint endeavours to establish a school or college on the plan of Kingswood School."[49] ("School" was Asbury's word, "college" Coke's, but like "superintendent" and "bishop" it was a distinction without a real

43. Asbury, *Journal*, I. 499, 510, 535–8; Coke, *Journals*, 1793, pp. 67–72; Lee, *Short History*, pp. 127–9; Sherman, op. cit., pp. 97–106.
44. Vickers, *Coke*, pp. 132–6.
45. Coke, *Journals*, 1793, pp. 8–10.
46. Jackson, *Early Methodist Preachers*, V, 283–4; Lee, *Short History*, p. 111.
47. Asbury, *Journal*, I, 324, 358.
48. G. P. Baker, op. cit., p. 66.
49. Coke, *Journals*, 1793, p. 16.

difference, a case of Tweedledum and Tweedledee.) Coke immediately put his charm to work in raising money for this cause. On December 14 they met at the future site, with enough money in hand to justify their laying the scheme before the preachers in Baltimore on January 1, 1785, after all the important constitutional matters were out of the way. The conference approved, added its own generous contribution to the fund, and after debate suggested a name which commemorated the two bishops,[50] who immediately went ahead and printed an eight-page *Plan for Erecting a College*.[51] The *Plan* shows how closely the institution was modeled upon Wesley's Kingswood School, but by the time it was approved by the Conference the provisions for Kingswood School made in the British *Minutes* had already been deleted, and were never restored to the *Discipline*, though the *Plan* itself was incorporated in the revised edition of 1787.[52] Henceforth the burdens and anxieties for the college were carried mainly by Asbury, who preached the foundation sermon on June 5, 1785, and welcomed the twenty-five students at the opening on December 6, 1787.[53] (On both occasions Coke was out of the country.) John Wesley also lent his aid, especially in securing the appointment and passage from England of the first President, the Reverend Levi Heath. Wesley continued to furnish financial support and friendly encouragement to Heath and his family, and even left money to Heath in his will.[54] In spite of its many problems, climaxed by its burning down in 1795, Cokesbury College was a significant beginning in Methodist higher education, and in this beginning Coke's enthusiastic drive undoubtedly bridged the gap between dream and realization. It is a somewhat strange irony that the general Methodist public see and hear the name of their first bishop most frequently in the title of this long defunct institution, taken over by the Methodist Publishing House.

That Coke's name should have been made memorable by the Pub-

50. See John Emory, *A Defence of "Our Fathers,"* pp. 93–4.

51. Coke, *Journals*, 1793, p. 22; Phoebus, *Whatcoat*, p. 23; Lee, *Short History*, pp. 113–18. A copy of the original *Plan* is at Randolph-Macon College, Ashland, Virginia. Coke seems to have been responsible for changing "School" in the title to "College": see the original text of Asbury's *Journal* for June 19, 1780, in *Methodist History*, IX, No. 2 (Jan., 1972), 42.

52. Sherman, op. cit., pp. 267–74.

53. Asbury, *Journal*, I, 490, 555. For fuller details see A. W. Cummings, *The Early Schools of Methodism*, pp. 20–34, and his main source, *The Methodist Quarterly Review*, 1859, pp. 173–88; cf. G. P. Baker, op. cit., pp. 65–73.

54. Frank Baker, "John Wesley and Cokesbury College's First President," pp. 54–9.

lishing House, however, is appropriate, for he himself was as experienced in that field as Asbury was inexperienced, and his own publications are far from exhausted by the sixty-two listed in John Vickers' valuable biography.[55] The first official publications of the new Church were the *Discipline* and two of Coke's Christmas Conference sermons, all probably not only written but underwritten and seen through the press by him personally.[56] On his first arrival in New York Coke had established a close rapport with John Dickins, the preacher there, and Dickins (as we have seen) had edited Asbury's rearrangement of the hastily prepared *Discipline* which was approved as the nucleus for the *Discipline* of 1787. One of the new sections in this revised *Discipline* was "On the Printing of Books," and both Coke and Asbury confidently placed the responsibility for the church's publications henceforth on the capable shoulders of Dickins. In 1787 Dickins combined publishing with preaching, but from Coke's next American visit in 1789 he became "Book Steward" in charge of the first "Book Room." Coke breathed a sigh of relief: "We have now settled our printing business, I trust, on an advantageous footing, both for the people individually and the Connexion at large."[57] Once again Coke had served as a major catalyst in the establishment of a lasting and important Methodist venture dedicated to the furthering of Christian concerns. One of the major early functions of the Book Room was the printing and distribution of religious tracts. Here again Coke was a pioneer, a moving power behind the Tract Society founded by John Wesley in 1782,[58] who during his first visit to America, while pleading for missions and education did not fail to put in a successful word—though in a lower key—for the cause of tract distribution.[59]

When Coke left for England after this first momentous tour Asbury

55. Vickers, *Coke*, pp. 375–82.

56. Pilkington, op. cit., pp. 72–3. Coke's itinerary furnishes a clue to the order of their publication: first came the *Discipline*, in Philadelphia; next was the *Sermon on the Godhead of Christ*, which Coke himself explicitly states that he published—"at the desire of the Conference"—while he was in New York, Jan. 22 to Feb. 6; lastly came the sermon on Asbury's ordination as superintendent, printed in Baltimore after Coke returned for a visit between February 26 and March 6—the dedication "To the Rev. Francis Asbury, Superintendent of the Methodist Episcopal Church of America" is dated "Baltimore, March 1, 1785."

57. Coke, *Journals*, 1793, p. 114; cf. Asbury, *Journal*, I, 598n.

58. *WHS*, XII, 136–8; XIX, 12–13.

59. Coke, *Journals*, 1793, p. 22. Coke felt that Mr. Gough was a poor steward of his wealth in that he would "only give thirty guineas towards the College and five guineas for tracts for the poor." See also Pilkington, op. cit., pp. 190–5.

said, "We parted with heavy hearts."[60] Upon his return two years later both Asbury and the American preachers seemed a little cool, partly because Wesley was directing that Whatcoat and Garrettson should be made superintendents, partly because Coke in Wesley's name had altered the arrangements made for the three Conferences. The first day of the major Conference at Baltimore, May 1, 1787, proved especially stormy, but on the second day Coke dissolved their fears about himself by apologizing, and when pressed by a few he also gave a written undertaking that he would exert no privileges as superintendent when absent from America, and none even when present except according to the regulations of the Conference itself.[61] Henceforth there remained no question about the supremacy of Asbury in American Methodism, even though in the amended *Minutes* there was no alteration in the order of their names: "Quest.1.Who are the Superintendents of our Church, for the United States? Answ. Thomas Coke (when present in the States) and Francis Asbury."[62] From this time onward Coke did little more during his brief biennial or quadrennial visits than tag along at Asbury's heels, like British royalty an impressive figurehead with little real power.

Coke also managed to rub the Americans the wrong way by his efforts to transform Methodism from the society which in practice it remained into a full-orbed church in closer association with the Church of England.[63] His attempt to promote liturgical worship failing, in 1791 he belatedly responded to earlier overtures from the Episcopalians in order to bring about a union between them and the Methodist Church. He as good as promised that most of the preachers would be prepared to submit to reordination, and hinted (though he did not demand) that, as the Episcopalians themselves had suggested in 1784, the present Methodist superintendents should be made bishops of the Protestant Episcopal Church. Wesley's death and Bishop Seabury's coldness to the scheme put an end to the matter, but when Coke's part in it came to light the preachers were furious. That was in 1806, however, and by that time Coke's effective links with America had been broken.[64]

60. Asbury, *Journal*, I, 490; cf. Coke, *Journals*, 1793, p. 49.

61. Asbury, *Journal*, I, 538; Coke, *Journals*, 1793, pp. 71–2; Lee, *Short History*, pp. 124–6.

62. *Minutes* (American, 1795), p. 95.

63. Cf. *HAM*, I, 422, and Sanders, op. cit., pp. 361–70.

64. Vickers, *Coke*, pp. 176–91. See also Edward J. Drinkhouse, *History of Methodist Reform*, I, 267–8n, 396–405; G. P. Baker, op. cit., pp. 73–4; Phoebus, *Whatcoat*, pp. 68–72.

COKE AND ASBURY

Coke's major contributions to American Methodism were not confined to his initial visit, however. He also proved of key importance in securing a workable system of centralized democratic control for the new church. A number of the preachers strongly disapproved of what William McKendree called Asbury's "poor miserable Council," which seemed to them disguised autocracy at worst and at best rule by aristocracy.[65] Jesse Lee made one protest to the Council itself in 1789, and another to Asbury in 1791, in each case suggesting as an alternative a delegated General Conference.[66] James O'Kelly first secured a group to support him in boycotting its meetings, and then wrote to Coke in England, seeking his support against Asbury.[67] As a result Coke came to America prepared to support the scheme for a General Conference in opposition to Asbury's Council. For Asbury this settled the matter. Although obviously distressed by Coke's change of mind, he found this strange alliance of Jesse Lee, James O'Kelly, and Thomas Coke too much for him, and "acceded to a General Conference for the sake of peace."[68] Ezekiel Cooper warned Coke that his support of O'Kelly must be handled carefully, because some of the preachers construed it, not simply as opposition to a faulty judgment on the part of Asbury, but as a deliberate attempt to undermine his authority, which O'Kelly himself might desire, but which the preachers in general would not tolerate.[69] Coke, however, was undoubtedly disinterested in his motives, and although he was not the originator of the quadrennial General Conference his episcopal advocacy carried the issue, so that this institution remains as another of the unmarked monuments to his American ministry.

The news of Wesley's death prompted Coke's hasty return to England from his fourth visit to America. Within eight months, however, he was back, rebuffed by the English preachers—who were determined that he should not step straight into Wesley's shoes, as he had expected—but courted by the dissident group in America. These he felt that he must both support and at the same time restrain by attendance at the first quadrennial General Conference of 1792, which

65. Tigert, op. cit., p. 250; cf. Ware, *Life*, pp. 181–2.
66. Lee, *Short History*, pp. 158–9; Asbury, *Journal*, I, 687.
67. Tigert, op. cit., pp. 250–2.
68. Asbury, *Journal*, I, 667–8.
69. Letter of Aug. 11, 1791, quoted in Scherer, *Cooper*, p. 69.

over Asbury's objections he had helped to secure. He did little more than attend that Conference.

His sixth visit was for the following General Conference, in 1796. At this Conference the two bishops were asked to prepare an annotated edition of the *Discipline,* and did so. The voluminous notes, in very small print, are almost twice as long as the *Discipline* itself, and though undoubtedly valuable, were never reprinted. For these Coke was chiefly responsible, though he incorporated some notes prepared by Asbury, while Asbury also "numbered the chapters" and "versed the Scriptures"—i.e., furnished seven hundred proof texts—and generally assisted. Both men thought highly of the work. Coke said, "If I ever drew up any useful publications for the press, this was surely one of them, and perhaps the best." [70]

Another matter of much greater moment was raised at this Conference. Because of ill health Asbury clearly needed help, and it was speedily resolved to "strengthen the episcopacy," though the method of so doing was the subject of lengthy debate. Coke offered himself to labor more fully among them, subject only to leaving them for the West Indies or France "when there is an opening." During the two-day debate—from which Coke absented himself—some preachers, led by Jesse Lee, argued instead for an additional American bishop, but Asbury's plea for Coke carried the vote. [71] Coke stayed in America a little longer for this visit—just over four months—before returning to tie up the loose ends in Britain, and finally pack his bags for America.

TRANSATLANTIC TUG-OF-WAR

In England he was greeted—somewhat belatedly, it must be admitted—with praise and pleas: "You are too valuable to us! Don't leave us! Ask our brethren in America to release you from your promise!" Seven years after Wesley's death they at length elected him President of the Conference, and almost immediately afterwards sent him back to America for a brief visit, stuffing into his pocket an appeal requesting—almost requiring—that he be released from his American agreement at least until they had found their way through the various post-Wesleyan crises which menaced the road to their becoming an

70. *The Doctrines and Discipline of the Methodist Church,* 10th ed., 1798; Coke, *Journals,* 1816, p. 249; Asbury, *Journal,* II, 117, 121; III, 159–60. Nearly sixty pages of extracts form an appendix to Sherman, op. cit. Cf. chap. 10, pp. 175–6.

71. Phoebus, *Whatcoat,* pp. 81–5; Lee, *Short History,* pp. 47–8.

independent denomination. The letter was presented to the Virginia Conference, and Asbury signed his consent to the British request, though at the same time he protested that his fellow-Englishmen did not appreciate the dire need for Coke's services in America. Nevertheless it is clear that Asbury had very mixed feelings as to whether in fact he wanted Coke as a permanent colleague, wondering both whether there might be some difficulty in assimilating him into a somewhat subsidiary role, and whether Coke's undoubted sincerity of the moment was a firm enough basis for prognosticating his future behavior. As a result Asbury never seemed quite sure for which side he was pulling in this strange transatlantic tug-of-war for Coke's services. The General Conference of 1800, for which Coke came over on his eighth visit to America, officially confirmed the decision of the Virginia Conference of 1797 by "lending" Coke "for a season, to return to us as soon as he conveniently can; but at farthest by the meeting of our next General Conference." This decision finally made it imperative to elect an episcopal assistant for Asbury, though instead of a vigorous native American such as Jesse Lee an ailing Englishman was chosen, Richard Whatcoat—a short-lived triumph for the old school, for he was already sixty-six, and died six years later.[72] Coke, therefore, stayed mainly in England, though he continued to protest, "In America only I consider myself at home."[73]

At last in 1803 came the time when Coke felt that the major British commitments preventing his emigration to America were out of the way, even though the British Conference still pressed for his return. He wrote to Ezekiel Cooper, who had succeeded John Dickins as Book Editor upon his death in 1798, "I am going to spend the remainder of my days with you."[74] The only obstacle remaining was in America itself. Coke had promised the British Conference that nothing but a clear assurance that his permanent residence in America was indeed the will of God would keep him there. He was preserving an escape route, and surely doing so because he was afraid he might need to use it. He needed a sign from heaven—which in effect meant from Asbury. But Asbury gave no sign. Probably Asbury was right, both from the reluctance of many Americans such as Jesse Lee to take Coke to their

72. Methodist Episcopal Church, *Journals of the General Conference*, I, pp. 31–7; cf. Lee, *Short History*, pp. 265–6.

73. Circular letter sent to many preachers, Feb. and March, 1802; see Vickers, *Coke*, pp. 242–3.

74. Vickers, *Coke*, p. 244.

hearts, and from Coke's own restless, unpredictable character. On arriving in Norfolk, Virginia, in October, 1803, Coke did not embark on the five-thousand-mile preaching tour suggested by Asbury, but impulsively went to assist his episcopal colleague in the Georgia Conference, and felt snubbed when he was by-passed at the discussion of the preachers' stations. He was not prepared to be "but a shadow of a bishop," "a *mere* preacher."[75] And so, after a preaching tour in the North, including a sermon in Washington before Congress,[76] he left the United States, never to return.

Not that he had completely written America off. On June 1, 1805, Coke sent a circular letter to Asbury and other preachers announcing his marriage. He reminded them of the "solemn engagements" made "on both sides" at the General Conference of 1796, and assured them that he wished still to fulfil those engagements, though not on any "transitory visit": "If we come to you at all, we come for life." But if they came for life it would be on condition that whenever Asbury was unable to travel throughout all the Conferences Coke should divide the territory with him, Whatcoat clearly being too frail to do so.[77] On receiving this letter Asbury made the wry comment: "Marriage is honourable in all—but to me it is a ceremony awful as death."[78] When indulged in by his preachers it also seemed to have a similar effect on Asbury—to him they were as good as dead. He was convinced that Coke's usefulness was now at an end—certainly his usefulness in America. In this the American conferences supported him, and politely replied that Coke's new status would not render him so well fitted to serve them. Although he later withdrew his conditions, their attitude did not change. The 1807 *Minutes* were the last to record his name as an effective bishop, and the 1808 General Conference elected an episcopal replacement in William McKendree, duly recording its gratitude for Coke's past services.[79]

Coke and Asbury continued to correspond, however, and when news came of Coke's death on May 3, 1814, en route to Ceylon to establish missionary work in Asia, Asbury preached a funeral sermon, adding a remarkable testimony to Coke in his *Journal*: ". . . a gentleman, a scholar, and a bishop to us; and as a minister of Christ, in zeal,

75. Ibid., p. 246.
76. Samuel Drew, *The Life of the Rev. Thomas Coke*, p. 316.
77. Asbury, *Journal*, III, 18–21.
78. Ibid., II, 474.
79. Vickers, *Coke*, pp. 254–8; M. E. Church, *Journals of Gen. Conf.*, I, 73–6, 79–81.

in labours, and in services, the greatest man in the last century."[80]

What does this signify? In penning such a tribute Asbury could hardly have overlooked John Wesley. Many, perhaps most, would not agree in ranking Coke above Wesley. Was this a faulty judgment on Asbury's part? Was it indeed a cold assessment? Or was it a posthumous expiation for having held Coke at arm's length during the past thirty years, thus denying him the opportunity to prove his constant assertion that he wished to live up to his full potential as the first bishop of the Methodist Episcopal Church? At the very least such a tribute emphasizes the fact that Thomas Coke hardly merits his status as the forgotten man of early American Methodism.

80. Asbury, *Journal*, II. 789. For a summary of the sermon itself, see John Wesley Bond's reminiscences, in *Methodist History*, IV, No. 1 (Oct., 1965), 18. Asbury certainly tried to be realistic, witness his words: "He was in his temper quick. It was like a spark; touch it and it would fly, and was soon off. Indeed it is natural in a Welshman to be quick. But jealousy, malice, or envy dwelt not in a soul so able as that of Coke."

10. THE DOCTRINES IN THE
DISCIPLINE

The hastily summoned Methodist preachers who huddled together in a wintry Baltimore that Christmas of 1784 issued their own declaration of independence. For all the thousands of miles of ocean separating them from England they had so far followed the precedents and accepted the oversight of Mr. Wesley. So it had been for more than a decade. Now, apparently with Wesley's agreement, and even on his suggestion, as transmitted by Dr. Thomas Coke, they made a deliberate attempt to erect a new American Methodist church, fraternally linked with British Methodism but quite independent of its control. Now at last they had their own spiritual leaders in Coke and Asbury—technically equal in authority, but far from equal in the allegiance of their colleagues. In 1784 the Methodist Episcopal Church secured its own national leadership, its own power to perpetuate a ministry, its own ecclesiastical organization, and also took an immense step forward in creating its own ethos.

A few of the preachers doubted whether the throwing off of parental restraints (and support) by this eager Methodist adolescent was wise and timely. Thomas Haskins spoke for others when he confided to his journal: "Oh, how tottering I see Methodism now!"[1] Their two bishops managed to hold a precarious balance on the ecclesiastical fence without falling off either on the one side of retaining full theoretical control of American Methodism for Wesley, or on the other of denying him any voice at all. At the very least they insisted that the decencies should be preserved, and that having successfully thrown Mr. Wesley to the ground they should not kick him in the stomach. He was therefore indulged with an occasional kindly reference, but no actual power. Not until 1787 did the preachers explicitly reject their 1784 agreement "in matters belonging to Church government to obey [Wesley's] commands." Perhaps, however, this original agreement should rather have been described as a courteous gesture than a firm commitment.

First published in *The Duke Divinity School Review*, XXXI (1966), 39–55.
1. Journal of Thomas Haskins at the Christmas Conference, Jan. 1, 1785, quoted in Sweet, *Men of Zeal*, p. 173.

A FORM OF DISCIPLINE

The first official document embodying the organization of the new church used the title, followed the pattern, and reproduced three-quarters of the contents of its British equivalent, though with the names of Coke and Asbury replacing those of the Wesleys. It was published in 1785 as *Minutes of several conversations between the Rev. Thomas Coke, LL.D., the Rev. Francis Asbury and others.* The extent to which this depended upon Wesley's so-called "Large Minutes" is convincingly demonstrated by the parallel arrangement of the two documents in the appendix to Bishop Tigert's *Constitutional History of American Episcopal Methodism.*[2] The ferment of independence was strongly at work, however, in what was omitted, what was altered, and in what was introduced, including especially the subtitle—"composing a Form of Discipline." The second edition appeared in 1786 as an appendix to the "American" edition of Wesley's *Sunday Service.*[3] This version also retained some reminiscence of the British prototype, but experimented with a different title, which retained little of Wesley's apart from the word "Minutes"—"The General Minutes of the Conference of the Methodist Episcopal Church in America, forming the constitution of the said Church." Thereafter for the remainder of Wesley's lifetime his example was completely forsaken, and the following five editions of the American Methodist preachers' ecclesiastical handbook discarded Wesley's title for their own subtitle, being published as *A Form of Discipline for the Ministers, Preachers, and Members of the Methodist Episcopal Church in America.*[4]

All this time the administrative discipline of American Methodism was evolving, and echoes of Wesley in new regulations steadily and inevitably diminished. The one area where his influence persisted was that of doctrine. Here conditions in America were not markedly different from those in England, and indeed some of the theological battles of the parent society were later re-enacted by her daughter

2. Tigert, op. cit., pp. 533–602. See also above, p. 151.
3. Wesley, *Sunday Service*, pp. 322–55. This particular edition is briefly described in Baker, *Union Catalogue*, p. 174, as No. 376 [E]. There were also "British" editions in 1786 ([C], [D]), and other years. These contained variants in the prayers and the Articles, suited to members who still owed allegiance to the British Crown, though otherwise the editions were the same.
4. See the editions of 1787, 1788, 1789, 1790, and 1791; cf. Baker, *Union Catalogue*, No. 425.ii, pp. 216–17.

church, when the old weapons forged by Wesley proved to have retained their cutting edge. The dependence of American Methodism upon Wesley's theology has been both deliberately obscured and strangely forgotten by succeeding generations, and only in our own day is it once more receiving careful attention. The extent of this dependence is somewhat difficult to trace, but one of the most interesting clues is to be found in the history of the *Discipline*.

We have seen that the founding fathers of the Methodist Episcopal Church transformed Wesley's *Minutes* into their *Discipline*. At the American Conference next but one after his death another significant change was made in the title. Instead of *A Form of Discipline* the eighth edition of 1792 introduced the one that became the standard or model for most branches of American Methodism until our own day—*The Doctrines and Discipline of the Methodist Episcopal Church in America*. The operative word in this change, of course, is "doctrines." The dead founder of Methodism is rarely mentioned in the volume, but in its doctrines, thus emphasized by the altered title, we become aware of his dominating though unseen influence, a ghost walking the *Discipline* for all succeeding generations, his teaching enshrined though his identity almost forgotten. Even when in 1812 Wesley's theological bones were disinterred from the *Discipline* and buried in a grassed-over grave exceedingly difficult for later Methodists to discover, his spirit could not fully be exorcised. Here, however, I suspect that my analogy is somewhat hard to follow for those who have not shared with me the excitement of searching out Wesley's doctrinal resting place in a mysterious publication entitled accurately but inadequately *A Collection of Interesting Tracts*. I will therefore return from the realms of fantasy to the prosaic task of the historian, endeavoring to trace the thread of Wesley's theology through the maze of the successive issues of the Methodist *Discipline*.

THE DOCTRINAL SECTIONS IN THE *DISCIPLINES*

The *Minutes* of 1785 contained no formal outline of belief, but the document did echo most of the doctrinal passages of Wesley's large *Minutes*. Three sections in particular call for mention. A verbatim reprint of Wesley's statement about the rise of Methodism, published originally in the annual *Minutes* for 1765 and incorporated with some minor changes into the large *Minutes* from 1770 onwards, appeared thus: "In 1729, two young men, reading the Bible, saw they could not be saved without holiness, followed after it, and incited others so to do. In 1737 they saw holiness comes by faith. They saw likewise, that men are justified before they are sanctified: but still holiness was their point. God then thrust them out, utterly against their will, to raise an holy people. When Satan could no otherwise hinder this, he threw *Calvinism* in the way; and then *Antinomianism*, which strikes directly at the root of all holiness." At the very least this makes clear the double Methodist emphasis upon evangelical theology and the pursuit of holiness, as well as drawing attention to some of the snares waiting to entangle the feet of unwary Protestant pilgrims who believe that salvation comes and stays by faith alone. Certainly it offers no encouragement to those Methodists who would banish theology from the pew and even from the pulpit, to languish only in the rarefied atmosphere of the seminary. The sentence about Calvinism and Antinomianism was omitted from the *Disciplines* of 1787, 1788, and 1789—presumably to remove an additional snare from the path of the unlearned rather than because Satan no longer wielded those weapons. In the 1790 *Discipline* this section was transferred to the opening address "To the Members of the Methodist Societies in the United States," though it was not made clear that the American Methodist bishops who signed that address were not in fact the authors of the statement, but had employed the services of a ghost-writer. Not until 1796 were quotation marks added, together with a footnote which stated, "These are the words of Messrs. Wesleys themselves." And not until 1948 was this "historical statement" replaced by one emphasizing Wesley's Aldersgate experience.[5]

Other unacknowledged statements from Wesley's publications, similarly stressing points of doctrine, were carried over from the 1785 *Minutes* into the later *Disciplines*. The two most important were deemed worthy of publication as separate sections in the volume revised by Asbury in 1787 and its successors. "Of the Rise of Methodism" formed Section I of the 1787 *Discipline*, "Against Antinomianism" Section XVI, and "On Perfection" Section XXII. Of these latter doctrinal sections the first emphasized the need for good works as at least a *condition* of entering into and remaining in a state of salvation.

5. Tigert, op. cit., p. 535. In 1876 the footnote was brought into the text. In 1892 this section was transferred to a "Historical Statement," where it remained until 1944, to be replaced at the following General Conference by a statement emphasizing Wesley's experience of May 24, 1738.

The second urged: "Let us strongly and explicitly exhort all believers to go on to Perfection." Both were taken almost word for word from Wesley's large *Minutes* by way of the 1785 American *Discipline*. Strangely enough, although these two important statements formed an integral element of the official constitution of American Methodism from 1784 until after the epochal General Conference of 1808, their existence was completely overlooked by the classic historians of the *Discipline*, Robert Emory and David Sherman, and only partly realized in the masterly work of John J. Tigert, who incorrectly speaks of them as having been introduced in 1792 and omitted before the passage of the restrictive rules by the General Conference of 1808.[6]

The *Discipline* of 1792 reorganized the numerous small sections of previous editions into three chapters, the third containing miscellaneous matter, mainly doctrinal, of which the retitled "Of Christian Perfection" was section 4, and "Against Antinomianism" section 5. This arrangement was continued in the *Disciplines* of 1797 and 1798. To that of 1798 were added "explanatory notes" by Bishops Asbury and Coke.[7] Those to these particular sections were very brief: "In respect to the doctrine of Christian perfection, we must refer the reader to Mr. Wesley's excellent treatise on that subject," and "The subject of antinomianism has been so fully handled by that great writer, Mr. Fletcher, that we need not enlarge on it, when it has been so completely considered by him." With the removal of the section on education in 1801 they moved up to become sections 3 and 4, and in 1804 were promoted to the head of Chapter 3, which was limited to doctrine and liturgy.

Again contrary to Bishop Tigert's statement,[8] this matter was still retained in the *Discipline* of 1808, when almost plenary powers were secured for General Conferences, subject only to a handful of restrictive rules. The first of these ran: "The General Conference shall not revoke, alter, or change our articles of religion, nor establish any

6. Tigert, op. cit., p. 146. Their place and manner of appearance varied greatly, however, so that omission and error can readily be understood. In the 1785 *Minutes* the doctrinal sections appear without any titles, the discussion of antinomianism forming the questions and answers of the two closing sections, 80 and 81, while the statement on perfection forms the lengthy closing paragraph of the answer to question 73 (see Tigert, op. cit., pp. 585–6, 600–2). In 1787 their order was reversed, "Against Antinomianism" forming section 16 and "On Perfection" section 22, as noted above. This remained true until 1790, when each was elevated one step, to slip back once more in 1791 through the insertion of a new section on Band Societies.

7. See above, p. 158.

8. Tigert, op. cit., p. 146.

new standards or rules of doctrine contrary to our present existing and established standards of doctrine."[9] This well-meant attempt to petrify the theological *status quo* left a heritage of uncertainty.

THE DOCTRINAL STANDARDS: THEIR NATURE AND IDENTITY

For one thing, the Articles appear by this time to have gained central importance, so that they alone must not be revoked or altered, whereas the other unspecified doctrinal standards must not receive contradictory additions.[10] Is the subtle ambiguity in wording deliberate—as we suspect—or merely careless? Surely it was not the intention of the drafting committee to imply that the Articles were in fact the *only* standards, with the mention of "our present and existing and established standards of doctrine" merely a legal device to cover all possible contingencies, with nothing concrete in mind? If not, what are these "existing and established standards" of Methodist doctrine which, like the laws of the Medes and the Persians, may not be altered? They are apparently like the common law, taken for granted by all, yet capable of accurate and complete definition by no one, and never summarized in any authoritative document.

At the present time the candidate for full connection in the United Methodist ministry undergoes an examination modeled on that given by John Wesley to his preachers. Questions 8–10 of the nineteen asked on this occasion run thus:

(8) Have you studied the doctrines of The United Methodist Church?

(9) After full examination do you believe that our doctrines are in harmony with the Holy Scriptures?

(10) Will you preach and maintain them?[11]

Similarly the British Methodist minister is challenged every year of his ministry with this question, asked at the May Synod: "Does he believe and preach our doctrines?" This sounds exemplary, but it does not answer the question, "What *are* these doctrines which we must believe and preach?"

The accepted practice of the Methodist Church was to treat the

9. M. E. Church, *Journals of Gen. Conf.*, I, 82–3, 89; cf. Tigert, op. cit., pp. 304–14.
10. The United Methodist Church, *The Book of Discipline, 1972*, pp. 21 (16, Article 1), 43–4.
11. *Discipline, 1972*, p. 157 (334).

Articles of Religion as "our doctrines," though with a vague suspicion that something additional was implied, or ought to be implied. With the formation of the United Methodist Church in 1968 a Theological Study Commission on Doctrine and Doctrinal Standards was appointed to clarify the situation, and (if it seemed desirable) to prepare "a contemporary formulation of doctrine and belief, in supplementation to all antecedent formulations."[12] Their report was presented to the 1972 General Conference, with the results noted below. The Methodist Church in Britain has continued to maintain a radically different approach, refusing to make a credal statement, taking general orthodoxy of Christian belief for granted, and regarding "our doctrines" as that something else implied but not stated in American Methodism. What is this "something else," then? Perhaps a closer look at the present position in British Methodism, clinging so much more tenaciously to ancient traditions, will enable us to visualize more clearly the doctrinal standards of our Methodist forefathers in this country, standards bequeathed to us, indeed forced upon us, by the first restrictive rule of the 1808 General Conference, and loyally accepted by the Uniting Conferences of 1939 and 1968.[13]

The doctrinal standards of British Methodism are set out in the Deed of Union adopted by the three uniting churches in 1932, and unlike everything else in that deed may never be altered by the Conference, though the Conference is the final authority in their interpretation. This is much the same as the position of the General Conference in the United States of America. Yet in this British Deed of Union the doctrines are never listed nor defined, no more than they were in any of Wesley's legislation—though he several times had the advice of capable lawyers. They are concerned with the spirit rather than with the letter of the law of God. It is taken for granted that the British Methodist preacher accepts "the fundamental principles of the historic creeds and of the Protestant Reformation," and he is expected to emphasize especially "the doctrines of the evangelical faith . . . based upon the Divine revelation recorded in the Holy Scriptures." Though these are never strictly *defined*, they are *illustrated*, in Wesley's manner, and from Wesley's writings: "These evangelical doc-

12. The United Methodist Church, *The Book of Discipline, 1968*, pp. 455–6 (1419).
13. Ibid., pp. 35–6, which make it clear that although the restrictive rule of 1808 is thus continued through 1968 the Wesleyan standards are to be interpreted as "negative limits of public teaching" rather than "the positive prescription of an inflexible system of doctrine."

trines to which the preachers of the Methodist Church both ministers and laymen are pledged are contained in Wesley's *Notes on the New Testament* and the first four volumes of his sermons." The Model Deed of the British Methodist Church stipulates that no doctrines contrary to these standards may be preached in any Methodist church. The significance of this lack of precision is thus spelled out in the Deed of Union: "The *Notes on the New Testament* and the *Forty-Four Sermons* are not intended to impose a system of formal or speculative theology on Methodist Preachers, but to set up standards of preaching and belief which should secure loyalty to the fundamental truths of the Gospel of redemption, and secure the continued witness of the Church to the realities of the Christian experience of salvation." [14] The voice is indeed Wesley's voice, though the words are those of his followers. For this was the principle on which he tried to ensure the loyalty of Methodism to its evangelical calling, and these were the very documents which he legally established as exemplars of evangelical doctrine.

Exactly this pattern was followed at first in American Methodism. Gradually, however, the Articles of Religion came to occupy a distinctive place as a formal and specific doctrinal standard, and eventually were regarded by many as the *only* genuine standard.[15] As a statement of the theological emphases of Wesley and his American followers, however, the Articles are clearly defective, for where is Christian Perfection to be found? The Methodist Protestant Church tried to remedy this defect by a twenty-sixth Article on Sanctification, but although this has been printed in recent *Disciplines* its status has been left deliberately vague, though clearly it does not have the same authority as the original twenty-five. In addition, from 1968 onwards the omission has been rectified by the adoption also of the Confession of Faith of the Evangelical United Brethren, whose Article XI, "Sanctification and Christian Perfection," is a careful and lengthy statement based solidly on Wesley's teaching.[16] Neither in the Articles nor elsewhere in the *Discipline*, however, were Wesley's *Notes* and *Sermons* mentioned until the 1968 *Discipline* at last reintroduced them by way

14. Harold Spencer and Edwin Finch, *The Constitutional Practice and Discipline of the Methodist Church*, pp. 276–7, 285.

15. Even the homespun evangelist Benjamin Abbott introduced an appeal for members by reading the Articles after preaching at a new place in 1792. (Benjamin Abbott, *Experience*, p. 204.)

16. *Discipline, 1968*, pp. 43, 47, and *1972*, pp. 60, 63–4.

of a reference to the British Deed of Union.[17] Eventually the 1972 *Discipline*, in adapting the report of the Theological Study Commission on Doctrine and Doctrinal Standards, inserted a careful discussion of the *Notes* and *Sermons* in a section on "Wesleyan Doctrinal Standards."[18]

The early neglect of these two "standards" does not seem to have been deliberate, but the result of the hasty preparation of the 1785 *Discipline* from Wesley's large *Minutes* of 1780—the reference to them was buried in a clause in the lengthy Model Deed, which was not reproduced.[19] This clause is finally included in the 1972 *Discipline*, with comments on its interpretation, along the same lines as the British Deed of Union quoted above, together with an evaluation of this unusual method of securing doctrinal orthodoxy: "The aim here was not to impose an inflexible system of doctrine or to inhibit responsible intellectual freedom, but rather to provide a broad and flexible framework of doctrine which would define the outside limits for public teaching in the societies, in disputed cases. These standards were more flexible than any of the classical creeds or confessions or articles, they gave the Methodists a measure of protection from doctrinal eccentricity, and they gave Methodist laymen a new role in the assessment of doctrinal standards. This particular collegial formula for doctrinal guidance was unique in Christendom. It committed the Methodist people to the biblical revelation as primary without proposing a literal summary of that revelation in any single propositional form. It anchored Methodist theology to a stable core, but allowed it freedom of movement in the further unfoldings of history."[20] Although the statement on the "historical background," including this clause and comment, is not itself either "part of the Constitution nor under the Restrictive Rules,"[21] it is of key importance in defining the doctrinal significance of the general phrase in trust clauses for United Methodist property, namely that the premises are "held in trust for the United Methodist Church and subject to the provisions of its *Discipline*."[22] Now at length Wesley is no longer present upon Meth-

17. Ibid., *1968*, p. 36.
18. Ibid., *1972*, pp. 40–3.
19. Tigert, op. cit., pp. 589–91. This Model Deed was earlier used by American Methodists, as in New York for John Street Chapel, and also for Old St. George's, Philadelphia. (See above, pp. 78, 87–8.)
20. *Discipline, 1972*, p. 41.
21. Ibid., p. 39n.
22. Ibid., pp. 484–6.

odist premises in concealment, a dusty skeleton in a dark cupboard.

To visualize the early American situation fully we need to go back behind 1784 to 1773, to the first Methodist Conference held on American soil. The preachers present agreed that "the doctrine and discipline of the Methodists, as contained in the *Minutes*," should be the sole rule of their conduct.[23] In thus accepting the *Minutes*, i.e., Wesley's *Minutes*, they knew that they were accepting the principle that the trust deeds of Methodist "preaching-houses" should contain a clause restricting those conducting worship therein from preaching any other doctrines than those "contained in Mr. Wesley's *Notes upon the New Testament, and four volumes of Sermons*." This, indeed, was there for those who wished to see it in the deed for the New York chapel.[24] To make sure that all the preachers knew what this implied Wesley presented a three-volume set of the 1760 edition of his *Explanatory Notes upon the New Testament* to all those present at the 1775 Conference, including the fourteen native preachers: William Duke's set, at least, has survived.[25] Their expected doctrinal loyalties were made slightly more specific in the challenging opening question of the 1781 Conference: "What preachers are now determined . . . to preach the old Methodist doctrine, and strictly enforce the discipline, as contained in the notes, sermons, and minutes published by Mr. Wesley?"[26] This same pledge was demanded by the Conference of April–May, 1784, as an essential prerequisite before any European preacher could be accepted into the American work.[27]

Unfortunately the *Minutes* of the American Conferences during the eighteenth century are little more than statistical bones with only an occasional shred of historical flesh clinging to them, so that they do not enable us to reconstruct the body of the primitive church. It is to the *Disciplines* that we must turn for fuller information. Even here, however, we find the merest crumbs of theological leaven scattered in the disciplinary lump. The Christmas Conference of 1784

23. *Minutes* (American, 1795), p. 5.

24. Seaman, op. cit., p. 421.

25. In the Methodist Publishing House Library, Nashville, Tennessee. Inscribed on the flyleaf of each volume: "William Duke/May 10th–1775/Mr. Wesley's Gift." Overleaf is a note by the Reverend J. B. Hagany describing how he received the volumes from Duke, who informed him that "Mr. Wesley sent over a copy of his *Notes* to each of the preachers who composed the Conference of 1775." It seems quite probable that Wesley also presented them with copies of his *Sermons*.

26. *Minutes* (American, 1795), p. 41.

27. Ibid., pp. 72–3. Cf. Wesley's 1783 charge to Asbury, quoted above, pp. 128–9.

asserted the virtual independence of American Methodism, instituting indigenous episcopal government and several modifications of Wesley's original discipline. But his theology remained untouched, almost unmentioned. A few incidental scraps of doctrinal teaching were specifically noted, such as the somewhat inadequate summary in a brief section on pastoral duties of "our doctrine" as "repentance toward God, and faith in our Lord Jesus Christ."[28] In general, however, Wesley's doctrines seem to have been regarded as almost inviolaable; the main thing was to give close attention to the discipline.

Both doctrine and discipline, however, were vulnerable. That this was realized may be seen from the wording of a caution against elaborate building plans for new chapels, which might give rich men undue influence—"and then farewell to the Methodist discipline, if not doctrine too."[29] One important omission from the 1785 *Discipline*, as we have seen, was the stipulation about naming Wesley's *Notes* and *Sermons* in trust deeds as the Methodist doctrinal standards, although there survived several incidental references to Wesley's publications both for the preachers' own study and for dispersal among the people.[30] To these was added in 1787 a recommendation that when preachers were not available, as during the sessions of the Annual Conference, "some person of ability . . . in every society should sing, pray, and read one of Mr. Wesley's sermons."[31] For a time, however, the Methodist Episcopal Church had no explicit doctrinal guidance apart from the three doctrinal sections carried over from the 1780 *Minutes*—"Of the Rise of Methodism," "Against Antinomianism," and "Of Perfection."

THE *DOCTRINAL TRACTS* INCORPORATED WITH THE *DISCIPLINE*, 1788–1808

This deficiency was in part remedied by the greatly enlarged fourth edition of the *Discipline*, published in 1788. The title page drew attention to "some other useful pieces annexed"—which in fact comprised two-thirds of the volume. These five "useful pieces" illustrated characteristic Methodist teaching from the writings of Wesley. The first addition was mainly historical and disciplinary in function— *The Nature, Design, and General Rules of the United Societies of the*

---

28. See Tigert, op. cit., p. 542.　　30. Ibid., pp. 562, 570, 576, 585, 600.
29. Ibid., p. 592.　　31. Sherman, op. cit., p. 200.

Methodist Episcopal Church in America—an almost exact reprint of Wesleys' *General Rules* of 1743, though their signatures are replaced by "Thomas Coke, Francis Asbury. May 28, 1787."[32] In 1789 this document was moved up into the general body of disciplinary regulations, and has remained there ever since, forming the subject of the fourth restrictive rule of the 1808 General Conference: "They shall not revoke or change the General Rules of the United Society."

The second tract appended in 1788 was "The Articles of Religion, as received and taught in the Methodist Episcopal Church throughout the United States of America." Once again this was in substance John Wesley's work, his abridgment of the Thirty-Nine Articles of the Church of England into the twenty-five appended to the *Sunday Service of the Methodists*. Once again this was incorporated into the general body of the *Discipline*, though not until 1790, along with other doctrinal tracts. Once again it was named as an inviolable part of the Methodist constitution by the restrictive rule of 1808.

The third tract dealt with Cokesbury College, and does not here concern us. The fourth was *The Scripture Doctrine of Predestination, Election, and Reprobation. By the Rev. John Wesley, M.A.*[33]—an antidote against some of the dangers of Calvinism noted in the statement on the rise of Methodism. Like the Articles, this was incorporated into the body of the *Discipline* in 1790, and was presumably part of the doctrinal standards set up in 1808 as inviolable. The same is true of the fifth tract. Once more it is Wesley, though Wesley in disguise. His original treatise had been entitled *Serious Thoughts upon the Perseverance of the Saints*,[34] but his editors apparently found it necessary for American consumption to expound the word "perseverance" and to expunge the word "saints." The resultant title appeared as "Serious Thoughts on the Infallible, Unconditional Perseverance of all that have once experienced Faith in Christ." (They nevertheless allowed the word "saints" to stand in the second paragraph, where Wesley defined the term.)

To the 1789 *Discipline* a most important addition was made, augmenting generously the tiny section on sanctification. This was no

32. There was one major and important change in this document—the addition of a provision against slaveholding. See above, n. 42, p. 152.

33. Actually it was not Wesley's own composition, but was extracted by him from *The Order of Causes*, originally published in 1654 by Henry Haggar, and first appearing in Wesley's abridgment in 1741. See Baker, *Union Catalogue*, No. 27.

34. Baker, *Union Catalogue*, No. 153; first published in 1751.

other than that spiritual classic, *A Plain Account of Christian Perfection, as believed and taught by the Rev. Mr. John Wesley, from the year 1725 to the year 1765*, which filled nearly ninety pages.[35]

The year 1790 saw an important change of policy. All the doctrinal tracts were included as numbered sections of the official constitution, and to signalize the change a parenthetical phrase was added to the title, which thus became, *A Form of Discipline . . . (now comprehending the Principles and Doctrines) of the Methodist Episcopal Church in America*. Once more an addition was made to these tracts, though this time it was not from the pen of Wesley. It was entitled *A Treatise on the Nature and Subjects of Christian Baptism. Extracted from a late Author*. This had in fact been published in Philadelphia two years earlier by Moses Hemmenway (1735–1811) as *A Discourse on the nature and subjects of Christian baptism*. John Dickins printed about half the contents as a separate work of 71 pages in 1790, and it seems quite possible that the perusal of Dickins' extract led to its official adoption by his colleagues as a doctrinal standard in this insufficiently covered area.[36]

The *Discipline* of 1791 continued to proclaim itself as "comprehending the Principles and Doctrines" of Methodism, but added nothing further to the doctrinal sections. In 1792 the parenthetical subtitle became a part of the main title, and from that year to 1964 the volume remained *The Doctrines and Discipline* of the church— on the title page at least. This same General Conference of 1792 rearranged the material in its newly designated *Doctrines and Discipline*. The formal statement of doctrine in the twenty-five articles was promoted to first place in Chapter I, after the description of the origin of the church, while the lengthier doctrinal commentary contained in the tracts was relegated to the closing sections of Chapter III. A further addition was made to these, in the shape of what we now

35. Ibid., No. 238, first published in 1766. An early edition was apparently used, for from the fourth edition onwards the terminal date was altered to 1777. In the 1789 *Discipline* the added tracts were paginated separately, but the signatures of the gatherings show that the work was printed as a unit: see *Union Catalogue*, No. 425.ii(5), p. 216.

36. That this was added to the printer's copy at the last minute, and presented some kind of a problem (perhaps its late substitution for other matter) is shown by the signatures of the gatherings. Up to this point they are signed A-P 6, and Wesley's *Plain Account* ends on pp. 177–8, sig. Q. The title page to the *Treatise* is apparently Q2— the matching chainlines confirm the conjugacy—but the drop title to the *Treatise* on p. (181) not only varies from the title page but begins a fresh gathering signed R, after which the book proceeds regularly R-Y 6, Z 2.

know as the Ritual, but which was then described as "Section X. Sacramental Services, &c." For some reason a few copies appeared without the bulky doctrinal tracts, so that "The End" could be printed on p. 72, though the full work contained 264 pages.

In their preface to the 1792 *Discipline* Bishops Asbury and Coke differentiated between the two parts of their doctrinal standards, though insisting on the importance of both, in what amounts to a recital of the titles of the Tracts: "We wish to see this little publication in the house of every Methodist, and the more so as it contains our plan of Collegiate and Christian education, and the articles of religion maintained, more or less, in part or in the whole, by every reformed church in the world. We would likewise declare our real sentiments on the scripture doctrine of election and reprobation; on the infallible, unconditional perseverance of all that[37] ever have believed, or ever shall; on the doctrine of Christian perfection and, lastly, on the nature and subjects of Christian Baptism." Nevertheless they were not prepared to treat this supplementary matter as sacrosanct. Early in 1797 Asbury wrote about a task apparently entrusted to him and Coke by the 1796 General Conference: "We have struck out many to us exceptional [i.e., exceptionable] parts of the tracts. These we did not hold as sacred as the discipline, which we did not alter a word."[38] In fact, however, the bishops' bark was worse than their bite. However vigorously they wielded the blue pencil the published results remained the same through subsequent editions, with the one exception that Hemmenway's treatise on baptism was removed from the 1797 *Discipline*.

The 1798 edition was unique in furnishing "explanatory notes" by Coke and Asbury, who estimated that the discipline proper occupied seventy pages and their notes one hundred pages, so that even with the removal of Hemmenway's treatise and the ordination services from the tracts the resultant volume would contain three hundred pages.[39] In the event, however, it was decided to publish the notes in very tiny print, and to omit the tracts from at least this edition, so that the 1798 *Discipline* turned out to have slightly fewer pages than that of 1797. Not everyone was happy about the changes, and at the General Conference of 1800 "Brother J. Stoneman moved that the explana-

37. Altered to "who" in 1798.   39. Ibid.
38. Asbury, *Journal*, III, 159.

tory notes be left out of the next edition of the form of Discipline, except the notes upon the articles of religion."[40] After pondering the matter for a week end the Conference reached a compromise —that the *Discipline* and the notes should each be printed separately, so that preachers could have the *Discipline* alone, or bound together with the notes if they so wished. In the following eleventh edition of the *Discipline* (1801) the notes were accordingly omitted and the tracts restored, and so it remained for the editions of 1804, 1805, and 1808. Nor do the notes appear to have been printed separately, in accordance with the Conference resolution; they simply disappeared without being missed.[41]

THE *DOCTRINAL TRACTS* SEPARATED FROM THE *DISCIPLINE*

Another major change was ordered by the General Conference of 1812, its manner apparently dictated by the first restrictive rule of the preceding General Conference of 1808. As we have seen, this rule sought to fix for all time the "present existing and established standards of doctrine." These clearly included the articles, and apparently also—though not quite so clearly—the doctrinal principles relating to *Notes* and *Sermons*, the doctrinal sections, and the doctrinal tracts—possibly even the Ritual. All these had been incorporated in the *Discipline* at the time of the restrictive rule. The mass of day-to-day legislation, however, was becoming embarrassingly large. (If only they could have seen the tightly packed little *Discipline* of a century and a half later!) To continue to publish these lengthy tracts in the *Discipline* was difficult, to add to them impracticable, to do away with them henceforth illegal. The delegates who met during May 1–22, 1812, eventually arrived at a neat solution for their dilemma, one foreshadowed and possibly suggested by the treatment of the bishops' "explanatory notes." They would publish their authoritative doctrinal commentary in a volume separate from their doctrinal creed. On the very last day of the protracted Conference Jesse Lee moved and Conference approved this resolution: "That the tracts on doctrine be left out of the future edition[s] of our form of Discipline, and that the

40. M. E. Church, *Journals of Gen. Conf.*, I, 40, 43–4.
41. Ezekiel Cooper had just taken over as editor and publisher upon the death of John Dickins, but his manuscript printing records for 1799–1804 reveal no such item. See Scherer, *Cooper*, pp. 116–17.

following tracts be printed and bound in a separate volume, viz.,: 'Predestination Calmly Considered,' 'Scripture Doctrines on Election and Reprobation,' 'On Final Perseverance,' 'A Predestinarian and his Friend,' 'Christian Perfection,' and 'An Antinomian and his Friend.' "[42] In effect it might be said that the *Doctrines and Discipline* was henceforth to be published in two volumes, Volume 1 dealing mainly with Discipline and Volume 2 with Doctrine.

Bishop Tigert did not seem unduly surprised to discover (as he thought) that at least the latter half of this Conference direction had been overlooked for twenty years[43]—and the neglect of the 1800 Conference's injunction to publish the bishops' explanatory notes in a separate volume would lend some color to this belief. (Indeed I understand that even in these enlightened and efficient days it is not unknown for a General Conference to pass resolutions which are immediately forgotten, even by their promoters.) In this particular instance, however, fairly prompt action was taken. The first thing was to issue the revised fifteenth edition of the *Discipline* without the tracts, and this was done that very year of 1812, followed up by a sixteenth edition in 1813. The unwary student tracing these volumes in a card catalogue, however, would hardly realize that extensive cuts had been made, for the volumes retained almost exactly the same number of pages, by the simple expedients of reducing the size of the paper and increasing the size of the type. With these two diminished *Disciplines* under his belt the Conference printer, John C. Totten, turned to the supplementary volume, which one hopes was eagerly awaited.

In 1814 there duly appeared the first edition of the "Doctrinal Tracts," and subsequent editions continued to be given that designation on their leather labels, though never on their title pages. The title remained constant (with minor variations in the second sentence) through at least fifteen editions covering the best part of a century: *A Collection of Interesting Tracts, explaining several important points of Scripture Doctrine. Published by order of the General Conference.*[44] The preface pointed out that these tracts had been omitted

---

42. M. E. Church, *Journals of Gen. Conf.*, I, 121.

43. Tigert, op. cit., pp. 145–8.

44. I wish to record here my indebtedness to the librarians of the following institutions, who made it possible for me to have access to their treasures, including the rare editions of the *Collection of Interesting Tracts* noted, for which see Baker, *Union Catalogue*, No. 425.ii(16), pp. 217–18: American Antiquarian Society (1814, 1817); Bangor

so that the quadrennial issue of the *Discipline* "might be small and cheap"—an unfortunate phrase which was amended in 1825 to "might still be within the reach of every reader."

This volume was almost twice the size of its companion *Discipline*, and contained 360 pages. The reason was that Jesse Lee's resolution had been followed not strictly but generously, even to the end of the second mile and beyond. In addition to the original three doctrinal tracts added by 1789, Lee had requested and been granted three more of Wesley's smaller publications (the dialogue between a Predestinarian and his friend, and the two between an Antinomian and his friend), and another of his major works, *Predestination Calmly Considered*.[45] So now there were seven—or would have been had not the two Antinomian tracts been forgotten, or deliberately omitted. Already there was matter here for a volume slightly larger than the *Discipline*. As if to atone for the omission with a work of supererogation, no fewer than nine other items were added, almost doubling the size of the volume. Like all those originally named by Lee, six of these were by Wesley, including his controverted sermon on *Free Grace*, his satire on Toplady's predestinarianism entitled *The Consequence Proved*, and a pinch-hitter for the tract on antinomianism (a word carefully avoided with the somewhat fanciful title *A Blow at the Root, or Christ stabbed in the house of his friends*.[46] The most considerable of the non-Wesleyan items was "A Short Method with the Baptists, by Peter Edwards, several years Pastor of a Baptist

Theological Seminary (1825); Library of Congress (1814, c. 1856–60 [Carlton and Porter], c. 1872–80 [Nelson and Phillips]); Depauw University (1836, 1856, c. 1856–60 [Carlton and Porter]); Drew University (1814, 1817, 1831, 1836); Duke University (1814, 1817, 1825); Emory University (1814, 1817, 1825); Garrett Theological Seminary (1817, 1861); The Methodist Publishing House, Nashville (1817, 1836, 1850, 1856, c. 1892 [Hunt and Eaton, etc.]); Methodist Theological School in Ohio (1847); Southern Methodist University (1814, 1834, 1850, 1854); Syracuse University (1825); Xenia-Pittsburgh Theological Seminary (1847); Vanderbilt University (1814, 1850). Dr Kenneth E. Rowe kindly informs me of several other insitutions who hold some of these editions, full details of which will be published in the forthcoming Methodist Union Catalog which he is preparing.

45. Baker, *Union Catalogue*, Nos. 24, 70–1, 155.

46. Ibid., Nos. 11, 274, 212; the other items were *Serious Considerations concerning the Doctrine of Election and Reprobation* (No. 16), abridged from *The Ruin and Recovery of Mankind*, by Isaac Watts; *Serious Considerations on Absolute Predestination* (No. 22), abridged from Robert Barclay's *Apology*; and *Thoughts on the Imputed Righteousness of Christ* (No. 211), an original work by Wesley. There were also two non-Wesleyan pieces, "A Plain Definition of Saving Faith," and "How the Doctrines of the Gospel come into the Succour of Morality," the latter being dropped after the 1817 edition.

Church, at Portsea, Hants.," which filled over thirty pages, and had originally appeared in England in 1793 as *Candid Reasons for renouncing the principles of Antipaedobaptism.* (Possibly a change in title was indeed called for!)

There must have been a reasonably good sale for this volume, because an unaltered second edition appeared in 1817. Eight years later yet another edition was needed. This time there was a general revision. The Methodists were still seeking an antidote to the pernicious doctrines and annoying success of the Baptists. Hemmenway's *Discourse* had been discarded. Now Edwards' *Short Method* was shed. Maybe Mr. Wesley could do as well; at least they would give him a try. And so the preface announced: "In the present edition some new Tracts are added, and Mr. Wesley's short Treatise on Baptism is substituted in the place of the extract from Mr. Edwards on that subject." As always, the preface was unsigned, though it was dated "New-York, October 5th, 1825." This volume was remarkable for the fact that each of the thirteen tracts was presented as a distinct entity, its pages numbered and its gatherings printed separately from its companions, though the gatherings were signed consecutively—with figures instead of with letters. Probably many of the items were in fact sold separately. This was certainly true of the last, Wesley's *Plain Account of Christian Perfection,* which was described on the title page as "Tract No. XXXVI of the New-York Methodist Tract Society." Any surplus pages at the ends of the tracts were filled with appropriate (though little-known) poems by Charles Wesley, or with additional prose material. Even more was added to Wesley's *Treatise on Baptism* (which is in fact mainly the work of his father); this was supplemented by another tract, an extract from William Wall's *History of Infant Baptism* which Wesley had published in 1751 under the title of *Thoughts on Infant Baptism,*[47] and by "Remarks on Infant Baptism, by H. S. Boyd, Esq." —an English patristic scholar.

The demand for these doctrinal tracts continued, and in 1831 this same collection appeared in consolidated form, the gapfilling Charles Wesley hymns omitted, and the other material printed consecutively on 388 pages. Strangely enough even the 1825 preface is reproduced exactly as in the original, complete with the earlier date and the statement that "two editions have been published and sold"—a statement which now contained the truth, but not the whole truth.

47. Ibid., Nos. 191.vi, 149.

The following year the lasting need for such a collection was recognized by the provision of a stereotyped edition. This followed the somewhat condensed pattern of 1831, still more compressed into 378 pages. The editor deserves a hearty pat on the back for at last restoring the original title of Wesley's *Serious Thoughts upon the Perseverance of the Saints*. The preface was almost unchanged except for the rewriting of two sentences, one about the two former editions, the other about "several new tracts" (a phrase replaced by "some new tracts") and the alteration of the date to "New-York, July 5, 1832." Indeed this change of date is the only evidence we so far possess that an 1832 edition was in fact published, no copy of the volume itself having been discovered. This preface appears in a reprint, presumably from the stereotypes, after a title page dated 1834. Copies are also known dated 1836, 1847, 1850, 1854, 1856, and one undated.

In 1861 the volume was once more revised, and the new preface closed somewhat optimistically: "We hope the circulation of the book will be extended until the errors it so ably explodes shall be fully banished from the Church. The Publishers. New York, January 1, 1861." This revision included a caustic defense of Wesley against an attack by a Presbyterian who had been misled by a misprint and his own ignorance. The main alteration, however, was once more in the area of infant baptism. Even Mr. Wesley had not won the day, and he in his turn was dismissed for an anonymous modern writer, apparently a Methodist, who cited not only a liberal Calvinist like Dr. Leonard Woods of Andover, but also long-discarded Peter Edwards. There were at least two reprints of this revised edition, one in the 1870's and another about 1892.

THE DISAPPEARANCE OF THE *DOCTRINAL TRACTS*

In the face of at least fifteen editions of the *Collection of Interesting Tracts* it is somewhat amazing that Bishop Tigert, writing his *Constitutional History of American Episcopal Methodism* in 1894, had never seen a copy, and in his revised issue of 1904 expressed surprise at meeting with even one edition. This contained the 1832 preface, from which he incorrectly deduced that the book agents had waited twenty years to carry out the Conference injunction—a somewhat excessive delay even in those unenlightened days. He decided to supply the supposed lack of early initiative by himself reissuing the original tracts in two small volumes of what he could then describe as the "well known series of 'Little Books on Doctrine,' " entitling the volumes, *The Doctrines of the Methodist Episcopal Church in America.* This was published in 1902.[48]

Methodism constantly needs Bishop Tigerts to reawaken us to our heritage. Our own generation seems at length to have realized that the methods of Methodism are far from being her only glory, that the *Discipline* may have more affinities with Leviticus than with Luke, and that the real secret of an effective Methodism is spiritual and theological. It is indeed a healthy sign that under the leadership of Dr. Albert C. Outler we have been summoned once more to study our evangelical foundations, so much taken for granted (until questions of church union force them upon our attention) that they have too often been neglected. As this has been done we have surely realized that John Wesley's gospel as well as his creed, not only in its spirit but even in its literary expression, long remained and apparently still remains an integral though frequently overlooked element in the "present existing and established standards of doctrine" which form an essential legal element in the constitution of the United Methodist Church. True, at first glance "present existing" might seem to refer to 1972, or 1968, or possibly 1939. In fact, however, these are the more recent successors in an unbroken line of exact quotations, all General Conferences having vowed to maintain the "present existing" standards of their predecessors, and thus in effect having vowed to maintain the doctrinal standards existing in 1808. Nor does any change seem likely in the foreseeable future. The report of the Theological Study Commission on Doctrine and Doctrinal Standards presented by Dr. Outler to the General Conference of 1972 pointed out that "despite continued and quite variegated theological development, there

---

48. *The Doctrines of the Methodist Episcopal Church in America, as contained in the Disciplines of said Church from 1788 to 1808, and so designated on their Title-pages. Compiled and edited with an historical introduction by Jno. J. Tigert, D.D., LL.D.,* 2 vols, Cincinnati: Jennings and Pye, 1902. Tigert does not print the complete contents of the 1814 doctrinal tracts, however, but only the four which had appeared by 1792, together with the two brief sections "On Christian Perfection" and "Against Antinomianism." The four presented comprise not only *The Scripture Doctrine of Predestination, Election, and Reprobation, Serious Thoughts upon the Perseverance of the Saints,* and *A Plain Account of Christian Perfection,* all by Wesley, but also Hemmenway's *Nature and Subjects of Christian Baptism,* even though this was dropped from the 1797 *Discipline,* and never restored, so that it could hardly have been included in the "present existing and established standards of doctrine" referred to by the restrictive rule of 1808, as the others surely were.

has been no significant project in formal doctrinal re-formulation in Methodism since 1808."[49] The Commission, however, suggested neither repeal nor revision, nor reformulation, because our doctrinal standards must not be regarded as inflexible legal instruments, but as a precious and inspiring heirloom, a heritage to be interpreted and reinterpreted in the light of Scripture, tradition, experience, and reason, so as to be kept continuously relevant to current needs and opportunities. To this the General Conference agreed.[50] In this heritage we should include, not only Wesley's *Sermons* and his *Explanatory Notes upon the New Testament*, but those other writings of his incorporated in the "Doctrinal Tracts," not only because a strong legal case could be made that these indeed formed a part of the "present existing . . . standards" named in the first restrictive rule of 1808, but because they were singled out by our forefathers as important illustrations of the essential spiritual and theological heritage of Methodism. In theory at least Methodist theology did not change its eighteenth-century oil lamps for gaslight in the mid-nineteenth century, nor for electricity in the twentieth. Like the Olympic runners, through the quadrennia it has handed on the torch kindled at John Wesley's warmed heart and theology of salvation. Nor need this cause us any impatience or distress. Methods may change, interpretations may vary, but the message of God's eternal saving love in Jesus Christ is the same yesterday, today, and forever.

49. The United Methodist Church, "The Theological Study Commission on Doctrine and Doctrinal Standards: A Report to the General Conference, April, 1972," p. 7; cf. *Discipline, 1972,* p. 44.

50. "The Theological Study Commission . . . ," pp. 13, 27–38; cf. *Discipline, 1972,* pp. 48–9, 75–82.

11. AMERICAN METHODISM: BEGINNINGS AND ENDS

> "The time has come," the Walrus said,
>   "To talk of many things;
> Of shoes—and ships—and sealing-wax—
>   Of cabbages—and kings—
> And why the sea is boiling hot—
>   And whether pigs have wings."

So wrote Lewis Carroll in *Alice through the Looking Glass*. It is the best example I know of combining things that have no logical connection. And I must admit at the outset that that is what I plan—in the title, at any rate. I am not playing fair with the English language, nor with you, until I have made this confession. For I use "beginning" in the dimension of time, and "end" in the dimension of purpose. I do not intend to describe how American Methodism began and then to prophesy when and how it must surely end. I want to look at its beginnings from the point of view of their ends rather than of their endings. Purpose is more important than power, and meaning more significant than money. Through two centuries Methodism has certainly grown bigger and richer. Has it grown better? Has it fulfilled its original purposes, even though transformed to meet the needs of changing generations? Sometimes we become so obsessed by size that we lose all appreciation of shape and color. I personally would rather contemplate a dandelion than the biggest aspidistra in the world.

In contemplating early American Methodism, I am traveling in my time machine way back beyond its birth to its conception. The bicentennial of Methodism's birth as a society was celebrated with some splendor in 1966, and in 1984 we shall surely commemorate its coming of age in the formation of the Methodist Episcopal Church. The conception occurred in 1736, when two Anglican priests, wedded to mother church, set up house with her on American soil, and began

Delivered in summary before the North Virginia Methodist Historical Society, March 30, 1967; first published in *Methodist History*, VI, No. 3 (April, 1968), 3–15, but now greatly expanded.

raising a spiritual family under the most puzzling as well as trying circumstances, some of which we have already studied. I plan to recapitulate a few aspects of this first beginning of Methodism as a movement under the Wesleys, briefly to note how these particular features developed during the second and third beginnings as an organized society and as a church, and then to add the briefest of comments about our present position.

The "beginnings" which I shall suggest as being among the more important "ends" of early Methodism are these: piety, evangelism, warmhearted worship—with a special emphasis upon spiritual song—Christian fellowship, discipline, lay leadership, and community service.

PIETY

The first characteristic of the brand of religion that John and Charles Wesley brought to Georgia was *piety*. This is not a word that we use much nowadays, no more than we do the other possible title for this section—holiness. Both seem to imply that we are better than other people because of our own efforts—and very proud of it:

> Little Jack Wesley
> Sat in the vestry
>   Looking for pie in the sky;
> He put in his thumb
> And pulled out a plum,
>   And said, "What a good boy am I!"

It is true, of course, that Wesley does tell us about his self-inflicted spiritual discipline; but he does it in no spirit of self-righteousness. At twenty-two he had been ordained a clergyman of the Church of England, and had sincerely dedicated himself to God, not only in his outward actions, but in his inward motives. At thirty-one, when he offered himself to Georgia, he was even more devout. Listen to his own critical appraisal of himself, written three years later: "I diligently strove against all sin. I omitted no sort of self-denial which I thought lawful; I carefully used, both in public and in private, all the means of grace at all opportunities. I omitted no occasion of doing good; I for that reason suffered evil. And all this I knew to be nothing, unless as it was directed toward inward holiness. Accordingly this, the image of God, was what I aimed at in all, by doing his will, not my own."[1]

Not many of us could in honesty echo such intense words. John Wesley meant business when he came to Georgia, and that business was to encourage the pursuit of holiness. It was not a popular goal for the busy and often materialistic colonists, most of whom had left debts behind them in England, and were now scraping a bare living by arduous labours, while threatened by aggression from the French and the Spanish alike. He met with occasional encouragement, however, especially at the deathbed of Henry Lascelles, to whom he surely alluded when he spoke of a dying parishioner who exhorted his friends, "Think of heaven, talk of heaven; all the time is lost when we are not thinking of heaven."[2]

Even after Wesley realized that spiritual peace does not come as an automatic byproduct of the pursuit of holiness, but from a humble acceptance of God's free and undeserved love as revealed in Jesus Christ, he still refused to deny the need for piety. Indeed he elevated it into one of the hallmarks of Methodist theology and devotion, and constantly urged preachers and people alike to seek holiness. It is perhaps significant that the American Methodist societies sprang up under the influence of British emigrants in the 1760's, in the very decade when that holiness or Christian perfection which Wesley had stressed from the beginning was developing into a controversial battle cry in Britain, leading many to extremes, but leaving none indifferent. Captain Thomas Webb made this the main challenge of his homespun but strangely moving sermons. In New York he urged upon his hearers that justification by faith was not enough, not even for the apostles: "You must be sanctified. But you are not. You are only Christians in part. You have not received the Holy Ghost. I know it. I can feel your spirits hanging about me like so much dead flesh."[3] The sincerity of such preaching often hit the target missed by more eloquent sermons. Joseph Pilmore wrote of Webb: "His preaching, though incorrect and irregular, is attended with wonderful power."[4]

The later American itinerants continued to sound the same note.

1. Wesley, *Journal*, I, 468.
2. Ibid., I, 225–6, 234, where Wesley calls him "Lassel"; sermon "On Love," *Works*, VII, 492–9, espec. 499, preached Feb. 20, 1737—not 1736, nor March 7, 1736, as claimed in Journal, I, 176–7. From Coulter and Saye, *List of Early Settlers in Georgia*, p. 29, "Lassel" must be Henry Lascelles, son of the surgeon of the same name who came over at the same time as the Wesleys, and though resident in Savannah, died in Frederica.
3. John Fletcher Hurst, *The History of Methodism*, III, 1252.
4. Pilmore, *Journal*, p. 30.

William Duke exclaimed in the privacy of his journal: "O may I always walk holy!" and "O that I had more gospel simplicity and sincerity!"[5] Freeborn Garrettson believed Christian perfection to be attainable in this life, and therefore "contended for it" "both in public and private," though he himself felt so unworthy that he almost "declined preaching so pure a gospel till the heart corruptions which [he] felt were washed away." He believed that he knew some who were indeed perfect in love, and even that he himself might possibly be, though this he never professed publicly.[6]

Those present at the Christmas Conference in 1784, therefore, found no difficulty in accepting one of the regulations passed over from Wesley's large *Minutes* of 1780 into the first American *Discipline*: "Strongly and explicitly exhort all believers to 'go on to perfection.' "[7] Nor was there anything more than minor verbal change in the opening statement about "God's design in raising up the preachers called 'Methodists,' " namely "to reform the continent, and to spread scriptural holiness over these lands."[8]

A century later the Methodists, both in Britain and America, became too respectable for holiness, especially when it was overemphasized and underillustrated by fanatics. It is good to know that after the passage of still another century Methodist theologians are once more exploring the important truths underlined in Wesley's teaching on Christian perfection. So much for our thinking. But what about our Christian living? Do we not still place too much importance on respectability, rather than on warm piety? Let us remember that piety does not mean a particular set of supposedly religious actions, but lives completely integrated with God's purposes, or (as Wesley once described it), "loving God with all our hearts, and serving him with all our strength."[9] In that sense our Methodist forefathers—even John Wesley before his heart was strangely warmed—can furnish us with both a message and a challenge.

5. William Duke, MS journal, July 3, Aug. 15, 1775; cf. Sept. 5, 1775—"It is no hurt to my soul when I moderate it by intervals of humble prayer."

6. Bangs, *Garrettson*, pp. 67–8; cf. Garrettson, *Experience*, pp. 72–81.

7. Tigert, op. cit., p. 585; cf. p. 579, where "Are you 'going on to perfection?' " was one of the questions asked of those proposed as preachers. Wesley reinforced this in his private letters, such as one of Feb. 1, 1775, to Samuel Bardsley, "Wherever you are, vehemently exhort the believers to 'go on to perfection.' " (*Letters*, VI, 137.)

8. Tigert, op. cit., p. 535.

9. Wesley, *Letters*, III, 168.

EVANGELISM

From the beginnings of Methodism in America, also—even under the Wesleys—the movement stood for evangelism. Whatever their own personal defects, both brothers were genuinely missionary-minded. We usually emphasize one half only of John's self-criticism as he returned to England: "I went to America to convert the Indians; but, O, who shall convert me?" [10] We gather that Wesley was not converted, but slide over the fact that he was nevertheless sincerely anxious to convert the Indians. He was doing what I have been doing—using the same word in two different senses. He had already completely dedicated his life to God, and thus experienced at least the measure of spiritual peace that comes from being a true servant of God. It was to this dedicated Christian life that he believed himself called to introduce the Indians, just as he had urged it upon his careless companions at Oxford, where he was regarded as a pious busybody, overzealous in his evangelism. This missionary zeal he characterized thus: "I advised others to be religious according to that scheme of religion by which I modelled my own life." [11] Eventually the Moravians showed him "a more excellent way." [12] Now he wished to become a *son* of God rather than a *servant*. Soon he had a richer gospel to preach, and immeasurably greater spiritual resources with which to drive his message home. Already he had been preaching the gospel as he knew it for ten years. Now, with a new dimension to his gospel, and with heart strangely warmed, he became an evangelist with spiritual power.

By that time Wesley had returned from Georgia to England, and his place had been taken by his Oxford pupil and disciple George Whitefield, who was far more the typical evangelist, and proclaimed the gospel in America with far more obvious success than Wesley. He not only kept alive the missionary enthusiasm of the Methodists which he had learned at Oxford, but immeasurably broadened and strengthened its appeal. Eventually some at least of those who formed the Methodist societies of the 1760's acknowledged that their spiritual impulses had originally come through him, so that they had fallen under Wesley's influence at secondhand long before they linked up with a society owing allegiance to him.

10. Wesley, *Journal*, I, 418.   12. Ibid., I, 470.
11. Ibid., I, 467.

Both the lay pioneers of American Methodism in the 1760's and the itinerant preachers sent by Wesley to consolidate the societies were zealous evangelists. When Joseph Pilmore first saw North Carolina, for instance, he exclaimed: "O that the great Master of the vineyard would raise up and thrust out laborers unto his field, such as will not hold their peace day nor night, but constantly run to and fro, that the knowledge of God may be increased, and poor wandering sinners brought into the fold of Christ!"[13] The revival was regarded as the natural climax of religious activities. Although he was critical of some aspects of the Virginia revival of 1775–6, Jesse Lee, writing in 1810, thus ended seven pages of rapturous description: "I have spoken largely of this revival of religion; but my pen cannot describe the one half of what I saw, heard, and felt. I might write a volume on this subject, and then leave the greater part untold."[14]

If anyone would read the saga of roughhewn American Methodist evangelism he cannot do much better than turn to the autobiographical *Experience and the Gospel Labours of the Rev. Benjamin Abbott*, first as a local preacher, from 1775, then as a regular itinerant, from 1789 until ill health caused his retirement in 1795 and his death a year later. Abbott's autobiography clearly demonstrates how among the most successful weapons of early Methodist evangelism in America the prayer meeting and the love-feast ranked with testimonies and exhortations in preaching services—where "Ye must be born again" was a typical text.[15] So strong was the spiritual expectation, indeed, that watchnight services in Baltimore might prove occasions for numerous conversions,[16] and a communion service in New Jersey might be attended with revival phenomena so rousing that communicants continued "shouting praises to God and the Lamb" long after the exhausted preacher had left.[17] Abbott was in his forties when he was converted and began preaching, so that others, preachers and laity alike, spoke of him as "Father Abbott."[18] Most of the preachers, however, were young. William Duke entered the itinerancy at sixteen. Although some of them faltered, or found that itinerancy and mar-

13. Pilmore, *Journal*, p. 169.
14. Lee, *Short History*, p. 59.
15. Abbott, *Experience*, pp. 55–7, 66, 129, 162–3, etc.
16. Phoebus, *Whatcoat*, p. 80; G. P. Baker, op. cit., pp. 76–7; Sweet, *Religion on the American Frontier*, IV, 79.
17. Abbott, *Experience*, p. 249.
18. Ibid., pp. 80, 86, 252.

riage did not make a comfortable mixture, many proved such untiring evangelists that they burned themselves out within one or two decades.[19]

It is good to know that in these present days the spirit of evangelism is still one of the signs of a good Methodist, even though that evangelism may assume—and indeed *should* assume— different forms to suit a different age. Men and women still long for victory over life's problems, a sense of purpose in living; one of those problems is still the evil in the heart of man, and there remains no more integrating goal in life than living to the glory of God. And if we have any experience of God helping us to solve our problems, any conviction of a God-given purpose, then surely we have good news to proclaim—surely we must be evangelists.

WARMHEARTED WORSHIP

Another hallmark of early Methodism in America was the revolution in worship. Wesley's Sunday program in Savannah involved one service after another, under peculiar difficulties. For one thing he was host as well as minister: until the church was built (for which he was raising money) all services were held in the parsonage. Most Methodist ministers today would shudder at the mere thought of his multilingual Sunday activities therein for the immigrants. Let Wesley tell his own story: "The English service lasted from five to half hour past six [A.M., of course; Wesley believed in early morning worship!]. The Italian (with a few Vaudois) began at nine. The second service for the English (including the Sermon and the Holy Communion) continued from half an hour past ten till about half an hour past twelve. The French service began at one. [N.B. Not much time for lunch!] At two I catechised the children. About three began the English service. After this was ended I joined with as many as my largest room would hold in reading, prayer, and singing praise. And about six the service of the Germans began: at which I was glad to be present, not as a teacher, but as a learner."[20]

Several different forms of worship found noteworthy expression during Wesley's Georgia ministry. His stress upon sacramental observance, an important feature of Oxford Methodism, was here con-

19. Cf. Lee, *Short History*, pp. 335–40.
20. Wesley, *Concise Ecclesiastical History*, IV, 174.

tinued. But Wesley sought to impart a warm, evangelical note into Holy Communion by grafting hymns onto the old stock of the liturgy in the Book of Common Prayer. Robert Strawbridge similarly trained his followers in the South to receive the sacrament frequently, even from lay hands—a true following of Wesley's spirit in the one respect, even though in the other a defiance of the letter of the ecclesiastical law. It was the desire for the Lord's Supper which almost led to a major schism within the American Methodist societies in 1779, when the preachers in Virginia decided to form a presbytery and to ordain each other; they were with difficulty restrained by Asbury, who pleaded patience pending an eventual appeal for help to Wesley.[21] Thus with the birth of the Methodist Episcopal Church there was little fear that the Lord's Supper would be slighted, even though the majority of American preachers instinctively sought Wesley's ends without the means of a liturgical observance, preferring a more extempore type of service.[22] This apparently still remains true at the grass-roots level; in spite of the developing liturgical appreciation among many church leaders, the average church member seems more drawn to spontaneity and human warmth than to the delicate patina of traditional language and ceremony.

Two of the three distinctive forms of British Methodist worship were transplanted in America. It was in Georgia that Wesley had first witnessed a Moravian love-feast, and this soon became one of the most moving religious occasions in English Methodism, when the sharing of bread and water furnished the hors-d'oeuvres for a solid meal of spiritual testimony and song.[23] Joseph Pilmore first introduced the love-feast to Philadelphia Methodists on Friday, March 23, 1770, and to those of New York on Sunday, May 13, that year.[24] In America the love-feast became a normal highlight of the occasions when Methodist preachers and lay leaders gathered together from a wide area for their quarterly meetings—patterned upon the quarterly meetings of English circuits, which originated in 1748.[25] The sometimes uproarious

21. Garrettson, *Experience*, pp. 171–8; Sweet, *Virginia Methodism*, pp. 79–86.
22. See above, note 5, p. 121.
23. Frank Baker, *Methodism and the Love-feast*, pp. 9–31.
24. Pilmore, *Journal*, pp. 40, 45. The "love-feast ticket" dated Oct. 1, 1769, noted by the editors on p. 53 does not invalidate Pilmore's statements about the priority of these services, for this was in fact a class-ticket.
25. See *HAM*, I, 118–20. William Duke's MS journal thus describes one held on Tuesday, Aug. 2, 1774: "Preaching began at 5 o'clock. A pretty large congregation attended. After preaching business began. About 12:30 the love-feast began, and in the evening

excitement of the love-feast was later taken over even more uproariously by the camp meeting, and gradually the love-feast pined away, except in a few centers such as New York—where such gatherings in 1818 celebrated both the last service in the old John Street Church and the first in the new[26]—and in the annual conferences, which took over some of the traditions as well as the functions of the circuit quarterly meetings.[27]

The second specifically Methodist form of worship imported to America was the watchnight. Again it was Pilmore who introduced this vigil of prayer and praise, first in New York on New Year's Eve, December 31, 1771.[28] Nor was it at first confined to New Year's Eve, no more than were English watchnights, but was observed on any night when traveling was simplified by moonlight. Pilmore conducted the first watchnight in Virginia, lasting from 8:00 P.M. until midnight, on Sunday, April 25, 1773.[29] Like the love-feast, the watchnight often formed one of the more public features of the quarterly meetings, though it was not quite so inseparable from them as the love-feast itself.[30]

The third characteristically Methodist form of worship, the Covenant Service, was a later development within English Methodism, was far less widespread, and no printed order for it was published until 1779—even then it was not so much an order of worship as a massive chunk of devotional reading for the occasion, extracted from John Wesley's *Christian Library*. It does not seem to have been introduced into American Methodism by the early British preachers, and has been added to *The Book of Worship* as recently as 1944. This order of worship is comparatively recent, as well as much more appropriate for our day, and it is a common error to believe that we are in fact using Wesley's own service, of which in fact only vestigial remnants survive in the opening hymn and the abridged covenant itself.[31]

---

the watchnight." Again on Tuesday, Dec. 5, 1775: "Our quarterly meeting—in forenoon business and a love-feast, and as usual had a watchnight."

26. Seaman, op. cit., pp. 203–4; cf. Wakeley, *Lost Chapters*, p. 485.

27. For love-feasts conducted en route to Conference, and the results of the love-feast at the 1790 Conference itself, see Abbott, *Experience*, pp. 162–3, 175–7.

28. Pilmore, *Journal*, pp. 70, 72; cf. p. 116 for the "annual" watchnight in New York.

29. Ibid., p. 194; cf. pp. 107, 217, and Asbury, *Journal*, I, 7.

30. The "moving season" when Richard Whatcoat preached in the new church in Baltimore on May 24, 1786, was probably a quarterly meeting—it was a Tuesday. See Asbury, *Journal*, I, 512. See also note 24 above.

31. *The Book of Worship*, Nashville, Tenn., The Methodist Publishing House, 1965, pp. 382–8. This derives from the British *Book of Offices*, London, Methodist Publishing

SPIRITUAL SONG

One of Wesley's most important ventures in Georgia was the introduction of hymn-singing both into the regular public services and at Holy Communion. During his Georgia ministry he published America's first hymnbook, largely in order to bring more spontaneity into worship. He loved the Book of Psalms, though he was not very fond of the metrical psalms. Sternhold and Hopkins' version he regarded as the direst doggerel, and although he never to my knowledge mentioned the *Bay Psalm Book*, which had sufficed New England for nearly a century, he would certainly not have considered it adequate for heartfelt spiritual song. He was one with Watts in wishing to spiritualize the Psalms, and to apply them to the situation of his own day, and he was also prepared to use hymns of human composition in public worship as a supplement to the Scriptures. He had long been of this mind, and hymn-singing was one of the regular devotional exercises of the Oxford Methodists.

Wesley's friendship with the Moravians on board the *Simmonds* and in Georgia introduced him to the great riches of German sacred song, and he began to select the most spiritual and to translate them into sympathetic English verse. These he introduced into his parish services in Savannah. Together with compositions from the pen of Isaac Watts and others—seventy in all—in 1737 he had them printed at Charleston, South Carolina, as *A Collection of Psalms and Hymns.* Two of the official complaints made against him by the ruling clique in Savannah concerned his enthusiasm for hymn-singing and his use of this book, even at the Lord's Table: he was charged with "introducing into the church and service at the altar compositions of psalms and hymns not inspected or authorized by any proper judicature."[32] This was far from the cold High Church ritualism of which with some justice we accuse Wesley. This was warmhearted and adventurous Methodism, unafraid to lay claim to the devotional aids of any wing of the church universal, from the hymns of a Roman Catholic priest, John Austin, to those of a rank Dissenter, Isaac Watts. Included in that pioneer hymnal was a hymn by Wesley's own father, "On the

House, 1936, pp. 119–33, a drastic revision which itself depends heavily upon the work of George B. Robson, who prepared and published a service for local use about 1921. See David Tripp, *The Renewal of the Covenant in the Methodist Tradition*, pp. 55–78, 104–7; cf. *HAM*, III, 562.

32. Wesley, *Journal*, I, 385.

Crucifixion," supposedly found on a loose sheet after the fire at the Epworth rectory in 1709, and here published for the first time. There is stirring pathos in this hymn, which Wesley's American congregations certainly sang at Communion:

> Behold the Saviour of Mankind,
>   Nail'd to the shameful tree!
> How vast the love that him inclin'd
>   To bleed and die for thee!

This breathes more than pathos, however. Here is the gospel: behold the Saviour, who died for thee. One wonders whether even in Georgia this hymn was used for evangelism. It was certainly so used shortly after the Wesleys returned to England.[33]

Evangelical hymnody was of late growth in America, mainly because of the strong grip of the metrical psalms in the few places where religious music was cultivated at all, especially in New England. The Great Awakening turned some attention to Watts, but Whitefield's own somewhat belated attempt to adapt the Wesleyan hymns had little effect in America.[34] The Methodists of the 1760's, however, did promote a singing faith as an adjunct of their evangelism. The first publication of Robert Williams, the Irish lay preacher from whose saddlebags sprang the Methodist Book Concern, was Charles Wesley's *Hymns for the Nativity of our Lord* (1769), and this was followed in 1770 by an edition of the Wesley's *Hymns for those that have and those that seek Redemption,* and in 1771 by a revised edition of John's *Collection of Psalms and Hymns,* as well as a fifteenth edition of what had become the major congregational hymnbook of Methodism— *Hymns and Spiritual Songs intended for the use of real Christians of all Denominations.* These three were all republished in 1773 and in 1781, in each case bound together in one volume.[35] The 1784 Conferences exhorted the preachers to improve the standards of congregational singing "by learning to sing true themselves, and keeping

---

33. Baker and Williams, *John Wesley's First Hymn-book,* pp. 46–7, xxxii. In the summer of 1738 Charles Wesley and John Bray, locked in a cell in Newgate prison with a group of criminals awaiting execution the following morning, sang this hymn with them. Wesley says, "It was one of the most triumphant hours I have ever known"—and so it proved for the penitent criminals, who faced eternity with a living faith. (Charles Wesley, *Journal,* I, 123.)

34. Louis F. Benson, *The English Hymn,* pp. 161–8, 358–61.

35. Baker, *Union Catalogue,* Nos. 30, 105, 165; cf. Benson, op. cit., p. 281—he knew only the 1781 volume.

close to Mr. Wesley's tunes and hymns." [36] Strangely enough Wesley's famous *Collection of Hymns for the Use of the People called Methodists*, which in 1780 completely replaced the *Hymns and Spiritual Songs*, was not reprinted in America. Instead a pirated and abridged version of the *Collection*, published by a British Methodist of York, Robert Spence, appeared on the American scene as *A Pocket Hymn Book: Designed as a Constant Companion for the Pious*, first in New York in 1786, and then in an ever-increasing flood, with a new edition almost every year, and frequently two editions per year. Its name changed in 1803 to *The Methodist Pocket Hymn Book*, it was the ancestor of all subsequent official Methodist hymnals, in spite of a valiant attempt by Coke to promote the *Collection of Psalms and Hymns for the Lord's Day* appended to the *Sunday Service*.[37]

Like Methodism in Britain, American Methodism was clearly born in song, even though it began somewhat sluggishly and exhibited a typical independence of approach. British Methodism as a whole remained much closer to Wesley's high standards of congregational singing, as well as to a much greater body of the Wesley hymns. The focal point in America seems to have shifted from congregation to choir. Many of us have become accustomed to much more decorous worship than our great-grandparents knew, and frequently to lovely choral singing. An expatriate Englishman, however, may voice some nostalgia for those four or five congregational hymns in which he would join at every service, for which the most tastefully rendered anthems prove an unsatisfying substitute. Securing a choir to sing your praises to God, after all, is like making love by remote control, and I for one believe in personal contact both in the physical and in the spiritual realms.

CHRISTIAN FELLOWSHIP

Even more significant than piety, evangelism, and warmhearted worship was another element planted in American religion by Wesley —Christian fellowship. Indeed, it is because of this rather than anything else that we can follow him in claiming that genuine Methodism began in Georgia in 1736. We have seen how when he looked back over the years in his *Concise Ecclesiastical History* he spoke of three

36. *Minutes* (American, 1795), p. 71.
37. Baker, *Union Catalogue*, Nos. 376, 378, pp. 183–4; cf. Benson, op. cit., pp. 285–9.

"rises" or experimental beginnings for Methodism. The first was in 1729, the Holy Club, as an extension of whose activities the young missionaries came to America. "The second," he continued, "was at Savannah, in April, 1736, when twenty or thirty persons met at my house," and the third in 1738, when he and Peter Böhler formed a religious society in London.[38] This was not regular church worship, but something both additional and different—a meeting for spiritual fellowship in a setting of devout informality. It was this that constituted the hallmark of Wesley's Methodism. His disciple George Whitefield, though he believed in Christian fellowship, and founded an occasional religious society, even in America,[39] saw his primary task as that of a preaching evangelist, and rarely took the immense pains necessary to give adequate spiritual oversight to his converts. The same temptation was always present for Wesley's preachers, for shepherding societies proved a more arduous and far less glamorous task than that of preaching, especially if one turned out to be a popular preacher.[40]

For Wesley Methodism was essentially neither a church, offering the full-orbed worship of Word and Sacraments, nor an evangelistic mission, but a society of those who were saved and those who were seeking to be saved, and who therefore needed spiritual intimacy in order to build each other up in the faith. This was not a religious duty imposed on everyone like public worship, but an additional opportunity only for those who realized their need for it. Wesley says of the first Methodist society in America: "I now advised the serious part of the congregation [only them!] to form themselves into a sort of little society, and to meet once or twice a week, in order to instruct, exhort, and reprove one another. And out of these I selected a smaller number for a more intimate union with each other: in order to which I met them together at my house every Sunday in the afternoon." This very small group was the "band" (though Wesley does not use the term), formed on the basis of the Moravian practice. Here is another impor-

38. Wesley, *Concise Ecclesiastical History*, IV, 175; cf. pp. 19–20 above.
39. See above, pp. 24–5.
40. Cf. Pilmore, *Journal*, p. 163: "Afterwards had two men to wait on me with an invitation to go and preach the gospel at Pasquotank in North Carolina. The longer I stay in these parts the more I am desired to preach, and have, by far, the greatest success. Frequent changes amongst gospel preachers may keep up the spirits of some kinds of people, but is never likely to promote the spirit of the gospel nor increase true religion. Had I left Norfolk when some persons would have had me I should have formed no Society either there or at Portsmouth, and now we have a goodly company in each place."

tant feature of later Methodist practice first tried out on American soil.[41]

The intimate and searching fellowship of the band never fully took on in American Methodism, although it was explained in the *Discipline*, urged by Coke and Asbury,[42] and maintained a struggle for existence in larger centers such as New York well into the nineteenth century.[43] The slightly more easygoing friendliness of the class-meeting proved more congenial, as indeed it did in Britain, where it had begun in 1742 as a byproduct of a fund-raising scheme. Members of the class, prompted by their respected leader, would in turn speak of their religious experience, and receive a suitable word of encouragement or advice.[44] The English class-meeting system was fully developed in the early American societies. Two regulations made at the 1775 Conference (though not reproduced in the printed *Minutes*) laid down that "every round [was] to be supplied with tickets and class-papers by the steward in Philadelphia," and that payment for these was to be brought to the Conference by the Assistants.[45] If William Duke's journal (1774–6) is any guide, however, lay class-leaders were harder to find than in England, for it abounds with such references as these: "To Philadelphia, and at night in meeting the class I was very happy"; "I preached, and met the little class"; "preached and met class. Then to R. Turner's and met class"; "went to Penn's Neck and met a class of seven or eight poor people"; "preached once, and met two classes."[46] It was in visiting a class-meeting that Freeborn Garrettson found himself warming towards the Methodists.[47] Forming and meeting classes frequently constituted the earliest pastoral activities of young preachers,

---

41. Wesley, *Concise Ecclesiastical History*, IV, 170. There is some confusion here, for the Sunday afternoon gathering described on p. 174 was apparently for the whole society, not for the band alone. Cf. p. 20 above for an independent description of the same events.

42. The 1785 *Discipline* contained a passage on bands brought over from the 1780 large Minutes (see Tigert, op. cit., p. 546), and to the 1791 *Discipline* was added a complete section, "Of the Band Societies," containing the rules which Wesley had drawn up for them in 1738, together with his directions of 1744; these were omitted from the *Discipline* in 1856 (see Sherman, op. cit., pp. 139–40). The annotated *Discipline* of 1798 included a lengthy explanation and commendation of bands by Coke and Asbury (pp. 151–3; cf. Sherman, op. cit., pp. 448–50).

43. Seaman, op. cit., p. 482.

44. Rupert Davies and Gordon Rupp, eds., *A History of the Methodist Church in Great Britain*, I, 222–3.

45. Gatch, MS minutes, 1775, p. 3; Duke, MS minutes, 1775, p. 3.

46. Duke, MS journal, Sept. 4, Dec. 21, 1775; Jan. 6, 13, Feb. 3, 1776.

47. Garrettson, *Experience*, pp. 37–9.

as in the case of Philip Gatch.[48] In their notes to the 1798 *Discipline* Coke and Asbury spoke of class-meetings as "the pillars of our work," and "in a considerable degree our universities for the ministry."[49] References to classes, class-leaders, class-meetings, class-papers, class-tickets, remained frequent in Methodist diaries until well into the nineteenth century.[50]

Here it seems clear that we have slipped from the high standards of our forebears—or at least have made considerable changes in their expression. Methodism both in Britain and America retains its strong emphasis upon social contacts, and seeks to create a friendly, "homey" atmosphere in its churches. But the class-meeting has completely disappeared in America, and almost disappeared in England; nor has its place been fully taken by anything else. Perhaps the nearest approach in America is the adult Sunday School class, where the emphasis is usually upon teaching and discussion rather than upon spiritual sharing. Maybe we still have something to learn about our Methodist heritage, and some new experiments to make in Christian fellowship.

DISCIPLINE

Another familiar feature of American Methodism was introduced in Georgia—discipline. Everybody knows that Wesley was compulsively addicted to rules. Only by spiritual discipline could a man be kept in God's ways. The Holy Club had rules for its members. In Savannah John Wesley kept a vigilant eye on the morals of his parishioners. He even made special rules for his own conduct in Georgia, including his relations with Sophy Hopkey. These are inscribed in shorthand and cipher inside the cover of one of his Savannah diaries. No. 3 reads: "Not to touch even her clothing by choice: think not of her."[51] Small wonder that Sophy herself was subject to discipline.

Everyone in Savannah knew that their minister was running his parish according to the strict time-honored regulations not only of the Church of England but of the Apostolic Church, so far as those regulations could be discovered. At the very outset of his ministry

48. M'Lean, *Gatch*, pp. 15–16.
49. *Discipline*, 1798, p. 148.
50. See Sweet, *Religion on the American Frontier*, Vol. IV, index. Seaman, *New York Methodism*, pp. 464–6, gives details of the classes, their leaders, their times and places of meeting, in 1793 and 1802—there were 27 classes in 1793, 45 in 1802.
51. MS diary, May 1, 1736 to Feb. 11, 1737, Emory University, Atlanta, Georgia.

Wesley had publicly announced his disciplinary principles, and had already repelled several people from communion before he took the crucial step of refusing the elements to Sophy Hopkey. The letter of the law was firmly on his side. If he avoided this painful and potentially dangerous step he might well ruin his whole insistence upon spiritual discipline. The actual result of repelling Sophy, however, was to begin a feud which in effect drove Wesley from Georgia. Yet though bitterly disappointed and distressed, he was not ashamed of himself. He had courageously done what he had to do. He had kept the faith as he knew it.[52]

Back in England, as the Methodist societies developed he realized even more clearly the need for discipline and in 1743 issued his famous *General Rules* for the Methodists, which went through over thirty editions during his lifetime and many more later. On the first Sunday evening after arriving in America as John Wesley's representative in 1769 Joseph Pilmore "met the little Society [in Philadelphia], and exhorted them to walk worthy of their high calling, and adorn the gospel of Christ." On the second Sunday evening he "read and explained the *Rules* of the Society to a vast multitude of serious people."[53]

There was a strong tendency under American conditions, however, for the rules to be applied in a more easygoing way than in England. This was true with Pilmore and Boardman. Rankin corrected this, and rigidly exercised his authority, as did Asbury, though more flexibly, and with more fellow-feeling. Nevertheless from time to time Asbury had sharp exchanges with both preachers and people, and made the comment in his Journal: "On my return [to Portsmouth, Virginia] some of the members appeared a little refractory in submitting to discipline. But without discipline we should soon be as a rope of sand; so that it must be enforced, let who will be displeased."[54] Their American colleagues eventually discovered from experience that societies where the application of the rules was relaxed gradually began to languish in spiritual vigor, and they too joined in the continuous

52. Cf. Wesley's comment after interviewing a somewhat lax freelance minister who visited Savannah and undermined his strictness about conducting baptisms and marriages: "O Discipline, where art thou to be found? Not in England, nor (as yet) in America." It was apparently this man who had irregularly performed Sophy Hopkey's marriage. See Wesley, *Journal*, I, 271.

53. Pilmore, *Journal*, pp. 24, 25.

54. Asbury, *Journal*, I, 159; cf. ibid., pp. 41–2, 45–7.

campaign of keeping the Methodist people on their toes.[55] As we have seen, from 1789 the *General Rules* were incorporated into the *Discipline*. About this section bishops Coke and Asbury waxed rhapsodical in their annotated edition of 1798, terming it "perhaps one of the completest systems of Christian ethics or morals, for its size, which ever was published by an uninspired [i.e., non-biblical] writer," and although they promised only to "touch briefly upon them," in practice "briefly" entailed well over five thousand words![56] It is not surprising, therefore, that at the General Conference of 1808 a motion to form a committee "to modify certain exceptional expressions in the General Rules" was lost, and that in its third restrictive rule the Conference agreed that no future General Conference should have the right "to revoke or change the 'General Rules of the United Societies.' "[57] Nor were these regarded as merely pious exhortations. For a generation after the death of Asbury Methodists convicted of immorality were expelled from the Church.[58]

Most of us are not familiar with the complexities of our official *Discipline*, and perhaps there is no need that we should be. Possibly we should regard the *General Rules* as a somewhat quaint survival rather than the living challenge which they can still prove for those who read them sympathetically. All of us, however, need to keep in spiritual training if we are to endure hardship as good soldiers of Jesus Christ. In these days of prosperity and "permissiveness" our eighteenth-century forefathers could certainly teach us something about discipline. The lesson might be of real profit.

LAY LEADERSHIP

One thing the story of early Methodism in America surely emphasizes—the importance of dedicated lay leaders. This was especially true of the beginnings of American Methodism as a society in the 1760's. In Maryland an immigrant Irish farmer preached and organized a class-meeting at his home in Sam's Creek, and built a log

55. See William Duke's MS journal for May 1, June 26, Sept. 29, 1774, and Oct. 31, 1775, when he confessed, after permitting a sinner to remain in society "upon condition," "I find it very difficult neither to be too severe nor yet too indulgent."
56. *Discipline*, 1798, pp. 135–45.
57. M. E. Church, *Journals of Gen. Conf.*, I, 89.
58. See James L. Lubach and Thomas L. Shanklin, "Arbitration and Trials of Members in the Methodist Episcopal Church, 1776–1860," pp. 30–49.

meeting-house for the growing congregation. His barn-storming preaching tours took him even into Delaware, Virginia, and Pennsylvania, so that his farm was neglected and his family were in need. He was a layman of courage and of independence—so much independence that he took it upon himself to baptize children and to administer the sacrament of the Lord's Supper. In New York an Irish carpenter who had turned his hand to teaching was roused by a pious housewife to begin preaching, and a Methodist society was born. In Philadelphia two of Whitefield's converts, a shoemaker and a soft-drink salesman, maintained a Methodist class-meeting until another layman, a retired British army officer, helped them consolidate the work. "Captain" Thomas Webb thus linked together the labors of Robert Strawbridge, Philip Embury, Barbara Heck, Edward Evans, and James Emerson. He was the chief agent of progress in the work both at New York, Philadelphia, and Baltimore, as well as the pioneer in other places, especially New Jersey.[59]

Another Irish layman with a wandering commission was Robert Williams, who sold his horse to pay his debts before embarking for the New World with the magnificent capital of a loaf of bread and a bottle of milk—and his trust in God. It was he, as we have said, who laid the foundation stone for the Methodist Publishing House. One more layman should be mentioned—Thomas Taylor, another British imigrant, a non-preacher this time. He served as a catalyst, pleading with Wesley to send full-time itinerant preachers to reap the harvest whose seed had so faithfully been sown by the laymen.[60]

From the ranks of such dedicated laymen came the itinerant preachers, who frequently returned after a few years to fulfill the more limited role of local preachers. The first such native American thus to graduate from local preacher to itinerant was William Watters, who tells how as converts he and others helped the British pioneers to build up the Methodist cause in Maryland: "On the Lord's day we commonly divided into little bands, and went out into different neighborhoods, wherever there was a door open to receive us, two, three, or four in company, and would sing our hymns, pray, read, talk to the people, and some soon began to add a word of exhortation. We were weak, but we lived in a dark day; the Lord greatly owned our labours, for though we were not full of wisdom, we were blessed with a good

59. See chap. 4 above, espec. pp. 56–9.   60. See chap. 5, pp. 72–83.

degree of faith and power. . . . Many will praise God forever for our prayer meetings. In many neighborhoods they soon became respectable, and were considerably attended to."[61] Other itinerants began their pastoral training as class-leaders. Many served both as class-leaders and local preachers. Nor must it be forgotten that for every class-leader or local preacher who entered the itinerancy, even for a brief time, there were unnamed and uncounted hundreds who remained in those less prominent but fundamental offices, men—and women, too—whose influence upon the vitality and growth of Methodism was incalculable.

While we are paying our tribute to the Methodist lay leaders of the 1760's and the 1780's, however, let us not forget that here again Wesley himself had led the way. One of his companions in Georgia was a layman—the other three were ordained clergymen. Charles Delamotte was a young sugar merchant who was coming out on business. He was American Methodism's first Sunday School teacher and lay leader—possibly her first lay preacher. Certainly he carried a heavy load of responsibility for Wesley's work in Savannah, especially after the departure of Charles Wesley and Benjamin Ingham for other areas. On February 16, 1737, John Wesley wrote to a friend in Oxford: "I have now no fellow labourer [in Savannah] but Mr. Delamotte, who has taken charge of between thirty and forty children."[62] These he not only taught "to read, write, and cast accounts," but also instructed in the Christian faith. After the three ministers one by one left Georgia it was Delamotte who kept the spiritual work going, and who welcomed George Whitefield as their successor.[63]

Truly the laity has played an honored part in American Methodist history. We cannot but rejoice to see how their dedicated labors at the present time lend strength to almost every major Methodist activity. It is largely to Methodism that people look when they seek to understand the full spiritual potential of the lay leader. Even here, however, we must not remain complacent. There is still more that lay people might do. I think especially of those many two- and three-point rural charges where too often a service is not held unless a minister can be present. This is neither original Methodism nor modern Methodism at its best.

61. Watters, op. cit., p. 18.   63. See above, pp. 29–30.
62. Wesley, Letters, I, 211.

COMMUNITY SERVICE

It would be comparatively simple to dwell upon other aspects of our continuing Methodist witness which were sketched out in those early days of the 1730's and the 1760's, such as the insistence upon a Bible-based religion, upon personal Christian experience, upon freedom of thought. I will be content with mentioning one more—service to the community. This, however, took many forms, even in Wesley's day, and takes far more now.

Wesley's career as a physician seems to have begun in Georgia. One aspect of his preparations as a a colonial missionary was research into medical literature and practice in order that he might be ready for those occasions when as the only educated man available he would have to deal with accident or sickness. His reading and experience were eventually gathered together in the well-known medical handbook *Primitive Physic*, which was reprinted in Philadelphia as early as 1764, and went through many American editions once Methodism was soundly established here.[64]

As we have seen, Wesley founded a school in Savannah, leaving much of the responsibility to Charles Delamotte, though he also taught a class himself. This was the forerunner not only of Wesley's schools in England, but of the wonderful educational program of American Methodism, from the founding of Cokesbury College to the present day. Wesley's genuine care for children, as well as his imagination, is revealed by an incident in Georgia. The school was intended for *all* children, and some were so poor that they came with bare feet, to be jeered at by the better shod. Charles Delamotte, unable to prevent this petty persecution, asked Wesley's advice. They changed classes, and the following morning Wesley himself appeared at school without shoes. A few days of this example put the better-provided children to shame. Even this incident was later turned against Wesley, however, the ruling clique criticizing his severe austerity in going about with bare feet, carefully ignoring the fact that this was undertaken as a silent rebuke to their own children.[65]

Wesley, in fact, earned a reputation in Georgia as a social reformer. He constantly attacked immorality, drunkenness, and the attempts

64. See Baker, *Union Catalogue*, No. 101.
65. This anecdote was related by Wesley himself in May, 1776, to one of his preachers, Thomas Rutherford—see *Methodist Magazine*, XXXI (1808), 490.

to introduce slavery. He urged a reform of the laws of inheritance so as to protect the smaller landowners. He even began to dabble a little in politics—another cause of criticism from some of his parishioners. In July, 1736, he wrote to a friend in England: "By what I have seen during my short stay here I am convinced that I have long been under a great mistake in thinking no circumstances could make it the duty of a Christian priest to do anything else but preach the gospel. . . . It is from this conviction that I have taken some pains to inquire into the great controversy now subsisting between Carolina and Georgia."[66] (He sided with Georgia in maintaining that by British law Carolina merchants had no right to trade with the Georgia Indians without first securing a Georgia license.) Once again he was endangering his reputation, but once again doing so at the call of conscience. Forty years later he rejoined the fray, and once more on the side of British law and King George—though history and the American love of liberty have proved him wrong. Nevertheless the courage to take an unpopular stand at the call of conscience, even in political matters, is something bred into our American Methodism, even from the early days.

Both in England and in America, however, it should be noted that the early Methodists were much more involved with philanthropy than with reform, with pastoral work to ameliorate unhappy conditions rather than with political agitation to change them. Every day Wesley was engaged in philanthropy of one kind and another; only rarely did he undertake or encourage political action. The same was true of early American activities. During the Revolution the preachers, with obvious prudence, tried to continue their evangelism without taking sides, though because their leaders came from Britain they were naturally classed as "Tories," and met with varying degrees of persecution. Even when they took oaths of loyalty before American magistrates they tried to remain aloof from both politics and war. It is normal to find in their journals entries such as those of William Duke: "reproved ferryman for swearing," "at night counseling alcoholic," "spoke with each prisoner," "visited sick man," "visited poor afflicted widow."[67] Less usual, but still an expression of the preacher's normal function, is this entry: 'I went (as I was desired yesterday) in the morning to open the Congress with a prayer suited to the occa-

66. Wesley, *Letters*, I, 201–2.
67. Duke, MS journal, Nov. 5, 22, 1774; May 14, July 10, Sept. 14, 1775.

sion."[68] Extremely unusual is an entry for March 25, 1775: "I was desired to address the congregations upon an uncommon subject (occasioned by the late disagreement between England and America), which is to recommend to the people the measures resolved upon by the Congress."

On a major social issue such as slavery the Methodist people were not ready for the advanced leadership of Coke, and even Asbury deemed it wise not to risk jeopardizing their spiritual progress even for such an important moral principle—though in fairness we should not expect a twentieth-century head on his eighteenth-century shoulders, even with the witness of Wesley and Coke to spur him on, for they, after all, were not so closely and permanently in touch with the problem of the conservative Methodists as he. (Nor indeed has this problem quite disappeared even in this enlightened twentieth century!)

Nevertheless across the centuries Methodists have continued to exert philanthropic leadership in the sphere of what is now a department of federal government—health, education, and welfare. They have also maintained standards of morality and social concern above the average, with a touch of puritanism which has probably done more good than harm, and a growing readiness to take political action in order to reform society; they have proclaimed a well-rounded social gospel closely allied with the good news of salvation by faith. In all this they have been working out in different terms, more suited to a changing culture, what they took over from John Wesley as the twin aims of Methodism: "To reform the continent, and to spread scriptural holiness over these lands."[69]

EPILOGUE

Wesley in Georgia, and our Methodist forebears of two hundred years ago, blazed many trails which we have followed to our advantage or deserted to our loss. Of not less importance than their examples in specific areas of worship and witness, however, was their attitude of mind—a reverence for the past, especially for the Bible and the primitive church, tempered by a readiness to venture forth

68. Ibid., June 1, 1775.
69. Tigert, op. cit., p. 535. See Richard M. Cameron, *Methodism and Society in Historical Perspective.*

into the religious unknown at the call of God. Wesley, staunch English monarchist and Anglican priest though he was, both respected and encouraged this urge for freedom to serve God in unaccustomed ways. His last official statement to his American followers, as they were on the verge of founding a church independent of his own control, recognized that an inscrutable providence might be at work even in the American Revolution. His final words, with which we may fitly close, contain both blessing and challenge: "As our American brethren are now totally disentangled both from the state and from the English hierarchy, we dare not entangle them again either with the one or the other. They are now at full liberty simply to follow the Scriptures and the primitive church. And we judge it best that they should stand fast in that liberty wherewith God has so strangely made them free."[70]

---

70. Wesley, *Letters*, VII, 239.

BIBLIOGRAPHY

Abbreviations used

HAM   Bucke, Emory S. (ed), *History of American Methodism.*
Minutes   (American, 1795)
        Methodist Episcopal Church, *Minutes of the Methodist Conferences,*
        1795.
Minutes   (English)
        Methodist Church (United Kingdom), *Minutes of the Methodist Conferences,* 1862
WHS   Wesley Historical Society, *Proceedings*

MANUSCRIPTS

Boudinot Correspondence, espec. April 7–Aug. 5, 1778 (New York Historical Society, New York City).

Coke Correspondence, espec. Thomas Coke to Mr. Holmes, Oct. 12, 1790 (Methodist Archives, London).

Cook, Jerry O'Neil, "The First Schism of American Methodism," research paper, Durham, N.C., Duke Divinity School, 1963. (Duke University, Durham, N.C.)

Duke, William, Journal, April 1, 1774–Feb. 3, 1776, Diocesan Library, Peabody Institute, Baltimore, Md.: abstract by Edwin Schell, Baltimore Conference Methodist Historical Society, 1958. (In author's collection.)

————, Minutes of the Methodist Conferences, 1774–7, Baltimore Conference Methodist Historical Society, 1964. (In author's collection.)

Evans, Edward, to John Wesley, Dec. 4, 1770 (Methodist Archives, London.)

Gatch, Philip, Minutes of Methodist Conferences, 1774–9, copied from the *Western Christian Advocate* of May 19 and 26, 1837, by the Baltimore Conference Methodist Historical Society, 1964. (In author's collection.)

Gilbert Correspondence: Mary Gilbert to Gilbert Webb, Feb. 9, 1797 (Library of Congress, Washington, D.C.)

Morgan, Steven D., "Lighting the Fire of American Methodism: Devereux Jarratt's Fostering Relationship with the Early American Methodists," research paper, Durham, N.C., Duke Divinity School, 1973. (In author's collection.)

Oglethorpe Correspondence, 1735–6 (Public Records Office, London, C.O. 5/636, 639, etc.)

Orpe, William, Correspondence, 1764–7, transcripts. (In author's collection.)

Rankin, Thomas, Journal, Aug. 29, 1773–Aug. 12, 1777 (Garrett Theological Seminary, Evanston, Ill.)

Smith, Warren Thomas, "Thomas Coke: the Early Years, 1747–1785" (unpublished manuscript, lent by author).

Strahan, William, Ledger (British Museum, Add. MSS. 48809).

Webb Correspondence: Chas. Webb to Gilbert Webb, Dec. 14, 1792; Thomas
   Webb to Chas. Webb, May 7, 1785 (Library of Congress, Washington, D.C.).
————. Mrs. Mary Webb with Morris and Dilwyn families (Historical Society of
   Pennsylvania, Philadelphia).
————. Thomas Webb to Daniel Montgomery, Dec. 27, 1771 (Drew University,
   Madison, N.J.)
————. Thomas Webb to Chas. Webb, n.d. (Lovely Lane Museum, Baltimore).
————. Thomas Webb to Chas. Webb, 1782–93 (Methodist Archives, London).
Wesley, Charles, Correspondence: to Joseph Benson, Jan. 19, March 6, 1773 (Duke
   University, Durham, N.C.).
Wesley, John, Diary, May 1, 1736–Feb. 11, 1737 (Emory University, Atlanta,
   Georgia).
Whitefield, George, Correspondence: James Bayard, May 10, 1749; James Wad-
   dell, Aug. 5, 1766 (Library of Congress, Washington, D.C.).

PRINTED WORKS

Abbott, Benjamin. *Experience and Gospel Labours*, ed. John Ffirth. New York:
   Waugh and Mason, 1833 (first published 1809).
Adams, John. *Diary and Autobiography*, ed. L. H. Butterfield. 4 vols. Cambridge,
   Mass., Belknap Press, 1961.
Ahlstrom, Sydney E. *A Religious History of the American People*. New Haven:
   Yale University Press, 1972.
Arminian Magazine. London: Paramore, etc., Vols. I–XX, 1778–97, continued as
   Methodist Magazine, Vols. XXI–XLIV, 1798–1821, continued as *Wesleyan
   Methodist Magazine*, XLV–CXXXVI, 1822–1913.
Arminian Magazine. Philadelphia: Dickins, Vols. I–II, 1789–90.
Asbury, Francis. *The Journal and Letters*, ed. Elmer T. Clark, J. Manning Potts,
   and Jacob S. Payton. 3 vols. Nashville: Abingdon Press, 1958.
Atkinson, John. *The Beginnings of the Wesleyan Movement in America*. New
   York: Hunt and Eaton, 1896.
Atmore, Charles. *The Methodist Memorial; being an Impartial Sketch of the
   Lives and Characters of the Preachers*. Bristol: Edwards, 1801.
Baker, Frank. *Charles Wesley as Revealed by His Letters*. London: Epworth Press,
   1948.
————. "Early American Methodism: A Key Document." *Methodist History*,
   VIII, No. 2 (Jan., 1965), 3–15.
————. "John Wesley and Cokesbury College's First President." *Methodist His-
   tory*. XI, No. 2 (Jan., 1973), 54–9.
————. *John Wesley and the Church of England*. London: Epworth Press, 1970.
————. *Methodism and the Love-feast*. London: Epworth Press, 1957.
————. *The Methodist Pilgrim in England*. London: Epworth Press, 1951.
————. *A Union Catalogue of the Publications of John and Charles Wesley*.
   Durham, N.C.: Duke Divinity School, 1966.
Baker, Gordon Pratt, ed. *Those Incredible Methodists*. Baltimore: Commission
   on Archives and History, Baltimore Conference, 1972.

Bangs, Nathan. *A History of the Methodist Episcopal Church.* 3rd ed. New York: Mason and Lane, 1840, Vol. I.

———. *The Life of the Rev. Freeborn Garrettson.* 3rd ed., revised. New York: Emory and Waugh, 1832.

Barclay, Wade Crawford. *Early American Methodism, 1769–1844.* 2 vols. New York: Board of Missions, The Methodist Church, 1949–50.

Benson, Louis F. *The English Hymn.* Richmond, Virginia: John Knox Press, 1962.

Bibbins, Ruthella Mory. *How Methodism Came.* Baltimore: Annual Conference Historical Society, 1945.

Blankenship, Paul. "Bishop Asbury and the Germans." *Methodist History,* IV, No. 3 (April, 1966), 5–13.

Bond, John Wesley. See Bull, Robert J.

Bradley, David H. "Francis Asbury and the Development of African Churches in America." *Methodist History,* X, No. 1 (Oct., 1971), 3–29.

Briggs, F. W. *Bishop Asbury.* London: Wesleyan Conference Office, 1874.

Brookes, George S. *Friend Anthony Benezet.* Philadelphia: University of Pennsylvania Press, 1937.

Bucke, Emory Stevens, ed. *History of American Methodism,* 3 vols. Nashville: Abingdon Press, 1964. (Cited in notes as *HAM*.)

Bull, Robert J. "John Wesley Bond's Reminiscences of Francis Asbury." *Methodist History,* IV, No. 1 (Oct., 1965), 3–33.

———. "Lewis Myers' Reminiscences of Francis Asbury." *Methodist History,* VII, No. 1 (Oct., 1968), 5–10.

Calkin, Homer L. "Henry Foxall." *Methodist History,* VI, No. 1 (Oct., 1967), 36–49.

Cameron, Richard M. *Methodism and Society in Historical Perspective.* Nashville: Abingdon Press, Board of Social and Economic Relations of the Methodist Church, 1961.

Candler, Warren A. *Life of Thomas Coke.* Nashville: Lamar and Barton, 1923.

Cannon, William R. "The Meaning of the Ministry in Methodism." *Methodist History,* VIII, No. 1 (Oct., 1969), 3–19.

Carroll, John. *Case and His Contemporaries.* 5 vols. Toronto: Rose, 1867–77.

Christian Advocate. Nashville: The United Methodist Church, 1971, etc.

Church, Leslie F. *Oglethorpe: A Study of Philanthropy in England and Georgia.* London: Epworth Press, 1932.

Church History. Chicago, Vol. XXVI (1957), etc.

Cliffe, Albert W. *The Glory of Our Methodist Heritage.* Philadelphia: 1957.

Coke, Thomas. *Extracts of the Journals of the Rev. Dr. Coke's Five Visits to America.* London: Paramore, 1793.

———. *Extracts of the Journals of the late Rev. Thomas Coke, L.L.D., comprising several Visits to North America and the West Indies. . . . To which is prefixed a Life of the Doctor.* Dublin: Napper, 1816.

———. *The Substance of a Sermon on the Godhead of Christ, preached at Baltimore . . . on the 26th Day of December, 1784.* New York: Kollock, 1785.

———. *The Substance of a Sermon preached . . . at the Ordination of the Rev.*

Francis Asbury to the Office of a Superintendent. Baltimore: Goddard and Langworthy, 1785.

———, and Francis Asbury. *Discipline*. See Methodist Episcopal Church.

———, and Francis Asbury. *A Plan for Erecting a College, Intended to Advance Religion in America*. N.p., n.p., 1785.

———, and Henry Moore. *Life of the Rev. John Wesley*. London: Paramore, 1792.

Collection of Interesting Tracts. See Methodist Episcopal Church.

Coulter, E. Merton, and Albert B. Saye, eds. *A List of the Early Settlers of Georgia*. Athens: University of Georgia Press, 1949.

Crook, William. *Ireland and the Centenary of American Methodism*. London: Hamilton, Adams, 1866.

Crookshank, Charles H. *History of Methodism in Ireland*. 3 vols. Belfast: Allen, and London: Woolmer, 1885–8.

[Crowther, Jonathan]. *The Life of the Rev. Thomas Coke. . . . Written by a Person who was long and intimately acquainted with the Doctor*. Leeds: Cumming, 1815.

Cummings, A. W. *The Early Schools of Methodism*. New York: Phillips and Hunt, 1886.

Dallimore, Arnold A. *George Whitefield*. Vol. I. London: The Banner of Truth Trust, 1970.

Daniel, W. Harrison. "The Methodist Episcopal Church and the Negro in the Early National Period." *Methodist History*, IX, No. 2 (Jan., 1973), 40–53.

Davies, Rupert, and Gordon Rupp, eds. *A History of the Methodist Church in Great Britain*. Vol. I. London: Epworth Press, 1965.

Davies, Samuel. *Diary*, ed. G. W. Pilcher. Urbana: University of Illinois Press, 1967.

———. *Religion and Patriotism the Constituents of a Good Soldier*. Philadelphia: Chatting, 1755.

Drew, Samuel. *The Life of the Rev. Thomas Coke*. London: Cordeux, 1817.

Drinkhouse, Edward J. *History of Methodist Reform*. 2 vols. Baltimore: Board of Publication of the Methodist Protestant Church, 1899.

Duke Divinity School Review. Durham, N.C., XXXI (1966), XXXIV (1969), etc.

Egmont, Earl of. *Diary of Viscount Percival, afterwards First Earl of Egmont*. 3 vols. London: Historical Manuscripts Commission, 1920–3.

Eller, Paul H. "Francis Asbury and Philip William Otterbein," in Godbold, *Forever Beginning*, pp. 3–13.

Emory, John. *A Defence of "Our Fathers."* 5th ed. New York: Mason and Lane, 1838.

Evans, Charles. *American Bibliography*. Chicago: for the author, 1903–59. 14 vols. with Supplement, ed. R. P. Bristol, 1962– .

Fanning, Samuel J. "Philip Embury." *Methodist History*, III, No. 2 (Jan., 1965), 16–25.

Garrettson, Freeborn. *The Experience and Travels of Mr. Freeborn Garrettson*. Philadelphia: Hall, 1791.

Gentleman's Magazine. London: Cave, etc., VII (1737), etc.

Georgia Historical Quarterly. Savannah, Ga., XL (1956), etc.

Gewehr, Wesley M. *The Great Awakening in Virginia, 1749–1799.* Durham, N.C.: Duke University Press, 1930.

Godbold, Albea. "Facts and Thoughts about Robert Strawbridge and His Work," in *Minutes and Papers of the Northeastern and the Southeastern Jurisdictions of the United Methodist Church*, ed. Norman C. Young. Portage, Pennsylvania, 1974.

―――. "Francis Asbury and His Difficulties with John Wesley and Thomas Rankin." *Methodist History*, III, No. 2 (April, 1965), 3–19.

―――. *Forever Beginning, 1766–1966.* Lake Junaluska, N.C.: Association of Methodist Historical Societies, 1967.

Green, Richard. *The Works of John and Charles Wesley: A Bibliography.* 2nd ed. London: The Methodist Publishing House, 1906.

Griffin, A. P. C., ed. *A Catalogue of the Washington Collection in the Boston Athenaeum.* Boston: Cambridge University Press, 1897.

Hammet, William. *Impartial Statement of the Known Inconsistencies of the Reverend Dr. Coke.* Charleston: Young, 1792.

Harris, Thaddaeus Mason. *Biographical Memorials of James Oglethorpe.* Boston: for the author, 1841.

Harvey, Marvin E. "He was Our No. 1 Layman." *Together.* Nashville: The Methodist Church, Oct., 1963, pp. 26–9.

―――. "The Wives of Thomas Webb and Their Kin." *WHS*, XXXIII (1962), 153–9.

Haskins, Thomas. MS Journal. See Sweet, *Men of Zeal*, pp. 169–75.

Henry, Stuart C. *George Whitefield, Wayfaring Witness.* Nashville: Abingdon Press, 1957.

Historical Magazine. Morrisania, N.Y., X, 1866.

Historical Manuscripts Commission. . . . The Manuscripts of the Earl of Dartmouth, Vol. II, American Papers, London, H. M. S. O., 1895.

Hurst, John Fletcher. *The History of Methodism.* 7 vols. London: Kelly, 1901.

Jackson, John W. *Margaret Morris, Her Journal.* Philadelphia: MacManus, 1949.

Jackson, Thomas. *Life of the Rev. Charles Wesley.* 2 vols. London: Mason, 1841.

―――. *Lives of Early Methodist Preachers.* 6 vols. 4th ed. London: Wesleyan Conference Office, 1872.

Jarratt, Devereux. *The Life of the Reverend Devereux Jarratt.* Baltimore: Warren and Hanna, 1806.

Jones, Charles C. (1831–93). *Historical Sketch of Tomo-Chi-Chi.* Albany, N.Y.: Munsell, 1868.

Kilgore, Charles Franklin. *The James O'Kelly Schism in the Methodist Episcopal Church.* Mexico 1, D.F.: Casa Unida de Publicaciones, 1963.

Knittle, Walter Allen. *The Early Eighteenth Century Palatine Emigration.* Philadelphia: 1936.

Lambert, A. J. *The Chapel on the Hill.* [Bristol, 1929.]

Lednum, John. *The Rise of Methodism in America.* Philadelphia: for the author, 1859.

Lee, Jesse. *A Short History of the Methodists.* Baltimore: Magill and Clime, 1810.

Lee, Leroy M. *Life and Times of the Rev. Jesse Lee.* Charleston: Early, 1848.

Link, John N. "Was Lewes before Philadelphia?" *Christian Advocate*, June 24, 1961.

Lockwood, John P. *The Western Pioneers; or, Memorials of the Lives and Labours of the Rev. Richard Boardman and the Rev. Joseph Pilmoor.* London: Wesleyan Conference Office, 1881.

London Quarterly Review. London, CLXXVI (1951), etc.

Lubach, James L., and Thomas L. Shanklin. "Arbitration and Trials of Members in the Methodist Episcopal Church, 1776–1860." *Methodist History*, IX, No. 4 (July, 1971), 30–49.

M'Lean, John. *Sketch of Rev. Philip Gatch.* Cincinnati: Swormstedt and Poe, 1854.

MacMaster, Richard K. "Liberty or Property? The Methodists' Petition for Emancipation in Virginia, 1785." *Methodist History*, X, No. 1 (Oct., 1971), pp. 44–55.

Maser, Frederick E. "Robert Strawbridge." *Methodist History*, IV, No. 2 (Jan., 1966), pp. 3–21.

Mathews, Donald G. *Slavery and Methodism.* Princeton: Princeton University Press, 1965.

Methodist Church (United Kingdom). *Minutes of the Methodist Conferences.* Vol. I (1744–98). London: Mason, 1862.

———. *The Book of Offices.* London: Methodist Publishing House, 1936.

Methodist Church (United States of America). *The Book of Worship.* Nashville: The Methodist Publishing House, 1965.

Methodist Episcopal Church. *A Collection of Interesting Tracts.* Various dates and contents from 1814–c. 1892. (See chap. 10, and note 44, pp. 177–8).

———. *Disciplines*:

Minutes of several conversations between the Rev. Thomas Coke, LL.D., the Rev. Francis Asbury and others. Philadelphia: Cist, [1785].

The General Minutes of the Conferences. . . . (pp. 322–355 of John Wesley, *The Sunday Service*, 1786).

A Form of Discipline. . . . New York: Ross, 1787.

A Form of Discipline. . . . Elizabeth Town: Kollock, 1788.

A Form of Discipline. . . . 5th ed. New York: Ross, 1789.

A Form of Discipline. . . . 6th ed. Philadelphia: Aitken, for Dickins, 1790.

A Form of Discipline. . . . 7th ed. Philadelphia: Aitken, for Dickins, 1791.

The Doctrines and Discipline. . . . 8th ed. Philadelphia: Hall, for Dickins, 1792.

The Doctrines and Discipline. . . . 9th ed. Philadelphia: Tuckniss, for Dickins, 1797.

The Doctrines and Discipline. . . .With explanatory Notes. 10th ed. Philadelphia: Tuckniss, for Dickins, 1798.

The Doctrines and Discipline. . . . 11th ed. New York: Conrad, for Cooper, 1801.

The Doctrines and Discipline, 12th (1804), 13th (1805), 14th (1808), 15th (1812), eds. etc. New York: various printers.

————. *Journals of the General Conference.* Vol. I, 1796–1836. New York: Carlton and Phillips, 1855.

————. *Minutes of the Methodist Conference, held annually in America, from 1773 to 1794, inclusive.* Philadelphia: Tuckniss, 1795.

————. *Minutes of the Methodist Conferences, annually held in America; from 1773 to 1813, inclusive.* New York: Hitt and Ware, 1813.

Methodist History. Lake Junaluska, N.C.: Commission on Archives and History of the United Methodist Church, 1962–.

Methodist Magazine. London. See *Arminian Magazine,* London.

Methodist Magazine. New York; various printers, 1818–27.

Methodist Quarterly Review. New York, 1859, etc.

Minutes. See Methodist Church, Methodist Episcopal Church.

Moore, Henry. *The Life of the Rev. John Wesley.* 2 vols. London: Kershaw, 1824.

Moravian Church, Bethlehem, Pennsylvania. Diary, quoted in *Bulletin No. 7 of the Association of Methodist Historical Societies,* 1939.

Morris, Margaret. *Journal,* ed. John W. Jackson. Philadelphia: MacManus, 1949.

Nayler, John. *Charles Delamotte.* London: Epworth Press, 1938.

Norwood, Frederick A. "James O'Kelly—Methodist Maverick." *Methodist History,* IV, No. 3 (April, 1966), 14–28.

Pascoe, C. F. *Two Hundred Years of the S.P.G.* London: S.P.G., 1901.

Peirce, William. *The Ecclesiastical Principles and Polity of the Wesleyan Methodists.* London: Hamilton, Adams, 1854.

Phoebus, William. *Memoirs of the Rev. Richard Whatcoat.* New York: Allen, 1828.

Pilkington, James Penn. *The Methodist Publishing House: A History.* Vol. I. Nashville: Abingdon Press, 1968.

Pilmore, Joseph. *Journal,* ed. Frederick E. Maser and Howard T. Maag. Philadelphia: Message Publishing Company, 1969.

Prince, H. H. *The Romance of Early Methodism in and around West Bromwich and Wednesbury.* West Bromwich: Tomkins, [1925].

Pritchard, John. *Sermon Occasioned by the Death of the Late Capt. Webb.* Bristol: Edwards, 1797.

Randolph, J. Ralph. "John Wesley and the American Indian: A Study in Disillusionment." *Methodist History,* X, No. 3 (April, 1972), 3–11.

Reeves, Joseph. MS History of Staffordshire, 1834, quoted by J. M. Day, brochure for official reopening of Asbury Cottage, Newton Road, Great Barr, England, Nov. 27, 1959, p. 7.

Reily, D. A. "William Hammett." *Methodist History,* X, No. 1 (Oct., 1971), 30–43.

Rogers, Charles A. "John Wesley and Jonathan Edwards." *Duke Divinity School Review,* XXXI (Winter, 1966), 20–38.

Rudolph, L. C. *Francis Asbury.* Nashville: Abingdon Press, 1966.

Sackett, A. Barrett. *James Rouquet and His Part in Early Methodism.* Publication No. 8 of the Wesley Historical Society. Chester: Taberer, 1972.

Sanders, Paul S. "The Sacraments in Early American Methodism." *Church History,* XXVI (1957), 355–71.

Schell, Edwin. "New Light on Robert Strawbridge." *Methodist History*, IX, No. 3 (Jan., 1971), 62–4.

Scherer, Lester B. *Ezekiel Cooper, 1763–1847*. Jesse Lee Prize Essay, 1968. Lake Junaluska, N.C.: The Commission on Archives and History of the United Methodist Church, 1968.

Schmidt, Martin. *John Wesley: A Theological Biography*. Vol. I. London: Epworth Press, 1962.

Seaman, Samuel A. *Annals of New York Methodism*. New York: Hunt and Eaton, 1892.

Sheldon, W. C., "The Landmarks of Bishop Asbury's Childhood and Youth." *WHS*, XII (1920), 97–103.

Sherman, David. *History of the Revisions of the Discipline of the Methodist Episcopal Church*. 3rd ed. New York: Hunt and Eaton, 1890.

Simon, John S. *John Wesley and the Religious Societies*. London: Epworth Press, 1921.

Spencer, Harold, and Edwin Finch. *The Constitutional Practice and Discipline of the Methodist Church*. 4th ed. London: The Methodist Publishing House, 1964.

Sprague, William B. *Annals of the American Methodist Pulpit*. New York. Carter, 1861.

Steadman, Melvin Lee. *Leesburg's Old Stone Church, 1766*. Manassas, Virginia: Virginia-Craft Printing Company, 1964.

Stevens, Abel. *History of the Methodist Episcopal Church*. Vol. I. New York: Carlton and Porter, 1864.

Sweet, William Warren. *Men of Zeal*. New York: Abingdon, 1935.

———. *Methodism in American History*. New York: Methodist Book Concern, 1933.

———. *Religion on the American Frontier, 1783–1840*. Vol. IV. *The Methodists*. Chicago: University of Chicago Press, 1946.

———. *Virginia Methodism*. Richmond: Whittet and Shepperson, 1955.

[Taylor, Thomas]. *A Letter, &c* [i.e., to John Wesley, April 11, 1768]. N.p., n.p., n.d.

Tees, Francis H. *The Beginnings of Methodism*. Nashville: Parthenon Press, 1940.

Tigert, John J. *A Constitutional History of American Episcopal Methodism*. 6th ed. Nashville: Smith and Lamar, 1916.

———, ed. *The Doctrines of the Methodist Episcopal Church in America, as contained in the Disciplines of said Church from 1788 to 1808, and so designated by their Title-pages*. 2 vols. Cincinnati: Jennings and Pye, 1902.

Tipple, Ezra Squier. *Francis Asbury, the Prophet of the Long Road*. New York: Methodist Book Concern, 1916.

Tripp, David. *The Renewal of the Covenant in the Methodist Tradition*. London: Epworth Press, 1969.

Tyerman, Luke. *The Life and Times of the Rev. Samuel Wesley*. London: Simpkin, Marshall, 1866.

———. *The Life of the Rev. George Whitefield*. 2 vols. 2nd ed. London: Hodder and Stoughton, 1890.

————. *The Oxford Methodists*. London: Hodder and Stoughton, 1873.

United Methodist Church. *The Book of Discipline of The United Methodist Church, 1968*. Nashville: Methodist Publishing House, [1969].

————. *The Book of Discipline of the United Methodist Church, 1972*. Nashville: United Methodist Publishing House, [1973].

————. The Theological Study Commission on Doctrine and Doctrinal Standards: *A Report to the General Conference*, April, 1972.

Vickers, John. "Coke and Asbury: A Comparison of Bishops." *Methodist History*, XI, No. 1 (Oct., 1972), 42–51.

————. *Thomas Coke, Apostle of Methodism*. Nashville: Abingdon Press, 1969.

Wakeley, J. B. *The Heroes of Methodism*. 10th ed. New York: Carlton and Lanahan, n.d.

————. *Lost Chapters recovered from the Early History of American Methodism*. New York: Carlton and Porter, 1858.

Ware, Thomas. *Sketches of the Life and Travels of Rev. Thomas Ware, Written by Himself*. New York: Mason and Lane, 1839.

Watters, William. *A Short Account of the Christian Experience and Ministereal* [sic] *Labours of William Watters*. Alexandria, Va.: Snowden, n.d.

Webb, Thomas. *A Military Treatise on the Appointments of the Army*. Philadelphia: Dunlap, 1759.

Wesley, Charles. *Journal, 1736–39*, ed. John Telford. London: Culley, n.d.

————. *Journal*, ed. Thomas Jackson. 2 vols. London: Wesleyan Methodist Book Room, n.d.

Wesley, John. *A Concise Ecclesiastical History*. 4 vols. London: Paramore, 1781.

————. *John Wesley's First Hymn-book: A Facsimile with Additional Material*, ed. Frank Baker and George Walton Williams. Charleston, S.C.: Dalcho Historical Society, and London: Wesley Historical Society, 1964.

————. *Journal*, Standard Ed., ed. Nehemiah Curnock. 8 vols. London: Epworth Press, 1938.

————. *Letters*, Standard Ed., ed. John Telford. 8 vols. London: Epworth Press, 1931.

————. *Minutes of Several Conversations between the Reverend Mr. John and Charles Wesley and Others. From the Year 1744, to the Year 1780*. London: Paramore, [1780]. (The "large" *Minutes*, reprinted in Tigert, *Constitutional History*, pp. 533–602, and in parallel columns with the other editions published during Wesley's lifetime in *Minutes* (English), pp. 444–675).

————. *The Sunday Service of the Methodists*. London: n.p., 1784, 1786, 1788, 1790, 1792. (Titles and contents vary slightly; see Baker, *Union Catalogue*, No. 376.)

————. *To Dr. Coke, Mr. Asbury, and our Brethren in North-America*. (Circular letter, 4 pp., dated "Bristol, Sept. 10, 1784." See Baker, *Union Catalogue*, No. 376A.)

————. *Works*, ed. Thomas Jackson. 14 vols. London: Wesleyan-Methodist Book Room, n.d.

Wesley Historical Society, *Proceedings*, 1893.

Wesleyan Methodist Magazine. See *Arminian Magazine*, London.

Wesleyan Quarterly Review. 4 vols. Macon, Georgia: Wesleyan College, 1964–7.

Whitefield, George. *Journals.* London: Banner of Truth Trust, 1960.

——. *Works.* 6 vols. London: Dilly, 1771–2.

Williams, George Walton. *Early Ministers at St. Michael's, Charleston.* Charleston, S.C.: Dalcho Historical Society, 1961.

Wright, Robert. *A Memoir of General James Oglethorpe.* London: Chapman and Hall, 1867.

INDEX